Power and Protectionism

The Political Economy of International Change
John Gerard Ruggie, General Editor

Power and Protectionism

STRATEGIES
OF THE NEWLY INDUSTRIALIZING
COUNTRIES

David B. Yoffie

Columbia University Press

New York

Library of Congress Cataloging in Publication Data
Yoffie, David B.
    Power and protectionism.

    Bibliography: p.
    Includes index.
    1. Free trade and protection—Protection.
2. Commercial policy. I. Title.
HF 1713.Y63   1983   382.7'3   83-2125
ISBN 0-231-05550-1
ISBN 0-231-05551-X (pbk.)

Columbia University Press
New York   Guildford, Surrey

10 9 8 7 6 5 4 3 2

Clothbound editions of Columbia University Press books are
Smyth-sewn and printed on permanent and durable acid-free
paper.

For my parents
William A. Yoffie
and
Judith S. Yoffie

Contents

Preface

I started this book in 1978 just as the study of international political economy was becoming fashionable in the United States. For most scholars in this new area, political economy meant using economic variables to explain political outcomes. Whether you were interested in understanding international regimes, foreign economic policy, or domestic politics, economic analysis could be employed as a powerful tool. My aim in this book, however, was to develop a somewhat different approach to the study of international political economy. It seemed to me that political variables could be just as important to economic outcomes as economic variables were to political outcomes. In other words, political science had a great deal to contribute to the science of economics, if one posed a different set of questions.

To get a handle on these questions, I was immediately drawn to the work of Albert Hirschman—one of the best "political economists" of the last 40 years. In his 1945 book, *National Power and the Structure of Foreign Trade,* Hirschman set a standard for the study of political economy by demonstrating how structural weaknesses in the free trade system could be exploited by big countries for political purposes. This book, as well as Hirschman's subsequent work, had a major influence on my thinking. Accordingly, I decided to develop the same theme developed by Hirschman in *National Power*, i.e., the linkage between power, politics, and foreign trade. But while Hirschman sought to explain how trade patterns could affect power relations and politics, I chose to focus on how politics and power relations could affect patterns of trade.

My first cut at this problem was my doctoral dissertation, which examined how Japan, Hong Kong, Korea, and Taiwan managed to increase their export earnings in textiles, apparel, and footwear in the face of American restrictions. In the same way Hirschman questioned conventional wisdom about the free trade system, in the thesis I questioned conventional wisdom about who gains and who loses under protectionism. By building upon the political science literature on bargaining, political decision making, weak states, and transnational relations in addition to the economic literature on international trade and trade adjustment, I tried to demonstrate that the politics of protection could have a major impact on trade patterns.

While writing the thesis from 1978 to 1980 I was extremely fortunate to have an excellent doctoral committee and several colleagues that were willing to read and comment on my early drafts. In particular, my greatest thanks belongs to my thesis adviser, Robert Keohane, and to Alexander George. Both read every draft of the manuscript throughout the two years of writing. Their stimulating comments continually forced me to sharpen my analysis, clarify my prose, and reach beyond the obvious answers. In addition, Linda Cahn, Harry Harding, Ernst Haas, Donald Hellman, Stephen Krasner, and Dan Okimoto provided insightful suggestions on various chapters.

Yet like many studies done for a dissertation, the thesis required more reflection, refinement, and research before it could go to print. I therefore spent the better part of my first year and a half at the Harvard Business School writing new theoretical chapters, revising and updating the case studies, and adding new research on the color television and automobile industries. This gave me an opportunity to test further my hypotheses about the relationship between politics and protectionism in textile, apparel, and footwear, and to generalize those conclusions to other sectors. For this second cut at the problem, I received very constructive comments from an international political economy seminar that included Jerry Cohen, Tom Elgin, Peter Hall, Robert Keohane, Joseph Nye, John Odell, Jeffrey Sachs, and others. Two colleagues at the Harvard Business School, Malcolm Salter and Michael Rukstad, also deserve thanks for their reading of my final chapter.

None of the research would have been possible, however, without the generous financial support of several institutions. At the dissertation stage, I received travel and research funds from the Institute for the Study of World Politics and the Center for East Asian Studies at Stanford. While at the Harvard Business School, the Division of Research provided editorial assistance as well as the necessary funds to conduct the final round of interviews. My parents and the late Mrs. A. S. Persky also gave their financial and moral support, whenever it was needed and always at the right time. And last, but certainly not least, it is doubtful that this book could have been written without the assistance of my wife Terry. During all those nights and weekends devoted to writing and rewriting, her patience and encouragement were invaluable.

Power and Protectionism

Introduction

Political analysts are frequently caught by surprise when "weak" actors succeed in influencing "stronger" actors, and, particularly in international affairs, they tend to proclaim a paradox every time a country with few resources turns its adversity into advantage. Although scholars from the time of Thucydides have predicted that "the strong do what they can and the weak suffer what they must,"[1] examples abound of relatively weak states performing feats which are apparently beyond their means: during World War II, several small European nations managed to avoid the total devastation that engulfed their continent;[2] tiny Malta has bargained successfully with more-powerful Britain;[3] countries in Africa have discovered ways to extract concessions from the European Economic Community;[4] and "small allies" have had a "big influence" on American policies.[5] Regardless of the issue, traditional stereotypes about the weak and the strong rarely seem to hold.

My aim in this study is to explore similar asymmetrical relationships in the context of the world trading system. In the vast literature on North–South relations and dependency one finds the widely accepted thesis that developing nations are at a disadvantage in confrontations with the more developed countries, especially in the realm of international trade.[6]

On the one hand, most newly industrializing countries depend on exports of manufactured goods for their economic growth and well-being. On the other hand, the United States and Europe control the access to a large percentage of the world's markets. Since importers in these circumstances usually have the greater bargaining capabilities, we are told to expect the "weaker" developing nations to be more or less at the mercy of the "stronger" industrial ones.[7]

If trade operated on the principles of Ricardian liberalism, politics and asymmetrical power relationships might be unimportant. Weak countries and powerful countries could simply exchange goods. Unfortunately, protectionism has always been a problem in the modern economy—a problem that has had portentous implications for developing countries in recent years. As developing nations have become serious international competitors in a growing range of manufactured products, industrialized countries have erected import barriers to protect their established industries. Tariffs and quotas, however, have ceased to be the primary tool for reducing imports. Instead, the industrial nations have discovered a "new protectionism" that uses "voluntary export restraints" and "orderly marketing agreements" to discriminate against developing states. The United States and Europe prefer to avoid restricting each other while they simultaneously single out products from the most successful developing countries for protection. Trade has consequently become an urgent problem of politics and power, pitting the weak directly against the strong. According to the United Nations Conference on Trade and Development (UNCTAD), this new protectionism may lead to "irreparable damage to the world economy [and] in particular to the developing countries."[8]

In this book I shall explore the political economy of this new protectionism and its implications for developed and developing states. Since the foundation for much of the postwar economic growth has been the phenomenal expansion in world commerce, the origins and development of contemporary trade barriers are matters of great concern. Developing countries have a huge stake in the system because many altered their development strategies to take advantage of the explosion in world markets. At the same time, the United States and Europe have become increasingly dependent on trade as a component of their national growth.[9] If protectionism spreads throughout the international trading system, the integrity of the world economic order and the future of many industrializing countries could come into question.

I shall take an in-depth look at this new protectionism. My central objective, however, is more fundamental: I plan to expose what Albert Hirschman has called the "countertendencies" in asymmetrical trading patterns—the political and economic dimensions of protectionism that create opportunities as well as dangers for exporting countries.[10] Are there any weaknesses in the structure of modern protectionism? Under what conditions might industrializing countries be able to capitalize on these weaknesses? And what strategies can exporting nations employ to turn the tables on importing states? Very little attention has been focused on this side of the protectionist problem. Yet it is crucially important for importers, exporters, and the trading system as a whole.

The first step in my analysis will be to outline in the remainder of this chapter the background of the new protectionism and its potential threat to exporting countries. Chapter 1 follows with a discussion of the policies and prerequisites that industrializing countries need in order to overcome contemporary trade barriers. I will argue that the political nature of protectionism has opened opportunities for less-powerful exporting nations. Despite the appearance of severe restrictions, industrializing countries can take advantage of loopholes in modern protection to avoid the damage of trade restraints. Moreover, under certain conditions and with an appropriate strategy, exporting nations may not only dissipate the effects of trade barriers, they may dramatically increase their export earnings.

In chapters 2 to 5 I will explore these propositions on trading strategies, drawing on empirical research in the tex-

tile, apparel, and footwear industries. I will use comparative
case studies in these chapters to examine American trade with
exporting nations in East Asia from the mid-1950s to 1982.
In chapter 6 I will try to generalize my findings by examin-
ing patterns of protectionism in color televisions and automobiles. I will pose the question in this concluding chapter
of whether the strategies of industrializing countries in the
1950s, 1960s, and 1970s will still be viable for the exporters
of the 1980s and beyond. To a large extent, exporters managed to mitigate the effects of United States trade barriers by
taking advantage of the accommodating nature of American
protectionist policies. Hegemonic objectives and bureaucratic
politics constrained United States bargaining and implementation during most of the postwar period. As American hegemony declines and decision makers learn from their experience in various sectors, the future remains an open question.

The Origins of Modern Protectionism

The new protectionism comes in many forms and guises. The
most important policy tools of these modern trade barriers
are voluntary export restraints (VERs) and orderly marketing
agreements (OMAs). Neither tariffs nor global quotas, VERs
and OMAs are bilateral arrangements that attempt to bias
consumption in the importing country in favor of domestic
producers. VERs and OMAs have become so widespread in
the postwar period that they have come to rank equally with
tariffs and quotas as the most widely used foreign commercial policies. As early as 1971, the dollar value of goods coming to the United States subject to export restraints surpassed
the value of goods subject to import quotas.[11]

Orderly marketing agreements, voluntary export restraints, and their equivalents have three basic characteristics.[12] First, they are bargained accords between an importing
and an exporting country. Through a process of negotiation,

the exporting partner agrees to restrict shipments of a particular product to a level lower than one might otherwise expect in a competitive market. Second, OMAs and VERs are
quantitative limits, based on the type of good, not on its price.
And third, these agreements are *selective* restrictions, applying only to a limited number of producers. This last feature
is critical because it introduces an element of discrimination
into world commerce. Under the most favored nation (MFN)
provision of the General Agreement on Tariffs and Trade
(GATT), all countries are to be treated equally in international trade relations. MFN has been the core principle of the
postwar trade regime. Because VERs and OMAs single out
individual exporters for restrictions, they violate the spirit if
not the letter of GATT's first and most important article.

The history of these export arrangements goes back to a
time when discrimination and the flagrant use of trade barriers were not that uncommon. During the depression of the
1930s, several importing nations chose to negotiate the level
of goods entering their markets rather than set those levels
independently. Holland agreed to limit its exports of agricultural commodities to France; Japanese textile manufacturers
set their exports at a level acceptable to American textile producers; and German coal mine operations restrained their
shipments to Belgium after a series of bilateral negotiations.[13]
These so-called bilateral quotas were preferred by importers
because bilateral arrangements were not as likely to provoke
trade retaliation. Furthermore, some importing nations
thought that bilateral quotas would be implemented more effectively than global quantitative restrictions (QRs). Exporters were willing to accept these negotiated restraints because
the alternatives always seemed worse.

Bilateral quotas virtually disappeared after the outbreak
of World War II, and it was not until the late 1940s that export restraints re-emerged. When the United States Department of Agriculture considered instituting QRs on Canadian
potatoes, Canadian exporters offered to restrict "voluntarily"
their potato shipments.[14] Fearing the possible longevity of

American import quotas, the Canadians saw a VER as the lesser of two evils; at the same time, the Department of Agriculture was satisfied because the restraint minimized its administrative responsibilities. VERs in potatoes, however, were not a central concern for the international trading system. Special provisions in the GATT exempted agricultural policy from unconditional most favored nation treatment. In addition, potatoes were not a major item in world commerce. Controlling trade in manufactures, on the other hand, was the backbone of the GATT. Restrictions in the manufacturing sector would be a problem to be reckoned with.

Ironically, it was the leader of the postwar movement for free trade, the United States, that reintroduced VERs for industrial products. During the early 1950s, American textiles and apparel producers found the cotton segment of their industry under pressure from Japanese imports. This was in part due to a shift in comparative advantage to lower-wage countries, but it was largely a function of United States government cotton-exporting policies that caused disadvantages for American manufacturers.[15] The increase in imports led industry leaders to lobby hard for protection. Even though Japanese market penetration was only 2 percent of the apparent consumption in 1956, the pleas of the textile industry were hard to ignore. With the power of almost two and one-half million workers behind them, textile and apparel producers had little difficulty mobilizing support in Washington.

American decision makers faced the fact that tariffs or quotas would hardly have been appropriate for a government promoting freer world trade. The United States was the most ardent advocate of abiding by GATT rules, and protectionist policies were circumscribed by the international organization. The American answer to this dilemma was to revert to a VER. The Department of Commerce informed the American public on January 16, 1957, that Japan would "voluntarily" restrict its exports of cotton textiles and apparel to the United States for five years. This allowed the Americans to disavow responsibility for an agreement they actively negotiated.

Once this precedent was set by the United States, VERs proliferated. Many importing countries found export restraints to be an excellent mechanism for bypassing GATT regulations. Several European nations negotiated "voluntary" restrictions with Japan in a wide range of commodities; Britain arranged an interindustry agreement with Hong Kong and India in cotton textiles; and the United States aborted an attempt to negotiate a VER with Hong Kong that would complement its agreement with Japan.[16] Yet few countries were satisfied with this piecemeal approach to trade controls, especially in this most sensitive area of cotton textiles. Importing governments wanted a more systematic means to deal with market disruptions. Therefore, the United States led the charge in the late 1950s and early 1960s to extend textile VERs to many producers. In 1961, an international conference sponsored by the United States produced a "Short-Term Arrangement" legitimizing textile VERs. By 1962, thirty-one countries signed a "Long-Term Arrangement Regarding International Trade in Cotton Textiles," which made bilaterally negotiated export restraints an institutional feature of world commerce.

Textiles and apparel remained the only major global industry protected by VERs until the late 1960s.[17] By then, other sectors felt import competition, and industrialized countries again found export restrictions a convenient way to accommodate domestic political pressures without directly violating the GATT. Between 1968 and 1981, the United States alone negotiated VERs or OMAs in steel, multifiber textiles, color televisions, nonrubber footwear, and automobiles. At the same time, the Europeans took over 100 actions to restrict imports—most of them directed against developing countries and frequently in the form of VERs and OMAs. The irony behind all of these protectionist policies was that they were done in the name of free and orderly trade. The argument was that the only way to avoid a return to the tariff and quota protectionism of the 1930s was to adopt these supposedly temporary measures.

The perils of these new protectionist trends are shared by the entire international community. But the spread of negotiated export restraints seems especially worrisome to the less-powerful, developing countries because of their unique discriminatory qualities. VERs and OMAs have been directed most extensively at labor-intensive, low-priced goods—products such as textiles and footwear, where a developing country has the greatest comparative advantage. In addition, because they are negotiated accords, VERs and OMAs may lead to political tension in the process of bargaining. This outcome differs from most tariffs and quotas, which are implemented unilaterally. And lastly, they usually involve bilateral negotiations which isolate the weak, developing country in a one-on-one confrontation against a powerful developed state, like the United States, or an organization, like the European Economic Community. From the perspective of organizations such as UNCTAD, this final feature is the most disconcerting. Since the industrializing nations are in a substantially disadvantageous bargaining position, "unable to retaliate" and "fearful of more severe restrictions," they are supposedly doomed to suffer in their foreign trade.[18] UNCTAD fears that the proliferation of these "restrictionist regimes" is a "grave threat to the trade and development of developing countries and would undermine their reliance on international trade as an engine for growth."[19]

Yet despite dire predictions, protectionism has not always been translated into disaster. An increasing number of rapidly developing nations—the so-called newly industrializing countries (NICs)—have found ways to avoid the damaging effects of import barriers. Despite rising protectionism and the odds against them, this heterogeneous group of nations has made a significant contribution to the volume of world trade. If, for example, one were to look at the ten NICs examined by the Organization of Economic Cooperation and Development (OECD)—Spain, Portugal, Greece, Yugoslavia, Brazil, Mexico, Hong Kong, Korea, Taiwan, and Singapore—one would find that from the early 1960s to the late 1970s these economies almost doubled their share of the world's industrial production, tripled their share of OECD imports (see figure A), and expanded their share of world exports by 170 percent (see table A).[20] This dramatic growth all took place while VERs and OMAs were aimed at key NIC products. Some nations have not performed well under this protectionist system. Countries such as India and Egypt have had difficulties responding to trade restrictions. At the same time, others such as Korea and Hong Kong have rebounded resourcefully and minimized the damage of protectionism. As table B illustrates, even the most severely restricted sector of textiles and apparel has not been an impenetrable barrier to some.[21]

The reason for this apparent anomaly is that there are political and economic weaknesses in the structure of modern protectionism. The industrial nations, particularly the United States, have not employed orderly marketing agreements and voluntary export restraints as well-conceived tools of industrial intervention. On the contrary, OMAs and VERs have been used as ad hoc, short-run political policies that may not be as dangerous as UNCTAD and others believe. By emphasizing adjustment in their trade relations rather than intransigence, bargaining rather than coercion, and the substance of international agreements rather than their form, these less-powerful exporting countries have found a way to turn an adverse situation into advantage. As I will show in the next chapter, the politics of trade have paradoxically created opportunities for the "weak" to beat the "strong" at their own game.

Figure A

OECD Imports of Manufactures

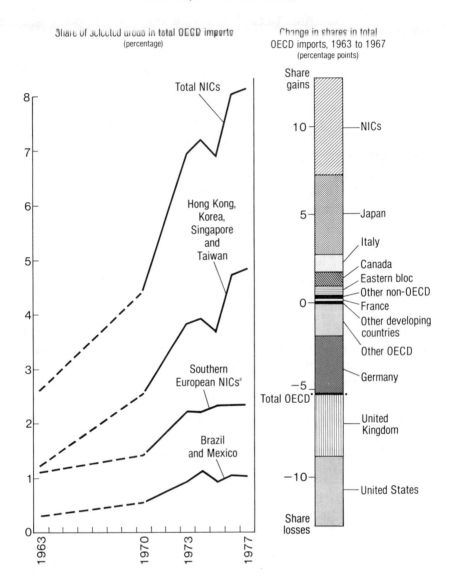

Share of selected areas in total OECD imports
(percentage)

Change in shares in total
OECD imports, 1963 to 1967
(percentage points)

Share
gains

Total NICs

NICs

Hong Kong,
Korea,
Singapore
and
Taiwan

Japan

Italy

Canada
Eastern bloc
Other non-OECD
France
Other developing
countries

Southern
European NICs[a]

Other OECD

Germany

Brazil
and Mexico

Total OECD

United
Kingdom

United States

Share
losses

[a]Greece, Portugal, Spain and Yugoslavia.

Source: *The Impact of the Newly Industrializing Countries* (Paris: OECD, 1979), p. 7.

Table A Geographical Distribution of World Exports of Manufactures (percent)

	1963	1973	1976
Canada	2.61	4.16	3.32
United States	17.24	12.58	13.55
Japan	5.98	9.92	11.38
France	6.99	7.26	7.41
Germany	15.33	16.98	15.81
Italy	4.73	5.30	5.49
United Kingdom	11.14	7.00	6.59
TOTAL OECD	80.49	82.25	82.76
Brazil	0.05	0.35	0.41
Mexico	0.17	0.64	0.51
Hong Kong	0.76	1.05	1.15
Korea	0.05	0.78	1.20
Taiwan	0.16	1.04	1.23
Singapore	0.38	0.46	0.52
TOTAL NICs	(2.59)	(6.29)	(7.12)
Other LDCs	2.70	2.34	1.55
India	0.85	0.45	0.49
Argentina	0.01	0.21	0.17
Eastern Bloc	13.35	10.00	9.65
WORLD TOTAL	100.00	100.00	100.00

SOURCE: *The Impact of the Newly Industrializing Countries* (Paris: OECD, 1979), p. 19.

Table B United States Textile Quotas for Selected Exporters, 1956–1976 (in millions of square yard equivalents)

	First United States VER [a]	First United States Multifiber VER [b]	Quantitative Increase	Percent Growth
Japan	245	1,737	1,492	609
Taiwan	56	562	506	903
Korea	26	403	377	1450
Mexico	75	278	203	270
Philippines	45	189	144	320
Pakistan	55	181	126	229
India	79	152	73	92
Egypt	43	105	62	144
Colombia	24	91	67	279

[a] Cotton textiles only, negotiated in 1956 for Japan, and between 1963 and 1965 for the other nations.

[b] Cotton, synthetic, and wool textiles, negotiated in 1971 for Japan, Korea, and Taiwan, and in 1975 and 1976 for the other nations.

SOURCE: U.S. International Trade Commission, *The History and Current Status of the Multifiber Arrangement.*

Chapter 1

Politics
as an Instrument
of Foreign Trade

Classical theories of international commerce have traditionally emphasized that free trade maximizes global social welfare. David Ricardo and his successors have persuasively argued that free-trading nations can escape the confines of their limited resources when they lower trade barriers and specialize production under the principle of comparative advantage. Since countries differ in their relative resource endowments, unfettered trade is supposed to relieve an individual nation's shortage of land, labor, or capital. A free world market, like a free domestic market, should improve efficiency and welfare for the greatest number.

With 150 years of economic theory behind them, economists and international organizations such as UNCTAD have felt they were on firm ground when they decried the use of trade barriers by industrial nations. According to Ricardian logic, protectionism in general, and voluntary export restraints in particular, should cause exporting nations to lose markets for their goods, reducing production and lowering economic growth. At the same time, trade limits should impede structural adjustments in the importing economy as well as force consumers to pay higher prices for restricted goods. Special groups *within* a protected country may benefit from restricted trade, but both importing and exporting economies should lose overall income and output from protectionism.

If trade barriers are clearly mistaken policies, several questions arise. How is it possible for a newly industrializing country to prosper in a protectionist system? With VERs and OMAs aimed directly at their key products, why are the NICs posting huge economic gains in world trade? Have David Ricardo and company failed to take something into account in their discussions of trade theory?

The problem with traditional approaches to international trade is that they have lacked perspective on politics. Trade barriers are erected for political reasons, and they operate in a political environment. This means that who gets what, when, and how is a function not only of the market but also of bargaining, implementation, coercion, and the use of symbols.[1] Because international trade relations *are* political, the theory and practice of world commerce usually diverge. Upon closer examination of the practice, one discovers that NICs can potentially achieve their foreign trade objectives in more ways than by relying on a free market. The politics of international trade create opportunities that newly industrializing countries can exploit.

In this chapter I will construct a strategy for newly industrializing countries—a set of interconnected policies and prerequisites that an exporting state could employ to overcome the disadvantages of voluntary export restraints and orderly marketing agreements. The assumption underlying this strategy is that myopic decision making in the United States and Europe has created a deficient form of trade barrier. These OMAs and VERs are faulty agreements that inevitably have problems. If an exporting country has a dynamic economy, is skillful in bargaining and the manipulation of symbols, and is cunning enough to circumvent restrictions, then it can capitalize on the deficiencies in modern trade barriers. A newly industrializing country is not always subject to the whims of the market or the industrial nations that erect the trade barriers; with well-designed policies that are carefully implemented, a NIC can turn another's protectionism to its own advantage.

The Dependent Variables

The most important questions to ask about trade restrictions are: What are the direct and indirect consequences of protectionism? To what extent do the discriminatory tools of voluntary export restraints and orderly marketing agreements affect an industrializing country's trade earnings? Operationally, I define this first dependent variable as a newly industrializing country's export gains or losses. This variable will be measured by three types of changes in a nation's export earnings: (1) earnings in product areas specifically protected; (2) earnings associated with broader sectoral trade; and (3) earnings from the overall bilateral trade. In cotton textile protectionism, for instance, one would want to know if the exporting state can increase earnings in "cotton" textiles, in the broader segments of the industry that include noncotton wool and synthetic textiles and in the country's overall trading balance.

The second dependent variable is the trade relationship between the importing country and the newly industrializing state. Conceptually we can think of this relationship as the bilateral "regime"—the set of rules, norms, institutions, and/or concerted expectations designed to regularize behavior.[2] Regimes may vary a great deal in foreign commerce. In some cases an importer may be quite generous to its less-developed trading partners. The United States, for example, has provided industrializing countries with open markets and special tariff preferences, and allowed exporting nations to discriminate against American goods. Alternatively, a bilateral regime could become relatively closed, with high barriers to trade and norms that demand equal trading rights. Exporters always want to preserve a favorable commercial relationship and fight against the alternatives. Since most bilateral trade regimes with the United States began as advantageous ones after World War II, an industrializing state will optimally avoid any action that would damage this trade relationship.

The third and final object of inquiry is the actual protectionist accords: the VERs and OMAs themselves. Trade earnings, especially in restricted sectors, and the health of the bilateral regime may depend upon the restrictiveness or generosity of the protectionist arrangement. The more explicit a VER, for example, the more difficult it will be to increase sales in restricted segments of the industry. Likewise, the scope of coverage—whether it includes all textiles or only some—will have a direct impact on broader export earnings. And side payments or sanctions that may accompany an accord could be a factor in the stability of the bilateral regime. Hence, one can see these agreements as a composite intervening variable that will have an important influence on trade and political relations. The scope and explicitness of VERs and OMAs will tell us something about the sectoral prospects for restricted NICs; and the political and economic side effects of protectionism will affect the overall trading relationship.

Thus confronted with the new protectionism, an industrializing country would optimally want to minimize the scope and explicitness of the restrictions, receive side payments, increase the value of trade across all sectors, and simultaneously preserve its bilateral trade regime. The strategy elaborated below suggests how and under what conditions a weak, exporting country can bring about these results. Briefly, this strategy assumes two preconditions, two core policies, and several supplemental tactics. The prerequisites for increasing trade earnings are (1) accommodating protectionist policies by the importing nation and (2) an adaptable economy in the exporting nation. Assuming these conditions are met, the core of the strategy is (1) that the exporting country give priority to long-term rather than immediate political and economic interests and (2) that it bargain for certain short-run needs. Within this general policy framework, an exporting country can also try to supplement its earnings by linking issues, cheating on restrictive arrangements, and mobilizing transnational and transgovernmental allies on its behalf. When coordinated, these policies will exploit the political and economic weaknesses in the new protectionism and spell victory for the exporting country.

Prerequisites

The Political Basis of Trade

One of the most important conditions affecting a newly industrializing country's trade earnings is the constrained nature of international trade policies. From the close of World War II, the United States has promoted freer, nondiscriminatory world trade. American officials have believed that trade barriers would have to be eliminated and a set of international rules enforced if the world was to avoid returning to a depression like the 1930s. The United States has wanted a "Pax Americana," in which the "establishment of a liberal trading system and the attainment of an expanding world economy" would be the central theme.[3]

The American strategy to achieve these goals has been to promote long-range political objectives, even if that required sacrifices of specific economic interests. The United States thus committed itself to free trade while it sought to reduce others' trade restrictions. The dilemma for the United States has been that protectionism for American industries is grossly inconsistent with these broader political and economic goals. Few American presidents want to bear the political costs of refusing to protect a powerful domestic industry that is under pressure from imports. But at the same time, "no country with a claim to leadership in tariff reductions wants flagrantly to impose textile [or other] quotas."[4]

Thus when the United States employs VERs and OMAs

in a sector, it is usually an attempt to reconcile hegemonic interests in free trade with particularistic demands for import barriers. Rarely are VERs and OMAs the product of a unanimous consensus to combat "unfair competition," "market disruptions," or a real threat to a domestic industry. The decision for bilateral arrangements is a political decision—a compromise between free traders and protectionists. As Bauer, de Sola Pool, and Dexter have noted, "In foreign trade issues, foreign policy becomes domestic politics."[5]

Trade is inherently political, and there is little that a NIC can do to alter this situation. Yet as long as VERs and OMAs are principally political tools to appease domestic industries, and as long as other alternatives such as tariffs and quotas are costly from an international perspective, there will invariably be some degree of flexibility in the United States' protectionist position. When the sole purpose of import restriction is political appeasement, the exporter may be able to accommodate that purpose without reducing its rate of export growth. The importance of political symbols for American and other policy makers may allow the NIC to exchange deference on politically salient questions for tangible economic benefits in less sensitive areas. The political nature of trade constitutes the first and most important loophole in modern protectionism.

Factor Mobility

The sine qua non for any weak state that hopes to influence a more powerful state is flexibility. Without the ability to maneuver and adapt, success in virtually any issue-area is unthinkable.[6] In the realm of international trade, flexibility comes from factor mobility—the ability to divert capital goods to new purposes, to turn labor to different tasks, and to obtain access to the relevant technologies.[7] For basic light industries such as textiles, clothing, and footwear, technology and capital are not major difficulties. Production knowledge about these labor-intensive sectors is relatively standardized and available to all developing countries; capital requirements are also extremely low. An efficient labor force, however, with commercial and managerial skills, is frequently more problematic.

Factor mobility is essential because it provides the foundation for responding to protectionism. Unless a state is maneuverable—unless it can induce firms to alter their product lines and make adjustments—the strategy for maximizing earnings which is suggested below will be of little use. Yet factor mobility, by itself, does not guarantee success; having the necessary infrastructure does not mean a country will adapt in the right way. As Albert Hirschman pointed out in *The Strategy of Economic Development*, most countries possess the basic factors of production. What they lack is something equally important—a *strategy* that calls forth and enlists "for development purposes resources and abilities that are hidden, scattered, or badly utilized."[8] The same is true for increasing pains in the face of import barriers. Although many countries have what it takes to succeed, the key is to find a way to mobilize those resources in the best direction.

Core Policies

Pursuing Long-Run Gains *

Politically motivated protectionism is essentially a refusal to adjust to change.[9] An industrialized country imposes trade restrictions when a loss in comparative advantage creates difficulties for domestic industries and labor. Rarely is protectionism, particularly in the United States, part of an integrated package for positive industrial adjustment. Rather, protecting selective industries is an attempt to force the burden of adjustment onto others.

* Long run and short run are obviously related terms. For the purpose of this analysis they will be defined as they are in the business and economic literature: the short run will refer to a period of time in which certain types of inputs cannot be varied—a period of usually less than a year; the long run will refer to three or more years in the future, when all factors can be varied.

Protectionism, however, is filled with contradictions. It may provide immediate benefits to domestic groups, yet it is "a short-run and ultimately self-defeating alternative to the needed adjustment."[10] Protectionism alone does not foster increased productivity or movement of domestic firms into more dynamic sectors: its objective is to give domestic producers a breathing spell—a chance to operate under conditions of restricted competition. Furthermore, protectionist policies often come very late, with import barriers being implemented only after a market has become stagnant or has gone into decline. As a consequence, protectionism is fraught with dangers for the industrialized nation. Protectionism may actually slow the process of adjustment "by insulating the industry [and labor] from the very factors which encourage it."[11]

The very short-run nature of the industrialized state's policy has its benefits for the developing country. Protectionism is paradoxical: an immediate loss of trading gains for a newly industrializing economy can produce even larger long-term benefits if the country can make adjustments.[12] Firms in the newly industrializing countries are frequently short-run profit maximizers that fail to take into account changing costs and long-run market trends. Moreover, many foreign exporters operate under conditions of imperfect information. This helps to explain why NICs do not always produce an optimal product mix and why they often saturate relatively slow-growth markets in the industrialized nations. Protectionism by the importing nations in these market segments, however, can prod NIC governments to institute corrective policies; jolted by politically motivated, myopic protectionism, an exporting government and its producers can potentially enhance profits if they make economic and political adjustments. By pursuing *long-run gains from trade* rather than relying on short-run market signals, a NIC can facilitate a more efficient allocation of resources while it maintains political stability. If the exporting country can be flexible and make changes to slowly growing markets, while the industrialized nations become entrenched in the status quo, the power of the industrialized country to force others to change can ultimately be used by the NIC itself.

The Political Component. Politically, the best strategy is one of short-term compromise and a willingness to make concessions. Weak countries can occasionally win in a head-to-head confrontation with more powerful states, but such an approach is dangerous. If a NIC pursues a "maximizing strategy," trying to achieve favorable results on all or most of the major issues in contention, it is likely to exacerbate political tensions and damage the bilateral trade regime. A strategy of short-run sacrifices and concessions, on the other hand, is designed to avoid stronger action by the importing nations and to minimize potential losses. Accepting import restraints may appease an importing country's protectionist interest groups and extinguish the fires of a wider-spread protectionist movement. While this policy of accommodation is not meant to achieve desirable new objectives, the alternative—to reject protectionism forthrightly—can have much worse results. As game theory tells us, a weaker party may win in a "one-shot affair," but in a supergame, where the game is repeated, the more powerful actor is likely to carry out its threats.[13] An exporting country may win a single battle by fighting the importer with a maximizing strategy, but it may also lose the war if it stimulates protectionist groups into action.

The essence of a long-run political strategy is to prevent a crisis in the bilateral regime. When an importing state is intent upon protection via an OMA, an exporting nation's refusal can politicize the issue. Higher levels of the importing government must get involved if the domestic industry and/or the importing state's bureaucracy will not allow the issue to die. A crisis can then develop if the industrializing country still rejects the protectionism.

A crisis for these purposes can be defined as "situations in which the basic institutional patterns . . . are challenged and routine responses are inadequate."[14] In some instances, crises can have positive effects on a bilateral relationship. Routine interaction directed by bureaucrats may become rigid and stifling. When elites are able to find common interests in a crisis, they can exploit the situation for mutual gain.

More likely, though, a crisis will damage a weak state's position and the continuance of the bilateral regime. First, NICs have an advantage when dealing with issues in a non-politicized way. The top leadership of a NIC will normally be involved in many stages of the decision making and negotiations. These matters are of great importance to their economy. Meanwhile, lower-level bureaucrats will usually implement an industrialized state's protectionist policy. Under these conditions, an exporting nation has a disparity in authority and potential resources in its favor. According to Annette Baker Fox, Albert Hirschman, and others, the low-level bureaucrats in a big, powerful country are "no match" for determined high-level officials in a weaker country.[15] In a time of crisis, however, elites in an importing country become involved, and this disparity is wiped out.

Second, the most serious consequence of a bilateral crisis is the disruption of the trade regime. In a crisis, the mutual sensitivity that often characterized day-to-day contacts may be lost. When perceptions of conflicting interest dominate, there can be a systematic misinterpretation of motives. If rejecting an industrialized state's demands indeed politicizes the issue, then, according to Keohane and Nye, "the insulation between the structure of the system and the process breaks down: specific quarrels become linked to macro-level arguments about appropriate institutions and permanent arrangements."[16] Instead of limiting sectoral change with short-term sacrifices, a crisis can increase the risk of overall regime breakdown.

The Economic Component. If confrontation were necessary to preserve essential economic interests, it might be a worthwhile risk for the exporting country. But this is in general not the case. Indeed, accepting certain forms of protectionism may in the long run be *beneficial* for the economic development of a NIC. Myopic protectionism—oriented toward short-term political problems—by the importing state can have a twofold impact on bilateral trading patterns: first, it can impede adjustment in the importing country by encouraging production in slow-growth markets; and second, it can serve as a signal to the exporter to allocate resources more efficiently, diversify markets, and upgrade product lines. In the absence of trade barriers, a profitable NIC manufacturer will normally continue production in established product lines until it has fully exploited the available productivity gains; in the short run there is little incentive to shift production.

The calculus of profitability, however, changes with protection. If quantitative restrictions are imposed, exporters will need to sell fewer goods for more money, and will therefore seek to improve the quality of their exports. "Trading up" is standard wisdom in international trading circles, particularly for those exporters that produce low-quality, labor-intensive goods. This effect will be reinforced if controls are imposed on slowly growing market segments but not on more dynamic sectors. In this case, NIC producers will have even stronger incentives to upgrade their exports rapidly, which will be in the long run beneficial to their continued growth. NIC governments, meanwhile, will be able to promote this upgrading by pointing out that the protectionist measures are making these steps necessary in the short run as well as desirable in the long run. Although exporting governments may have planned to upgrade before protectionism, the external stimulus can help NIC leaders overcome any domestic resistance to adjustments as well as accelerate the diversification process. Finally, realizing that future market access is limited, an exporting country will also diversify *market outlets*. Small trading states should have as many markets for their goods as possible, according to classical mercantilism. Another twist in the new protectionism is that it encourages the opening of new markets, which ultimately decreases dependence upon one trading partner.

It is important to mention that this strategy of focusing on long-term gains from trade is not without risks. First, agreeing to accept protectionism should come only when restrictions are inevitable. An importing country may go through the motions of seeking protection to appease domestic interest groups, without ever intending to pursue it. In such a case, concessions by the developing nation would be premature. Second, accepting protectionism in one sector can establish a precedent for restricting other sectors in the future. To increase overall gains, developing states want to avoid a spillover into new sectors. Moreover, if restrictions become more comprehensive, the economic benefits diminish over time; there will no longer be the prospect of diversifying.

These potential dangers, however, do not outweigh the benefits of this approach. It is critical that NICs maintain good relations with major importers. The costs to the exporting nation of the collapse of trade regimes are extremely high. Furthermore, over the long run NICs must be prepared to give up their market share in labor-intensive protected sectors. If their economic growth is to continue, they cannot indefinitely rely on textiles, footware, and similar products in their foreign trade.

Bargaining

The essence of a long-term strategy is to avoid overspecialization, encourage export diversification, and simultaneously minimize political tensions. On the economic front, this is consistent with Schumpeter's conception of industrial growth as involving "creative destruction." Economies must continually adjust, supplanting the old with the new. Yet long-run plans must be consistent with short-term needs. A country cannot simply respond to protectionism by immediately diversifying product mixes and markets. Economies need time to adjust to these changes, and the more severe the short-run dislocations, the harder the long-run adjustment. The dilemma for the NIC is how to meet short-run requirements without jeopardizing long-run objectives.

This dilemma can be resolved for a NIC if an importing state is willing to bargain. Ironically, this is another "advantage" of the new protectionism. In the past, trade barriers in the form of tariffs and quotas were implemented unilaterally, leaving an exporter with little choice. Today, even when a NIC decides that it has to accept a VER or an OMA, it can try to obtain its short-run objectives through the bargaining process. Bargaining allows an exporter to influence the nature of an agreement and therefore reduce the severity of its short-run impact. Bilateral negotiations usually lead to higher import levels, greater flexibility, and more growth than unilaterally imposed programs. Moreover, protectionism can be more restrictive in form than in substance, and effective negotiating can help to assure this result.

The Problems of Negotiations. There are several specific factors that determine whether or not a developing state can reach its export goals. These include: (1) market conditions in the importing country; (2) a product's competitiveness; (3) the base levels of imports and growth factors; (4) the scope of protection—that is, the number of products included in the restrictions; (5) the way the products are defined; (6) the transferability of one restricted good for another—that is, flexibility; and (7) the sanctions against circumvention. Numbers (1) and (2) are necessary conditions for export success, regardless of protection, but they are not sufficient. Assuming these conditions are held constant, all of the remaining factors are important to a developing country's short-term trading prospects. Each is also a direct product of bilateral bargaining.

The problem, of course, is that as weak states, NICs have relatively little leverage. They will often have the least control over the most basic questions, such as the aggregate levels of imports or the scope of protection. Exporters may occasionally be able to stall the negotiations to provide time to raise their export levels and/or stockpile future supplies. Sometimes, threats and retaliations will also work. In a study of trade conflicts between the United States and Latin America, John Odell found that these tactics were relatively successful in a few cases.[17] But in most instances, aggregate numbers are highly visible and are the most obvious target of attack for dissatisfied domestic interests. If a NIC tries to gain significant advantage on these politically sensitive issues—if, in other words, the NIC tries to "win" in the bargaining with a maximizing strategy—it will jeopardize its long-run goals.

This does not mean, however, that industrializing countries are helpless. NICs do not always need to follow a purely accommodating approach. Within the above constraints, NICs can push hard for critical concessions while they control the risk of breakdown. By using a negotiating strategy that might be called a "controlled risk" approach, industrializing nations can reduce the restrictiveness of protection with two bargaining policies.[18] The most important of these negotiating tactics is to try to foster ambiguity in the agreement as well as bargain for flexibility. To supplement this policy, a NIC may be able to link unrelated issues to the negotiations at hand to compensate for possible losses.[19]

Ambiguity and Flexibility. The key to a weak state's bargaining success is to negotiate for loopholes. Appearances can be deceiving in politics. A restrictive arrangement on paper may be an unworkable arrangement in practice. Therefore, the optimal agreement for an exporting state to seek is one that is impermeable and restrictive in form (thus satisfying potential political problems) but porous and unrestrictive in substance—an agreement so filled with loopholes that it is impossible to implement.

In protectionist accords, ambiguity and flexibility are the most desirable loopholes. Ambiguity is the ally of a restricted party because an ambiguous agreement—like ambiguous legislation—is difficult to implement.[20] Ambiguity can conceal substantive differences between governments as well as allow the exporter to ship more goods than interest groups within the importing country are led to expect at the time of an agreement. And unlike negotiating over numbers, bargaining for ambiguity is much easier for an exporting country, particularly in agreements with the United States. Sometimes ambiguity will be mutually agreed upon; at other times it will be an unintended consequence of the bargaining. But if NICs make ambiguity a priority, many issues—particularly technical and complex ones—can be easily clouded in the negotiation process. Furthermore, definitions of products can provide sizable loopholes for exporters. American customs definitions are often so antiquated and/or so complicated that they verge on uselessness. Thus, classification of a shoe as rubber or nonrubber, a fabric as cotton or synthetic, or a television set as an incomplete set or a subassembly can be as important to the eventual export figures as the base levels, growth rates, or numerous other clauses which a NIC cannot control.

Flexibility provisions can have advantages similar to ambiguity. Trade agreements usually include some limitations on switching between categories, borrowing against future quotas, and carrying over unused quotas to future years. When these flexibility clauses are too restrictive, an exporting country may be unable to meet aggregate quotas. If market conditions change quickly, rigid restraints will inhibit effective responses. But generous flexibility will not only overcome these problems, it may also allow an exporter to compensate for low aggregate limits. By borrowing against future years and exploiting various other technicalities, an exporting country can sometimes overship allotments legally and find a great deal of freedom to maneuver. Moreover, like ambiguity, bargaining for flexibility is feasible for a weaker country. In many cases, flexibility provisions are politically less salient than issues such as overall quotas. As John Odell found in his Latin American cases, exporters that mastered technical details frequently achieved positive results.

A variety of opportunities for an industrializing country are built into the bargaining process. As long as NICs do not try to "win" with maximizing strategies or give in too easily with accommodating strategies, they can have a significant impact on the structure of protectionist arrangements. The greater the success of the NICs in blurring the clarity and consistency of a protectionist accord, the less likely the country will suffer short-term losses. And bargaining, even very tenacious bargaining with controlled risk strategies, does not jeopardize long-run goals. It is part of the rules of the game.

The biggest danger of this strategy is that the importing state will later close loopholes, leaving an exporting nation with low quotas and no other compensation. Earlier concessions on overall limits in exchange for flexibility and ambiguity could therefore have a devastating impact. Yet fortunately for the NICs, the technical complexity of most manufacturing trade is too great to plug all the loopholes. Even if agreements become complex and comprehensive in labor-intensive sectors, more loopholes are likely to open up. It is rare, indeed, to find a truly restrictive agreement, completely devoid of some exploitable ambiguity.

Supplemental Policies

Pursuing long-run objectives and bargaining for ambiguity and flexibility are the core of a weak state's strategy because in combination they should always lead to an increase in trade earnings, preservation of the bilateral regime, and a minimally restrictive protectionist accord. Yet an exporting country need not stop here. Under certain conditions, a NIC may be able to link issues, cheat, and mobilize transgovernmental allies to make additional profits. Although these strategies entail higher risks than the core policies and they cannot be used at all times, they can still be useful in supplementing a long-run-oriented, loophole-seeking approach.

Issue Linkage

Reliance on an ambiguous agreement and diversification is not always sufficient for an exporting state's short-term or long-term needs. If bargaining for loopholes does not yield an acceptable accord, then the NIC can try to broaden the arena of negotiation to other issues, with the hope of using leverage from other areas to counterbalance weakness in trade. In the nineteenth century, it would have been inconceivable for weak states to link issues to trading benefits. Under the balance of power system, and British hegemony in particular, force was a real and usable threat in bargaining over trade.[21] Under American hegemony, however, the declining utility of force has strengthened the hand of many developing countries.[22] Militarily powerful states no longer have undisputed control over all issue-areas.

Linkage strategies are nonetheless risky for a NIC. Once an exporter broadens the bargaining agenda, a Pandora's box could potentially be opened, as both sides have the opportunity to introduce new issues into the negotiations. Thus linkages can be profitably pursued only under certain conditions. All other things being equal, the more broadly the importing country defines its interests, outside of narrow protectionist ones, the greater the developing state's potential leverage. When the importing country is a hegemonic state, for instance, it usually identifies its interests with the interests of the trading system.[23] Unlike an importing country that is worried exclusively about its domestic industry or nationalistic goals, a preponderant state will try to avoid a protectionist stigma. Such a state is the most likely to give side payments to cushion the impact of a particularistic policy.

The best linkage opportunities exist when the importing state has strong extracommercial bilateral ties to the exporting country. The United States has military bases, intelligence operations, and other important stakes all over the world. If an industrializing country has a relatively narrow range of interests, and controls one of these vital assets, its bargaining power is increased. The more "powerful" country is more constrained in using its overall capabilities for particularistic gains, and the exporting country has additional bargaining chips for advancing its own interest.

Furthermore, linkages are most likely to succeed during a crisis in the negotiations. Bargaining theorists who study conflictual or distributive negotiating situations have put forth the plausible hypothesis that bargainers will start to search for new alternatives only when negotiations near default.[24] Under normal circumstances, importers and exporters prefer to resolve differences in negotiating positions with a limited agenda. When an impasse is reached, however, both sides will recognize that innovation may be necessary to avoid a stalemate and breakdown. Therefore, crises in a negotiation are a two-edged sword: they risk disrupting the trade regime, but they also provide opportunities for NICs to demand compensation.

Types of Linkages. Two kinds of linkages are beneficial under these circumstances: an exporting state can link outside issues to benefits within the VER or OMA; or it can link outside issues to some form of side payments. For the first type of linkage, a developing state would argue that the industrialized country must moderate its negotiating position to preserve the overall bilateral relationship. This means convincing the importing nation that its demands are so unreasonable that the bilateral regime, military-security ties, and the like would otherwise be damaged. Similar bargaining advantages might be obtained if the developing country can manipulate its bilateral (albeit asymmetrical) interdependence with an importer such as the United States. Export-oriented sectors in America have a great interest in increasing trade with rapidly developing countries—not restricting it. These types of cross-cutting pressures can also provide a linkage possibility.

The second type of linkage uses the same leverage but for different purposes. Domestic politics may constrain the importing government's willingness to compromise on trade restrictions, even if the linkage is convincing. If the importing country insists upon short-run protectionist goals, a linkage strategy could profitably be used by the exporting country for gaining assurances against protectionism in other sectors, obtaining special trading preferences, or demanding unrelated side payments, such as additional military and economic aid.

Although linkages can have highly lucrative payoffs, it must be remembered that linkages are hazardous. In most instances, it requires a developing state to conduct a sort of brinkmanship. Moreover, the conditions for linkages do not remain constant over time. If the global and bilateral commitments of a hegemonic state shrink, there is a greater likelihood that the more-powerful state would use its own linkage strategies, especially if the NIC helps to create the opportunity. Hence, linkages are best used selectively and only as a means of last resort.

Cheating

Once the bargaining has been completed (and assuming an agreement is signed), importers and exporters move into the phase of implementation. Critical questions arise at this point for a weak state. Does the exporting nation have to abide by the terms of a restrictive accord? What alternatives are open to it? What types of opportunities and constraints does a NIC face when pondering the prospects of implementing a VER? Perhaps the most obvious answer for an industrializing state in these circumstances is to "cheat." Yet despite Machiavelli's advice, that "men from obscure conditions . . . have succeeded by fraud alone," cheating has remained one of the most neglected arts in the study of politics.[25]

Cheating can be defined as the evasion of regulations— the achievement of some outcome through a process not explicitly permitted by the rules of the game. Operationally, cheating extends along a spectrum of evasion from legal circumvention to illegal acts clearly specified as improper by an agreement or statute. This definition is broad, but cheating is a multifaceted phenomenon. Even illegal evasion and circumvention are not always possible to identify; what is legal is often a matter of perception. The legality of a particular action in international affairs is easy to identify only at the extremes.

Circumventing restrictions is an ancient art in international trading circles. Dating at least back to the interwar period, exporters and importers have found numerous ways to sidestep bilateral protectionism.[26] One of the easiest forms of evasion is transshipment—exporting to an uncontrolled third party en route to the final destination. Another common method is to substitute a freely exportable or partially finished good for the restricted product. When a cotton product is protected, a producer simply adds a little wool and it is no longer "cotton." Dutch, Swiss, and Belgian exporters were well known for such tactics in the 1930s.

As the methods of restricting and monitoring trade become more effective, the methods of cheating can become more subtle and complex. In international coffee trade, for example, attempts to circumvent export quotas in the 1960s were accomplished with the help of minor technicalities.[27] A shipment of coffee had to be accompanied by "a" certificate of origin to prevent transshipment. The regulations did not specify, however, whether a given certificate had to be valid. Any certificate, even a forged one, was sufficient. In manufacturing trade, cheating can range from commercial fraud (for example, the mislabeling of goods to avoid classification) to establishing assembly facilities in quota-free countries.

Under some conditions, exporters may have little incentive to circumvent quotas. As mentioned in the previous section, prices generally increase under a quota, and the net results may benefit exporters, particularly if these firms have other markets available or can switch part of their capability into more sophisticated products not covered by import restrictions. Incentives to cheat arise when losses from quotas exceed price benefits. Low quotas may lead to underutilized capacity in the short run, inducing firms to cheat temporarily while restructuring production. Or, if there is concern about elasticity of supply, exporters may not receive high enough prices as a result of quotas; in this case, both importers and exporters will have a strong incentive to cheat. Finally, when restrictions become comprehensive, cheating may be the only way to avoid surplus capacity. As one observer commented, "It is economic forces, and not an aversion to the principles of international law, that are at the root of cheating." [28]

Cheating can also be encouraged or tacitly approved by the *restricting party*. The importing country may realize that strict enforcement is oppressive and unfair. At the same time, the more powerful state also recognizes that cooperation is necessary to make a pact work. Cheating can thereby satisfy legitimate grievances of the restricted nation, and simultaneously keep the protectionist system largely intact. As George Kennan noted in his *Memoirs*:

> International political life is something organic, not something mechanical. Its essence is change; and the only systems for the regulations of international life which can be effective over long periods of time are ones sufficiently subtle, sufficiently pliable, to adjust themselves to constant change in the interests and powers of the various countries involved. [29]

If the importing country does not allow the exporting nation to cheat, the exporter may become frustrated and refuse to participate on any level.

While some cheating may be necessary, too much cheating can be dysfunctional. Restrictions are politically passable only if they give the appearance of being successful. Too much cheating will undermine this image and possibly lead to retaliation or crackdowns by the importing state. Instead of reinforcing short-term profits, excessive cheating can result in a more restrictive system. For stability, cheating must remain within bounds. Regimes, treaties, or laws no longer function as a guide to behavior when cheating goes beyond tolerable levels.

Cheating and Reputation. The most prominent constraint against cheating and circumvention in world trade is reputation. A reputation as a cheater in trading issues can have severe political consequences for some exporting countries. A great deal of emotionalism characterizes the debate over protectionism, especially in the United States. Claims about exploitation of cheap labor and unfair competition pervade the arguments. If protectionism is accepted under these conditions to avoid a spillover into other sectors, an exporter's reputation for honesty may be critical in preserving economic peace. Cheating, even in small amounts, can upset a precarious political balance, bringing short-term and long-term strategies directly into conflict.

A reputation for cheating can also affect one's bargaining position. Domestic interest groups may pressure their government to tighten loopholes and enact special monitoring procedures with cheaters. The more the country is thought to cheat, the more restrictive protectionism becomes. The same would be true of a business. When a known shoplifter walks into the store, greater protective measures are likely to be taken.

A cheater's reputation, however, is not without advantages. Known cheaters, for instance, are not always held accountable for their actions. An importing government may think the exporting nation is incapable of controlling individual producers. If the importing country is also unable to limit the cheating, the developing state doubly benefits: it obtains the gains from additional trade, but it is not politically liable. Known *successful* cheaters may also attract business. Importers unable to find producers with quota allocations are most likely to seek out a cheater to obtain the products.

The greatest practical problem with cheating is that the efficacy of the strategy declines over time. Importing countries and their interest groups may learn that their restrictions are inadequate. If this leads to the implementation of more effective sanctions, the costs of cheating will increase for the exporter. The result would be that the short-term benefits of cheating may no longer outweigh the uncertainty associated with getting caught.

To Cheat or Not to Cheat? Interesting moral issues are also raised by cheating. Some people might be inclined to justify the practice on the grounds that industrializing countries are poor relative to the importing nations, or that they have been denied, through the exercise of power, their "natural right" to free trade. Coffee exporters in the 1960s, for instance, asserted that they had a "moral right" to cheat.[30]

Although one might not want to go this far, cheating can be thought of as a sort of ironical justice. The French philosopher Guez de Balzac suggested that "prudence must come to the aid of justice in many things."[31] Cheating in this context is a way for the weak to beat the strong at their own game. It comes in response to restrictive and possibly oppressive states of affairs. Machiavellian prudence was justified as a means for equals to obtain advantage. Cheating, by contrast, provides an opportunity for the *unequal* to *recapture* a relatively small gain.

Mobilizing Transnational and Transgovernmental Ties

In its struggle to shape the form of protectionism, a NIC is not limited to formal diplomatic channels. This is particularly true in the United States, since the American government is rarely united on protectionist issues, and its bureaucracy is relatively open to transnational and transgovernmental contacts. The State Department and Treasury will usually argue for free trade; Labor and Commerce normally insist on import restraints, and when the Special Trade Representative's Office is involved, it often takes a middle ground. Strong lobbying with sympathetic agencies can reinforce bureaucratic splits. Such lobbying can be particularly effective if the NIC forms coalitions with organized domestic interest groups such as trade associations or with multinational corporations.[32]

Transnational and transgovernmental allies can provide numerous services for a weak state. First, transnational alliances can constrain American protectionist policies by exacerbating Congressional–Executive conflicts. Coalitions with free-trade¬s in Congress can affect legislation or limit an administration's freedom of action. Second, transgovernmental ties can exploit differences within the American bureaucracy. If bureaucrats disagree with their government's negotiating position, they can help the exporter by leaking bargaining instructions, arguing for bargaining concessions, and the like. Third, transnational and transgovernmental connections can ease some of the burdens of implementation. Friends in high places can warn of an impending crackdown, thus warding off costly embargoes.

Transnational and transgovernmental lobbying efforts, however, cannot be pushed too far. Dramatic efforts may politicize an issue, strengthening the resolve of higher-level officials. If the importing state's decision makers perceive the foreign government as "meddling" in its internal affairs, it can unite an otherwise divided government. A transnational and transgovernmental approach is best viewed as a supplementary means to other tactics for subtly influencing domestic policy processes.

Summary of Strategy

The strategy for maximizing an exporting country's earnings against protectionism is briefly summarized in table 1.1. The central purpose of this ideal typical set of policies is to hypothesize the relationship between trading gains for a newly industrializing country and politics. The argument is that a long-term-oriented, loophole-seeking strategy, which can be supplemented by other tactics, can exploit the weaknesses in the new protectionism. As long as an exporter has factor mobility and the importer is making protectionist decisions based on short-run political imperatives, it is possible for a NIC to use this strategy to increase its export earnings, preserve its bilateral trade regime, and operate under a minimally restrictive protectionist accord.

Yet few, if any, countries wholly adopt this approach to dealing with the new protectionism. Industrializing nations

Table 1.1 Summary of Exporting Strategy

Context	Strategies	Policies	Benefits	Risks
Core Policies	Pursuing long-run gains	Making political sacrifices and shifting production	Minimizes political tensions, avoids overspecialization, encourages export diversification	Setting precedents
	Bargaining	Negotiating for ambiguity and flexibility with "controlled risk" strategy	Minimizes short-run dislocation, provides loopholes and protectionist "image"	Low quotas, no compensation if loopholes closed
Supplemental Policies	Cross-issue linking	Demanding compensation for restrictions	Provides added long-term and/or short-term compensation	Reversed linkage
	Cheating	Evading regulations	Minimizes short-run dislocations, provides added profits	Sanctions and damaged reputation
	Mobilizing transgovernmental and transnational allies	Reinforcing bureaucratic splits	Fosters importing state's shortsightedness	Fosters importing state's coherence

do not always recognize this strategy as the best one, and not all exporters are sufficiently free from their own domestic political pressures to follow such a bold design.[33] Moreover, the success of the strategy assumes relatively stable markets and technologies as well as a continuing high degree of myopia on the part of the importer. As I begin the empirical study of protectionism in chapter 2, I will take these other factors into account.

Case Selection

Only a handful of studies have systematically examined the new protectionism. The majority of political and economic analyses of NICs and trade barriers have emphasized the negative aspects of VERs and OMAs without delving into the details of sectoral trade. Even in individual sector studies, analysts have examined aggregate trends rather than national performance and bilateral conflicts.[34] Both the record of NICs in confronting protectionism and the process of trade bargaining have been understudied.[35]

To fill this gap, I shall adopt a comparative case study approach.[36] In chapters 2 through 5 I will explore the process of bargaining and the implementation of protectionism in the postwar period using a series of standardized questions.[37] The participants in the cases are the United States and the four major exporters in East Asia: Japan, the Republic of Korea, the Republic of China (Taiwan), and the British Colony of Hong Kong. I chose these countries for both theoretical and methodological reasons. First, the strategy in chapter 1 was designed for NICs that have been subject to protectionist demands by the United States. Since I was drawing on the period between 1955 and 1982, this narrowed the universe of cases to about fifteen nations. Second, I sought countries that succeeded as well as failed to increase their trade earnings in response to import restraints. In other words, I needed variance on the dependent variable. The only nations that potentially fit both the first and the second categories are Japan (in the 1950s and 1960s), Brazil, Hong Kong, Korea, Mexico, Taiwan, and, to a lesser extent, Israel, the Philippines, and Singapore. The four Asian countries were chosen from this group for two important reasons: they are the only states which have maintained competitive capabilities throughout the twenty-five years; and during this period, these countries have been subject to the greatest number of restraints in the most sectors.

The critical variable to control in this analysis is the production and marketing capabilities of a NIC. When an exporting nation has domestic economic difficulties and lacks factor mobility, it is impossible to distinguish between protectionism and an inability to adjust as the cause of a decline in export earnings. These four Asian countries have been the only nations (with the exception of Singapore) that have exhibited a high degree of factor mobility and have consistently (and usually successfully) adapted to American protectionism.

Furthermore, in the 1970s, Hong Kong, Taiwan, and South Korea "are involved in the most sectors and hence have borne the brunt of protectionist pressures."[38] Among the NICs, only Taiwan and Korea have negotiated bilateral export restraints with the United States in several sectors. Brazil and Mexico have been subject to numerous countervailing duty actions and antidumping charges (which are largely technical in nature), but Brazil's negotiating experience on export restraints with the United States is limited to cotton textiles, and Mexico's trade restrictions are principally confined to apparel. Singapore is not considered because it, too, has been subject to relatively few American import restraints.

Hong Kong provides a useful comparison to Taiwan and Korea because it is not under the United States' security umbrella. The Hong Kong case will allow examination of the importance of bilateral ties in modern protectionism to see if allies are treated differently from nonallies, and if so, in what ways.

The case study of Japan was chosen for the historical dimension it will add to the analysis. In 1952, Japan's gross national product (GNP) was one-twentieth of the United States', and its per capita GNP was below that of Brazil, Malaysia, Chile, and other less-developed countries. In addition, during the 1950s and 1960s, Japan was subject to the greatest trade discrimination of all the world's export economies.[39] As noted in the Introduction, the first important VER negotiated after World War II was between the United States and Japan in cotton textiles and apparel. The in-depth study of American–Japanese trade bargaining, however, will end in 1972, even though the studies of the other countries will continue until 1982. Although Japan was no longer a developing country by economic criteria in the late 1960s, its export pat-

terns and protectionist treatment remained relatively constant through the early 1970s. It was not until Nixon termi-
nated the Bretton Woods system in August 1971 that Japan
politically, as well as economically, began to enter the ranks
of industrial nations.[40]

The Sectors
    The four country studies are organized around four prod-
uct sectors: textiles and apparel, footwear, color televisions,
and automobiles. Sectoral analysis is valuable because it will
allow control and study of the effects of technological change
and market structures on policies. For analytical purposes the
studies are further divided into subcases of individual bargaining episodes. Since 1956, American negotiators have bargained with representatives of the Japanese, Hong Kong, Taiwanese, and Korean governments well over fifty separate
times in these industries.[41]
    I chose textiles and apparel because this sector has been
the most important trade issue in each of the bilateral relationships. These products accommodate themselves extraordinarily well to the low-capital and plentiful-labor characteristics of most NICs.[42] As a result, textiles and apparel have at
times dominated the foreign trade of each Asian exporter, occasionally accounting for up to 50 percent of total exports.
As late as 1976, textiles and clothing products represented
44 percent of Hong Kong's exports, 35 percent for Korea, and
28 percent for Taiwan.[43] In addition, the GATT has sanctioned (under certain conditions) the use of unilateral and
bilateral restrictions in cotton textiles since 1961, and in synthetic and wool fibers since 1974.[44] Since textiles and apparel
have the longest history of trade controls in manufactured
products, this sector will be the principal focus for the empirical chapters.
    I selected footwear because it has many of the same char-
acteristics as textiles, such as labor intensiveness and low
capital and technology requirements. Footwear protectionism, however, has a much shorter history. An analysis of the

Table 1.2 Overview of Cases (Values Estimated as High, Moderate, or Low) [a]

Bargaining and Implementation Episodes	Prerequisites		Dependent Variable I		Dependent Variable II
	United States Accommodation	Factor Mobility	(Protected) Sectoral Earnings [b]	Overall Sectoral Earnings [b]	Bilateral Trade Regime
Cotton Textile VERs					
Japan 1956–60	Moderate	High	Low	Moderate-High	High
Hong Kong 1959–61	High	High	High—1960 Low—1961	High—1960 Low—1961	Moderate
Short-Term Agreement					
Japan 1962	High	High	High	High	High
Hong Kong 1961–62	Low	High	Low	Moderate	Moderate
Long-Term Agreement					
Japan 1962–	Moderate	High	Moderate-Low	High	High
Hong Kong 1962–	Moderate-High	High	High	Moderate-High	High
Taiwan 1962–	Moderate-High	High	Moderate-Low	High	High
Korea 1963–	Moderate-Low	Low—1963 Moderate—1964 High—1965	Moderate-Low	High	High
Wool					
Japan 1965	Moderate-High	High	Moderate	High	Moderate
Multifiber VERs					
Japan 1969–75	Low, Moderate, High	High	High 1969–71 Low 1972–75	—	Low
Taiwan 1969–81	Moderate-High	High	High	—	High
Korea 1969–81	Moderate-High	High	High	—	High
Hong Kong 1969–81	Low, Moderate, High	High	High	—	Moderate-High
Footwear OMAs					
Taiwan 1977–81	High	High	High	High	High
Korea 1977–81	High	High	High	High	High

[a] For scoring techniques, see note 45.
[b] Protected sectoral earnings and overall sectoral earnings are the same under the multifiber textile VERs.

footwear orderly marketing agreements negotiated in 1977 with Taiwan and Korea (and the failure to negotiate one with Hong Kong in 1978) will help to determine if strategies and outcomes are comparable across sectors and over time. Finally, I will review briefly the OMAs in the color television industry and the VER in automobiles to illustrate the effects of the new protectionism in very diverse industries.

Out of the more than fifty negotiations in these sectors, I will analyze fifteen in depth. The minimum criterion for considering a case is that an Assistant Secretary or Under Secretary from the United States Commerce or State Department was involved in the decision making. Trade negotiations are often very technical affairs; unless higher-level political actors in the United States participate, one can generally assume the bargaining was of little overall political significance. About 50 percent of the negotiations fit into this category.

The selected fifteen cases represent a sample that has variance on independent and dependent variables. As one can see in table 1.2, American accommodation varied over time, as did the ability of the East Asian countries to increase trade earnings and maintain a stable bilateral regime with the United States.[45] The purpose of the case studies is to determine how much of the variance can be explained by the exporters' strategy.

Chapter 2

Textiles, Round 1:
The Move Toward Protection,
1955–1961

By the end of World War II, the United States had become the leader of the capitalist world and the prime mover behind the search for a more open international trading system. Among other goals, the United States assumed responsibility for breaking down the tariff and quantitative barriers that had been plaguing world trade since the 1930s. But in the summer of 1956, something changed. High-level American decision makers confronted the government of Japan with an unpleasant choice: the Japanese were told either to restrain their exports of cotton textiles or face the possibility of Congress passing quotas on Japanese goods, the spread of state and local boycotts against Japanese textiles, and the implementation of restrictive tariffs, which were likely to be recommended by the United States Tariff Commission.

Neither avenue, of course, was very attractive to the Japanese. On the one hand, textiles and apparel were the highest valued and single most important product Japan traded with the United States (see table 2.1). On the other hand, Japan was hardly in a position to resist. With its major alternative markets effectively closed in Communist China and Europe,

Table 2.1 Japan's Trade with the United States, 1956 (in $ million)

Total exports	$547.5
Total textile and apparel exports	203.8
Cotton textile exports	84.1
Wool exports	30.5
Synthetic textile exports	7.0
Textiles as a percent of total exports	37.0%
Cotton textiles as a percent of total textiles	41.0
Cotton textiles as a percent of total exports	15.3

SOURCE: Hunsberger, *Japan and the United States in World Trade*, p. 264.

the United States was virtually the only open market for its manufactured goods. Approximately 20 percent of Japanese exports were destined for the United States in 1956, and Japan's overall trade with the United States was eight times greater than with any other country.[1] Therefore, with nowhere to turn and great dependence on the American market, the Japanese followed the prudent path: they negotiated an agreement to limit their exports of cotton textiles and apparel for a period of five years. In retrospect, this was a turning point in the history of modern protectionism. This voluntary export restraint (VER) set the precedent for the next twenty-five years of trade restraints.

U.S.–Japan Textile Trade:
Setting the Precedent

American policy toward Japan in the 1950s was defined in the context of the Cold War. The United States wanted a strong Japan after World War II—one that would be a vital link in America's newly envisioned United States–East Asian security system. To that end, the United States sought to give Japan close to "total [economic] freedom" in return for cooperation in the political sphere.[2] The United States supplied Japan with a wide range of benefits, ranging from technological and military aid to cotton and agricultural credits. Furthermore, the two countries' bilateral trading regime stressed benefits favoring Japan. The United States allowed the Japanese to discriminate against American goods with high tariff and quota barriers while simultaneously opening its markets for all Japanese exports.

Why, then, in 1956 did the United States seek to limit Japan's single most important export? The answer can be found in America's domestic politics. Although the American Executive favored free trade and strengthening Japan, general goals can become subservient to particular ones when an interest group is powerful enough to force an exception. This is precisely what happened during the mid-1950s, when the American cotton textile industry suddenly entered the ranks of the most outspoken protectionists.[3] During the late forties and early fifties, textile manufacturers had only grumbled; they had never been a vociferous advocate of import barriers. As Japanese textile import penetration grew, however, American textile producers and unions began to envision a Japanese "invasion" of their market. Although Japanese textile imports represented a small portion of American consumption (approximately 2 percent), in a few categories such as gingham, velveteen, and women's blouses, Japanese sales were reaching two-thirds of apparent consumption and putting some American producers out of business.[4] Manufacturers responded to this loss by seeking protection. Mail flooded the offices of members of Congress from the South and the North alike, charging the Japanese with "unfair competition," "dumping," and "social exploitation."

The textile industry's large work force (over 2.5 million) and its wide geographic distribution meant that it was well endowed to exert pressure on government policy, particularly the Congress. In 1955, the industry proved to be a potent force in American trade politics by almost defeating the renewal of a major trade bill—the Reciprocal Trade Act. Although the textile lobby lost this first protectionist battle, it nonetheless carried the war forward. A variety of industry groups attacked Japanese textiles from every angle: they pressured members of Congress for quotas; they lobbied extensively with individual government agencies; they pleaded with the Tariff Commission for more protection; and they made public speeches in favor of local and state officials who advocated boycotts and rollbacks of Japanese goods. Over time, their efforts showed signs of success, as numerous bills were introduced in Congress that would have imposed quantitative restrictions on Japan's imports.

When the textile industry approached the State Department in mid-1955, it did not find a warm reception. Secretary of State John Foster Dulles insisted that American trade policy had to be integrated into America's overall goals to contain Communism. "Legislation to establish import quotas on Japanese textiles," he said, "would be unfortunate . . . it would serve to restrict trade at a time when the free world must depend for so much of its strength on the expansion of trade and economic viability of countries such as Japan."[5] Dulles was concerned that quotas would lead Japan to seek more trade with Communist China.[6]

Dulles changed his mind, however, when Senator Margaret Chase Smith, an influential voice from the textile-dependent state of Maine, told the Secretary she would support restrictive legislation if Japanese imports were not curtailed.[7] Fearing the implications of congressional action, Dulles concluded that Japan should cut back its exports. In a letter to Senator Smith, dated December 1, 1955, Dulles said, "I have personally advised representatives of the Japanese Government that they should exercise restraint in their exports and not attempt to capture so much of the American market that an American industry will be injured."[8]

The Japanese responded to this "advice" and the spreading adverse publicity with a flurry of activity designed to rationalize their export policy. Late in November 1955, the Ministry of International Trade and Industry (MITI) unilaterally suspended textile exports to the United States. A month later, Japan announced that it would "voluntarily" restrict its shipment of cotton textiles during 1956 to "promote mutually beneficial trade relations between the two countries."[9] Although some categories were to be cut back, this so-called voluntary export restraint actually called for an increase in Japanese sales above the all-time peak of 1955.

The textile industry, however, was by no means satisfied. Early in 1956, textile associations started to file "escape clause" applications with the United States Tariff Commission. According to the Reciprocal Trade Act, an industry that considered itself hurt by tariff reductions could appeal to the Commission to study its situation. If injury was indeed found, the Commission could recommend remedial policies to be taken by the President, who might or might not choose to act on the findings. Escape clause proceedings are troublesome to an exporting country because they add uncertainty to bilateral trade. Exporters and importers are wary of making long-term commitments after an escape clause application is filed, since the final outcome of an investigation can change the rules of the game on sectoral trade.[10]

Protectionism was also spreading to the state and local levels. Legislatures in South Carolina and Alabama passed laws that required retail stores handling Japanese textiles to display a sign at least four inches high that read "Japanese Textiles Sold Here." It was obvious to everyone, especially to the Japanese, that these regulations were designed to hinder, if not prevent, the sale of Japanese products. South Carolina urged other states to pass similar legislation, and this was attempted and narrowly defeated in Georgia, Louisiana, and Mississippi. In addition, there were boycott actions taken by individual communities and retail outlets, from North Carolina to Massachusetts. Boycotts usually involved stores refusing to handle Japanese textiles and advertising the fact in local newspapers.[11] Japan formally protested that these laws violated the Treaty of Friendship, Commerce, and Navigation of 1953, but the State Department did not take concrete action.[12]

To make matters worse, several pieces of legislation designed to limit Japanese imports were introduced into Congress. On May 16, 1956, the Japanese government tried to calm some of the growing tensions by publicly clarifying its voluntary restrictions for that year, and by reducing its voluntary quotas in a few sensitive categories.[13] Yet despite these efforts, the Eisenhower administration found itself increasingly under pressure to provide some relief for the textile industry. On May 17, the government promised "definite and concrete" moves, a promise which was followed a month later by a statement from the Secretary of Agriculture saying he was in favor of quantitative restrictions.[14] On June 28, a Senate motion to impose rigid import quotas on textiles failed to pass by only two votes.

The final decision to negotiate a voluntary restraint arrangement emerged as the only reasonable compromise the American government could find. Quantitative restrictions or tariffs, which would have been the most effective and most satisfactory to the domestic industry, were undesirable to American leaders. Above and beyond the Cold War concerns already mentioned, American government accession to the textile industry's demands could have had far-reaching implications for the General Agreement on Tariffs and Trade (GATT) and America's goal of freer world trade. The United States originally helped design the GATT to achieve free and nondiscriminatory trade; in principle, nontariff barriers, especially quantitative restrictions, were to be abolished and all nations were to adhere to the principle of most favored nation. Three exceptions were to be allowed: quantitative restrictions (QRs) could be maintained for balance of payments purposes; QRs could be used to support certain domestic agricultural programs; and less developed countries were permitted to impose QRs in response to foreign exchange problems or to further economic development.[15] In other words, the purpose of the GATT was to limit the possibility of unilateral action on noneconomic grounds. Ironically, this meant that countries like Great Britain and France could invoke GATT Article XII (QRs for balance of payment reasons) with impunity in the 1950s and early 1960s, whereas the United States had no such legal option. If the United States wanted to pursue this course within the GATT, it would have had to receive Europe's permission. This was a "galling prospect," according to Gerard and Victoria Curzon, because the United States was urging Europe to open its markets to more Japanese goods.[16]

The only viable option that the GATT provided the United States was to invoke Article xix. If a domestic industry was harmed by a tariff cut, a country could alter (with consultation) its past concessions. But even this avenue would not give the United States the right to act unilaterally—it necessitated time-consuming negotiations. Moreover, Article xix did not assure adequate protection; it only allowed for the return to a former level of tariff walls, which was not likely to stop Japanese imports. Thus the United States had the "capability" to erect import barriers, but there were significant international costs for doing so. Import restraints against Japan were contrary to overall American foreign policy goals as well as America's international trading obligations.[17]

The magnitude of these constraints explains why the Eisenhower administration resisted protectionism for so long. But late in the summer of 1956, congressional officials warned that restrictive legislation was going to be pushed through the next Congress—regardless of which party won the 1956 presidential election.[18] In such a case, there would be no guarantee that the restrictions would be limited just to cotton textiles. The domestic textile industry was gaining enough strength, especially combined with other import-sensitive industries, to force a general exception to free-trade policies. Furthermore, the Tariff Commission would soon release its findings; if injury was found, there would be direct pressure on the President to aid the industry. To diffuse this political time bomb, *before the upcoming election*, the idea of the "voluntary export restraint" was put forward.[19] Not only did it seem like the perfect compromise, but there was also a precedent. A VER in textiles had been negotiated with Japan in the 1930s; and then, as now, the VER could avoid stronger congressional action in addition to reducing the movement toward wider-spread protectionism.[20]

When the Americans finally approached the Japanese government, they sought to integrate all of these competing interests. On the one hand, the Eisenhower administration did not want to damage Japan's economy or its overall trade. Yet at the same time, it had to appease the textile industry. Therefore, the administration put together a plan for a comprehensive "voluntary" quota that would cover most Japanese textile exports. The perceived problem for American planners was that Japan was focusing its manufacturing capacity too narrowly on a few goods. Government officials hoped that an extensive export quota system could force the diversification of Japanese product lines and thereby minimize the complaints of any one segment of the domestic industry. The bottom line was that the United States would try to *accommodate* Japan's general needs, but only as long as it could solve the domestic political problem. This meant that on many "sensitive" issues, the United States would not compromise.[21]

Japanese Goals

Not surprisingly, the Japanese government became acutely concerned in 1956 about the prospect of spreading protectionism and its impact on overall United States–Japan relations. The *Japan Times* suggested that the "Japanese side is anxious to . . . go as far as they can without unduly sacrificing the national interest."[22] The Japanese, like the Americans, had a two-fold set of goals: on the one hand, they wanted to assure the maintenance of the bilateral regime with the United States and to preserve broad market access; on the other hand, they felt constrained about how much they could reasonably give up, since textiles were a significant component of their overall trade.[23] Their dominant concern, however, was parallel to that of the United States: they wanted to be accommodating.

On the surface, the prospects surrounding the limitation

of cotton textiles were unsettling. Japan had a balance of payments deficit with the United States, and limiting an export which represented 15 percent of overall trade would surely aggravate the situation. Yet the constraints were not as significant as they first appeared. *Before* the rumbles of American protectionism were heard in Japan, MITI recognized that the world cotton textile industry was declining. Japanese government projections in the Five-Year Plan announced at the end of 1955 confirmed this trend. World consumption of cotton was expected to decline in absolute and per capita terms; Japanese cotton output would therefore drop approximately 11 percent, while exports would fall by 14 percent.[24] Synthetic textiles, in contrast, were designated as a "promising" industry, with consumption and production of synthetics projected to grow by leaps and bounds.[25] Hence, Japanese government planners decided as early as 1955 that there would be a subtle but distinct effort to encourage the diversification of textiles away from cotton and into synthetics. Not only was cotton seen as a dying market, but an emphasis on synthetic fibers would help reduce import dependence, complement the growing Japanese chemical industry, and meet the growing international and domestic demand.[26]

Despite the fact that the Japanese had a certain comparative advantage in cotton textiles, they were willing to take the risk and venture into an untried area. To encourage synthetic production, the government limited cotton textile production, gave loans at favorable rates to synthetic plant expansion, and approved foreign technical assistance contracts. MITI's eight-year plan called for an increase of 118 percent in synthetic fiber production between 1954 and 1963, while cotton was to expand only 2 percent.[27] Furthermore, large companies within the industry were concerned with the poor reputation of Japanese products. Late in 1954, the Japan Cotton Yarn and Cloth Exporter Associations recommended a curb in production of low-quality cloths to force a general upgrading of Japanese textiles.[28]

The Japanese bureaucracy was also well suited to pursue such industrial rationalization in the mid-1950s. Although far from being a "Japan, Incorporated," the Japanese had a relatively coherent policy network at this time. Through the mid-fifties, MITI was extremely powerful in relation to industries such as textiles. MITI issued all licenses, allocated export promotion funds, and had tight control over raw material and international procurements.[29] In addition, the government was effective in using the threat of international intervention (the United States, for instance, imposing unilateral restrictions) to build a consensus around the need for compromise and adjustment.[30] Although the Japanese textile industry had a large number of firms and was by no means easy to control, it grudgingly accepted restrictions as inevitable.[31] The relative concentration of power at the top combined with the shared perception of economic weakness in the first ten years of postwar Japan allowed the government to exercise a high degree of control that would not be exhibited in later years.

Although America's efforts to limit cotton textiles were in many ways consistent with Japan's long-run policies, this did not mean that the two sides were in total agreement. The Japanese did not plan to phase out cotton textiles overnight; they hoped for a gradual decline and the continued contribution of textiles to export earnings. The Japanese saw voluntary restraints as a way to foster the adjustment of their own industry, but they preferred to set the limits themselves in order to minimize the short-run sacrifice. Furthermore, even if a VER was consistent with certain objectives, the Japanese still disliked the idea. According to Leon Hollerman, the Japanese did not find the concept "congenial," it offended their "free-trade" principles, and they were uncomfortable with the discriminatory aspects.[32] A bargaining range clearly existed between the United States and Japan, but there were areas of substantial conflict that would not be easily solved.

The Negotiations

Setting the Agenda. In the early stages of the negotiations, the Americans and the Japanese quickly agreed on two points. First, some type of restraint was necessary to prevent greater damage to United States–Japan relations and overall Japanese trade. Second, they agreed that the exports should be controlled from Japan. America would not have to shoulder the burden of violating the GATT, and it would be easier for Japan to force textile adjustment. The Japanese wanted to use these restraints to shift from quantitative growth to qualitative improvements in cotton products.

Beyond these common interests, however, there were substantial conflicts. The initial American proposal called for the rollback of Japanese exports and for "several hundred" types of cloths and fabrics to be under separate quota.[33] The Japanese, on the other hand, originally sought a "gentlemen's agreement"—one similar to its present arrangement that would informally restrict exports with as few specifics as possible.[34] Both sides eventually scaled down their demands and issued a compromise agenda on September 27, 1956. In a carefully worded statement, the United States officially requested from the government of Japan "plans for future controls." In response, the Japanese reaffirmed their desire for export diversification. Emphasizing the "voluntary" nature of the discussion, Japan acceded to the American demand that the agreement be more concrete than the restraint program of the previous year. In addition, the Japanese agreed to use the 1955 level of exports as a base, which would be accompanied by specific reductions in the most sensitive areas.

These concessions, however, came with a price. The Japanese insisted, and the Americans agreed, that such a plan would be implemented only if the United States government took "all feasible steps . . . to solve the problem of discriminatory state textile legislation and to prevent restrictive action with regard to the importation of Japanese textiles into the United States."[35] For the Japanese this linkage confined the areas of protectionism from the outset, limited future spillovers, and safeguarded long-run interests.[36] The Americans would not make any promises earlier in the process because it would have offended the textile lobby; moreover, it was precisely the threat of restrictions that the negotiators used as their leverage.[37] Yet once an acceptable solution could be found, it was in the United States' interest to prevent further restrictions. Presidential assistant Sherman Adams defended the principles of the agreement as the "best arrangement possible." As part of the administration's efforts to legitimize the policy, Adams said that he could not see how a "better plan could be negotiated with another country."[38]

The Bargaining. Once the agenda was outlined, several issues remained in contention. First, what were the 1955 levels of trade, and what would be appropriate for the aggregate limit in 1957? Second, which items were to receive specific ceilings and at what levels? Third, how long would the agreement last? And fourth, how much flexibility would Japanese exporters be given?

Initially, both sides hoped that the differences could be rapidly resolved. On October 3, 1956, the Japanese Finance Minister, Ichimada, said that the consultations could bring a quick end to the textile problem. Ichimada felt that "relations between the United States and Japan are so important, we should avoid creating any appearance of controversy."[39] Unfortunately, this hope was shattered when the Japanese presented their first proposal; the scope of the disagreement appeared vast.[40] The Eisenhower administration was in the midst of a presidential campaign. American officials wanted symbolic concessions from the Japanese, particularly in weak market segments, to "ease pre-election pressures."[41] But many small- and medium-sized Japanese producers had invested heavily in specialized equipment for producing the most sensitive items (such as gingham and velveteen). These firms as well as industry associations were thus pressuring their government for high quotas. There was little room, therefore, for compromise and few acceptable tradeoffs.

In an attempt to narrow the difference, the United States used several sticks and one carrot to influence Japan's position. First, immediately following the September agreement,

Eisenhower invoked the "Geneva wool-fabric reservation." By increasing the *ad valorem* rate of duty applying to most woolen and worsted imported fabrics, the President sought to appease domestic producers and to convince the Japanese that the United States was willing to act unilaterally.[42] Second, the Tariff Commission announced in mid-October that it was recommending a substantial increase in the tariff on velveteen. The administration remained strategically silent about what action it would take. It left open the possibility of a tariff increase in case the Japanese would not come to terms. Lastly, the State Department took no concrete steps to prevent local discrimination against Japanese goods. The only carrot offered by the Americans was an Executive Order to postpone another Tariff Commission hearing from late October to early December. This was done for the expressed purpose of allowing time for a "solution with Japan."[43]

The problem was that even if Japan wanted a compromise, international and domestic pressures made Japanese officials increasingly defensive. After Japan had agreed in principle to a VER with the United States, Canada and West Germany inquired about the possibility of similar arrangements. In addition, pressure from the Japanese textile industry for high quotas made it difficult for the Japanese government to formulate a consistent and flexible bargaining strategy. Textile analysts in Japan were insisting that local firms did not have the productive capacity to expand their quantitative share of the United States market at that time.[44] Yet instead of negotiating for the critical concessions that would minimize short-run dislocations—that is, how the categories were to be broken down and what flexibility provisions would be provided—the Japanese government bargained most vigorously over the areas of greatest importance to the American government.

In November, the Japanese finally lowered some of their demands in response to American pressures.[45] Meanwhile, Tokyo's ability to influence Washington was very limited. Japan's negotiating tactics consisted largely of technical persuasion, as Japanese experts argued that American statistics were inaccurate. Since the Americans remained unconvinced, the negotiations stalled. Each side continued to submit new plans, but the same issues were repeatedly left unresolved. On November 27, the Japanese threatened to break off the negotiations unless the United States showed some degree of compromise.

In response to this threat, the Americans softened their stance. They finally recognized that their demands were beyond Japanese tolerance. In an attempt to break the deadlock, the United States proposed a higher aggregate total and asserted its willingness to accept a higher limit for velveteen, if the government of Japan would agree to scale down the quota for 1958.[46] Yet this was still unsatisfactory to Japan. Japanese negotiators told the Americans that they could not justify to their industry reduced quotas after 1957. In addition, they were concerned over the velveteen tariff decision and a few clauses in the American draft agreement.[47]

The impasse reached a head around December 18. The Japanese and the Americans were in agreement on most of the substantive issues, but the Japanese wanted to wait until Eisenhower disclosed his position on the Tariff Commission recommendation to increase the tariff on velveteen. The President was committed to making such a decision by December 23. The Japanese said that an affirmative decision by the White House would defeat the entire purpose of the VER.

Japan's growing obstinancy during this period can be partly attributed to a process of transition going on *within* its own government. Bureaucratic differences were constraining the bargaining: the Foreign Ministry was anxious to settle the controversy, but MITI was taking a maximalist position.[48] Resolving these conflicts became problematic when Prime Minister Hatoyama announced his retirement in late November 1956. This complicated the bargaining because MITI Minister Ishibashi was the front runner for the Prime Minister's post. In addition to favoring a forceful position on textiles, Ishibashi was known for his interest in promoting Japanese trade with the People's Republic of China. Therefore, when Ishibashi won the election for Prime Minister in December, a new set of issues suddenly entered the negotiations.

There was growing apprehension in the American State Department that the Japanese would not follow through with the VER if Eisenhower approved the tariff increase on velveteen—a perception that the Japanese sought to reinforce.[49] One source said that Japan would consider "other steps" if the tariff was raised.[50] The linkage was never made explicit, but it was clear that these "other steps" included a price war to undercut the tariff and increasing trade with Communist China.[51] Ishibashi stated that he would honor America's ban on strategic material exports to China but noted that "textiles do not normally come under that category."[52]

The Decision Phase. On December 21, Eisenhower postponed the tariff decision to avoid a rupture in the negotiations. Although he left open the possibility of a tariff increase if negotiations broke down, his action ended the miniature crisis and sent both sides back to the bargaining table. Within a short period of time, the major issues appeared to be settled. The Japanese accepted an American compromise for an aggregate limit of 235 million square yards; and the United States compromised on a 3.5 million square yard figure for velveteen for 1957 and a 2.5 million limit for 1958. Essentially, the differences were split down the middle. Gingham also was set at a compromise figure, which left only technical details to be worked out.

During Japan's ten-day year-end holiday, however, disaster struck. Someone in the Japanese government leaked the tentative agreement to industry officials and the Tokyo News Service.[53] The leak provoked massive criticism from both sides. The American textile industry, in particular, was unhappy with a report that its government had promised to veto the velveteen tariff, and the industry had expected the aggregate limit to be closer to 200 million square yards.[54] On January 3, 1957, industry leaders told Sherman Adams that the velveteen limit was unsatisfactory.

The news leak forced the American government to revise its position. Suddenly the domestic constraints on the negotiations had changed, and the legitimacy of the government's policy had temporarily broken down. Since the industry would not be appeased by the agreement, a stiffer quota would be necessary.[55] American officials then lowered a "Cotton Curtain" over the talks and called the Japanese ambassador to the White House.[56] Sherman Adams told the Japanese ambassador that the 3.5 million figure for velveteen was no longer acceptable following the Japanese press leak, and Japan would have to accept a 2.5 million square yard quota in its place.

The Agreement

On January 16, 1957, the Departments of State, Commerce, and Agriculture released a joint statement concerning the "details of the Japanese program for the control of exports of cotton textiles to the United States." The communiqué emphasized the "voluntary" nature of the package and the "constructive" contribution it would make to overall United States–Japan trade relations. On the one hand, the magnitude and explicitness of the new restrictions were somewhat severe compared to the restraints of the previous year. The overall quota, as well as several categories, was cut sharply, and a large number of specific items were to be separately restricted for the first time. A more serious problem was that flexibility was limited. The arrangement provided only 10 percent variance between categories, and no provisions for exceeding the aggregate total. Moreover, the agreement was quite explicit about circumvention and the possibility of future reductions if there were "excessive concentrations" or "changing conditions."

On the other hand, the scope of the agreement critically omitted any mention of synthetic or wool fabrics.[57] In addition, the side payments accompanying the accord were among the most important benefits. Several days after the news release, the Eisenhower administration assured the Japanese that it would oppose any attempt by Congress to implement quotas.[58] Although an explicit connection to the VER was denied, this was a welcome assurance to the Japanese, because numerous new quota bills had been introduced in Congress since early January. Furthermore, the VER met most of the industry's proclaimed needs.[59] Therefore, the agreement was highly successful from the Japanese perspective on those questions concerning their long-run trading objectives. But at the same time, it was relatively restrictive and unsuccessful on matters related to their short-term trading requirements.

Implementation and Adjustment

The first important test of the VER came on January 22, when Eisenhower formally rejected the Tariff Commission's recommendation for higher duties on cotton velveteen imports. The President explicitly noted that Japan's willingness to restrain "voluntarily" its exports would provide the industry with all its needed relief.[60] In addition, in early February, the Georgia State Senate, responding to pressure from Washington, postponed consideration of a bill that would have required merchants to display special signs similar to those in South Carolina and Alabama.

Yet some concern was expressed by the American textile industry that Japanese exporters could easily cheat on these arrangements—a concern shared by the Japanese government. On the American side, the Commerce Department indicated that it would check on compliance; on the Japanese side, the government instituted a stringent program for controlling exports. Japan's decision makers were highly sensitive about allegations of cheating. During the 1930s, Japan had a notorious *reputation* for ignoring international trading regulations. Its alleged transgressions included violating copyrights, using false marks of origin, and sudden flooding of markets to destroy competition.[61] The result of these prewar misdeeds was widespread discrimination against Japanese goods throughout the 1950s. Since the purpose of the VER was to assure that the same thing would not happen in the United States, the Japanese sincerely wanted to prevent further cheating.[62] In addition, the Japanese government wanted the VER to force producers to upgrade and diversify poor-quality and inferior goods. Officials noted that inadequate enforcement of restraints "can lose not only good friends, but valuable markets as well."[63]

The structure of Japan's textile industry was also well suited for a system of export controls. A few large firms exercised a great deal of influence in textile production and to a limited extent in clothing manufacture. Through the help of trade associations, the government set up an allocation system to maximize orderly marketing and minimize the balance of payment problems. Initially, allocations to individual exporters were based on a producer's previous quantities or market share. Over time, however, the Japanese became more sophisticated. Thirty percent of the allocation formula became based on price or the income generated from textile sales. This gave exporters an incentive to sell goods at a maximum price to maintain or increase their individual quotas; it also guaranteed that the artificial limitation on quantity would not damage Japan's export earnings. Furthermore, the government provided strong incentives for companies to fill their quotas. Heavy penalties were to be assessed on all manufacturers that were unable to dispose of their allotment (either alone or through subcontracts).[64]

Despite these adjustments, the quota took a toll in its first year. In 1957, Japanese cotton exports dropped from their 1956 high of $84 million to $66 million. Part of the reason for this decline can be attributed to a recession in the United States, which led to a decline in all United States cotton imports and domestic production. Japanese world exports of cotton textiles nonetheless increased as the manufacturers expanded their markets in Asia, Africa, and Europe, and shifts into wool and synthetic exports to the United States partially offset the quota's effect (see table 2.2). Finally, there were a few administrative difficulties that worked in Japan's favor, and despite the government's efforts, unauthorized transshipments occurred. Both in gingham and velveteen—the major issues of contention during the negotiations—Japan shipped over 120 percent of its quota in 1957.[65] Japan acknowledged the existence of the transshipments, but refused to count them against the quota. In addition, the United States later discovered that Japan was not charging certain exports to its gingham quota

Table 2.2 United States Imports from Japan, 1956–61 (in $ million)

	1956	1957	1958	1959	1960	1961
Textile fibers and manufactures	$203.8	$189.9	$201.2	$266.0	$297.2	$238.8
Cotton manufactures	84.1	65.7	71.7	76.9	73.4	69.7
Wool manufactures	30.5	34.4	41.5	55.6	67.6	57.2
Silk	62.6	61.8	55.2	77.8	75.6	59.1
Synthetic fibers and manufactures	7.0	8.6	11.2	29.0	33.5	27.6
Overall Imports	547.5	602.2	674.0	1018.0	1126.5	1075.9

SOURCE: Hunsberger, *Japan and the United States in World Trade,* p. 264.

because of definitional ambiguities. Thus, in an ironic way, Japan got most of what it had failed to achieve in bargaining by *unintentional* cheating.

Late in 1957, Japan used the consultation process provided in the VER to seek an upward revision of the quota. Given the transshipment problem and lingering protectionist sentiment (twenty protectionist bills were introduced into the 85th Congress), the Japanese government decided not to press the issue. The Japanese government also learned that it needed to appeal more directly to American public opinion and to lobby with members of Congress.[66] This led to creation of the United States–Japan Trade Council—the first official transnational organization sponsored by the Japanese government for the explicit purpose of actively lobbying in America. The Council was designed "so that the Japanese can grasp beforehand the moves to impose restrictions on Japanese goods in the United States and to study appropriate countermeasures."[67]

During 1958, the end of the recession in the United States brought an increase in cotton imports from all sources and a renewed effort by Japan to obtain an increase in its quota.[68] MITI, however, had not learned from its previous bargaining experience that flexibility and ambiguity were the critical variables. Japan had not reached its overall quota limits in 1957 and 1958, and transshipments had accomplished many of Japan's bargaining goals. Nonetheless, in the renegotiations MITI emphasized the same issues on which it had failed two years earlier: it asked again for an increase in aggregate totals and higher quotas for velveteen and gingham.

Similar to the 1956 negotiations, the Japanese side was constrained by domestic pressures and splits between the Foreign Ministry and MITI. Tactics, however, differed. MITI warned the Americans that unless Japan received an increase in the aggregate total, some "unscrupulous Japanese traders might be encouraged . . . to exploit loopholes in the present arrangement."[69] After four months of bargaining, the two sides eventually agreed to a 5.2 percent increase in total shipments, but at the price of substantially reduced flexibility.[70] The benefits barely exceeded the costs; the reduction in flexibility made it harder for Japan to fill their quotas in the remaining years. There were few other significant changes during the life of the quota, and as table 2.2 illustrates, Japanese cotton textile exports remained relatively constant through 1961.

Evaluation

The Japanese agreement to a voluntary export restraint in 1957 was the key to keeping exports flowing within politically tolerable limits. There seems to be little doubt that "textiles, especially cotton textiles, were by far the most important single apprehension creator among Japanese exports" to the United States market.[71] The consensus among Japanese experts and political analysts of the day is that if there had been no VER, the outcry and restrictions against Japanese goods would have been much worse. The Japanese kept their trade regime largely intact by making political and economic compromises. At the end of the fifties, Japanese imports generally and cotton textiles specifically were no longer a hot political issue. The ultimate success of the VER was to defuse an explosive problem and to achieve an acceptable political outcome without unreasonable economic damage. For example, while American producers had filed four escape clause applications in the first six months of 1956, not one application was submitted for three years after 1957.

The essence of Japan's economic strategy during this period was to guide its firms toward *long-run gains* from trade and shifting market dynamics.[72] Despite the fact that cotton exports to the United States suffered as a result of the VER, Japan successfully diversified into growing markets. Between 1956 and 1960, overall textile earnings averaged 9.9 percent compounded growth. Exports of synthetic products increased by almost 400 percent, as wool shipments nearly doubled (see table 2.2). In addition, a decline in cotton exports was likely, regardless of restrictions. As market demand rose in synthetic fibers, Japanese firms increasingly de-emphasized their cotton textile exports on a worldwide basis. Cotton production in Japan decreased from 35.3 percent of total textile production in 1958 to 26.9 percent in 1962. Ironically, the VER accelerated the movement toward synthetics, which was indeed the most dynamic market segment. Finally, and perhaps most important, overall Japanese gains from trade increased dramatically during this period. Despite the threat of widespread protectionism in 1956, the value of Japanese exports to the United States *doubled* by 1961.

Japan lost in its short-run gains from cotton textiles for two important reasons. First, the Americans outbargained the Japanese in the negotiations over the voluntary restraints. The Japanese negotiators did not sufficiently appreciate the subtleties of negotiating these arrangements. Moreover, their own domestic political constraints limited Japanese ability to formulate a completely coherent, and internally consistent, bargaining strategy. Secondly, Japan's former reputation for cheating, and its decision makers' fear that circumvention would bring retaliation, compelled the government forcefully to implement the restrictions. Low levels of cheating had rel atively minimal costs, but large-scale cheating was politically out of the question.

What disturbed Japanese officials and textile manufactur- ers most in the late 1950s was their *relative loss* in the Amer- ican market (see table 2.3). Other producers quickly capital- ized on Japan's restraints after 1957. Its market share of American imports in cotton cloth, for example, declined from

Table 2.3 United States Imports of Cotton Manufactures, 1956–61 (in $ million)

	1956	1957	1958	1959	1960	1961
Total Cotton Manufactured						
Imports	154.3	132.2	150.0	201.3	248.3	203.3
Japan	84.1	65.7	71.7	76.9	73.4	69.7
Hong Kong	0.7	5.8	17.4	45.8	63.5	47.0
Other Asian countries	15.3	13.0	14.3	24.0	34.0	25.0
Egypt	0.4	0.5	0.3	0.3	5.9	1.0
Spain	0.3	0.3	0.4	1.6	7.2	3.2
Portugal	0.0	0.1	0.3	1.0	5.2	2.3

SOURCE: Hunsberger, *Japan and the United States in World Trade*, p. 325.

over 70 percent in 1956 to 35 percent in 1961.[73] In effect, the Americans were holding down Japanese cotton exports while they allowed other foreign competitors free access to the United States market. To rectify the situation, American offi- cials returned to the concept of the voluntary export restraint. It had worked so well in one case that American officials thought it might work again. Since Hong Kong was the larg- est new entrant into the market, it was the most obvious tar- get for restrictions.

The American Failure with Hong Kong

The Americans opted for a VER with Hong Kong in 1959–60 for almost the identical reasons that they had pursued restrictions against Japan: domestic interest groups were pressuring for quotas and finding congressional support, but international obligations limited unilateral action. American imports of cotton textiles rose by over 50 percent in the two years following Japanese restraints, and Hong Kong accounted for almost 25 percent of the increase. Not surprisingly, the textile industry did not remain quiescent about the situation. Late in 1958, Senator Pastore of Rhode Island responded to industry pressure by establishing a special subcommittee to investigate the problems of domestic textiles. During the two months of hearings, textile and apparel manufacturers used this public forum to launch a fierce attack against imports. Although Japan was still their central target, Hong Kong had become the most important threat to the United States textile and apparel industry.

When the subcommittee recommended quotas for textiles, the Eisenhower administration was reluctant. Such action would still contradict America's commitment to free trade; and QRs would still violate the GATT. Therefore, a "voluntary" export restraint seemed to be the perfect compromise, again. The United States could build on the precedent it had set with Japan; moreover, Hong Kong had a precedent of its own. During 1958, Hong Kong's cotton textile industry negotiated a VER with the British textile industry—an arrangement which had striking similarities to America's agreement with Japan.[74] Domestic cotton textile producers in England were pressuring their government for quantitative restrictions on imports. London nonetheless preferred bilateral arrangements as a way to maintain the basic principles of free trade within Commonwealth countries. At the same time, Hong Kong eventually agreed to the voluntary restraint measures because it feared the British might impose unilateral quotas.[75] American officials hoped that Hong Kong would see yet another voluntary restraint agreement in its interest.

For the United States, however, there were significant differences between negotiating an agreement with Japan and negotiating an agreement with Hong Kong. Patron–client relationships, such as the United States–Japan case, have a dialectical nature. On the one hand, a patron has responsibilities to its clients. The United States wanted to build up Japan's economy and provide the Japanese with economic benefits in return for political services. On the other hand, a patron also has a wide spectrum of tools available to influence its clients' policies. The United States provided Japan with military, economic, and political goods that could be easily (and subtly) manipulated to extract concessions. A client stands to lose as well as gain in relations with a patron state.

Table 2.4 Hong Kong Exports, 1958–60 (in $ million)

	1958	1959	1960
World exports	$495.0	$543.0	$656.0
Exports to United States	54.0	98.0	136.0
Textile exports to United States	24.3	64.0	84.7
Cotton textile exports to United States	17.4	45.8	63.5
Cotton as percent of total exports to United States	32.2%	46.7%	46.7%
Cotton as percent of total textile exports to United States	72.0%	71.0%	75.0%

SOURCES: United Nations, *Yearbook of International Trade Statistics, 1960; Hong Kong Trade Statistics, 1959.*

Since Hong Kong was not a client of the United States, it did not receive the same American benefits as Japan, nor was it as vulnerable to pressure. The United States did not have security ties with Hong Kong as it did with other states in East Asia; and Hong Kong was not as dependent as Japan upon American markets. Hong Kong exported only 11 percent of its total exports to the United States in late 1958, when the first demands were made for voluntary restraints (see table 2.4). By comparison, Japan exported almost 20 percent of its products to America in 1956. Therefore, the United States lacked some of the basic tools required to pressure Hong Kong into a voluntary restraint agreement.

The United States bargaining position was also weakened by two additional factors. First, American policy toward Hong Kong was not constrained by bilateral considerations as it was with Japan, but Hong Kong did play a role in America's global, strategic objectives. Hong Kong provided a home for refugees from the People's Republic of China, and Hong Kong was the most accessible location for collecting intelligence on the Communists. Second, Britain provided Hong Kong with a small measure of commercial protection. Although Hong Kong was largely an autonomous actor in international economic relations, the United Kingdom has always tried to prevent discrimination against the colony. In other words, Hong Kong's patron would usually intervene on its behalf if there were serious threats to Hong Kong's trade.

Finally, the ideological orientation of Hong Kong's entrepreneurs and government officials distinguished negotiations with Hong Kong from bargaining with most other nations. Business and government officials alike in Hong Kong perceived the colony as a bastion of free trade and market capitalism. In the principle, they were strongly opposed to trade barriers, of any kind. Furthermore, the colonial bureaucracy did not intervene in the economy or attempt to plan it. Unlike the Japanese bureaucracy, Hong Kong's government was not concerned with long-run gains from trade or with forcing diversification. Thus despite the apparent precedent, despite the apparent logic for voluntary restraints from the United States' perspective, and despite the apparent disparity in power, Hong Kong was not likely to be a willing subject. Even the United Kingdom had had difficulty bringing its own colony into line.

American Goals

When the United States sent its first delegation to Hong Kong, its goals were quite modest. Lacking leverage, the United States could not deal with Hong Kong in the same way it had handled Japan in 1956. There were no boycotts of Hong Kong goods, congressional legislation was not a strong possibility at that time, and there were few broader values (such as the bilateral trade regime) at stake. Officials in the Commerce Department felt that Hong Kong was making the same mistake that Japan had made a few years earlier—it was concentrating too narrowly on a small number of exports. Hence America's initial objective was cooperation from Hong Kong officials in fostering the diversification of cotton products. With no real alternative available, the United States was offering a generous form of accommodation.

Hong Kong Goals

It is difficult to specify a unified set of goals for Hong Kong, because in 1959 there was no single organization that clearly represented the colony. Hong Kong's economy may be the freest on the planet.[76] The government had a minimal role in domestic economic activity, and unlike Japan, Hong Kong had no centralized bureaucracy for directing trade. Therefore, it was more important for Britain and the United States to negotiate with various private associations, such as the Chamber of Commerce and the Hong Kong Garment Manufacturers Union, than it was to deal with the government. Particularly in the late 1950s and early 1960s, colonial officials often abided by the majority will of the business community, and most of the time this meant maintaining a strong laissez-faire and free-trade orientation.

Before the United States Assistant Secretary of Commerce, Henry Kearns, first visited Hong Kong on February 13, 1959, the consensus among the government and business elite was that any American offer should be rejected with a "loud and emphatic No."[77] Already unhappy with their voluntary restraint with Britain, Hong Kong textile manufacturers were convinced that any concession to the United States would invite similar demands from other countries.[78] Furthermore, the United States was their most promising market. With the British market limited, Hong Kong textile producers worried about attempts to "nip in the bud Hong Kong's developing trade with the United States."[79] Hence, Hong Kong had little interest in even talking with the United States.

The Negotiations: Round 1

Agenda Setting 1. The outcome of the first round of negotiations reflected the great disparity in goals—the two sides could not agree upon an agenda. Assistant Secretary Kearns tried to reassure Hong Kong business executives that the purpose of his trip was simply to "meet merchants and manufacturers to discuss possible common ground."[80] Kearns asserted that he had no preconceived plans; he wanted only to discuss with Hong Kong on a "friendly basis" its need for diversification. The essence of Kearns' message was that unless the Hong Kong Chinese diversified, there would be rising domestic pressures in America for restrictions. Since the colony was a relative newcomer in United States textile trade, Kearns emphasized that Hong Kong would be the big loser.

Although the Hong Kong Chamber of Commerce said it would consider Kearns' proposals, the Hong Kong Cotton Spinners Association, the Chinese Manufacturers Association, and the most important textile organization in the American trade, the Hong Kong Garment Manufacturers Union, all flatly rejected American overtures. The Spinners Association said that it was certain that the United States would not limit Hong Kong exports because the United States was "imbued with a spirit of fairness."[81] And the Garment Union stated that "for the present we have chosen not to believe that the United States government would, in the interest of perhaps some short-sighted garment business in the states, adopt any measures which would lead to curbing the imports of Hong Kong-made goods."[82]

The results of the three days of talks were negligible. Kearns communicated American demands for diversification, but a bargaining range never existed. The United States had nothing to offer Hong Kong besides vague threats. Kearns himself recognized this fact. When asked about his opinion of the various Hong Kong statements, Kearns said that he was not the least bit surprised. He added that under similar conditions, he would have reacted in the same way.[83]

Upon his return to the United States, Kearns expressed "cautious optimism" about the problem of Hong Kong's overconcentration. But such hopes were more for public consumption than what Kearns actually believed.[84] In the months following Kearns' Hong Kong visit, it was business as usual in the Far East. In fact, the British colony increasingly focused on the United States as its principal textile market. By April, Hong Kong's exports were rising at a rate double the previous year's quantity and value.

The rapid expansion of Hong Kong's market penetration put American officials on the defensive. Domestic pressures were building again for import barriers. The Commerce Department countered the textile industry's charges by arguing that the negotiations with Hong Kong "did not flop."[85] Kearns even met with retailers and importers to urge them to use moderation in buying Hong Kong goods. Frustrated that the United States could do little with regard to Hong Kong, the Assistant Secretary tried to shift the blame for the overconcentration problem away from the colony and onto the importers.[86]

While American domestic politics were building a new case for import barriers, Hong Kong domestic politics were breaking up the united stance against voluntary export restraint. In the summer of 1959, certain groups within the Hong Kong textile industry began to see the "wisdom" of the American position. Internal discussions were held among several leading manufacturers in Hong Kong about the concept of "orderly marketing." The rapid growth in textile trade was heightening competition among local Hong Kong manufacturers. The fierceness of the competition was driving up wages (as the demand for skilled workers grew), increasing the prices of raw materials, and reducing profit margins drastically. Large firms and importers felt that voluntary restraints could act as an incentive to diversify orders and counter this "overcompetition."[87] In addition, these manufacturers began to understand the political value of a VER. It was suggested that a self-imposed ceiling might "pacify" "those Americans" complaining about the growth of Hong Kong sales. The Secretary of Commerce for the colony, Frederick Mueller, reinforced this position when he warned that "with 1960 a U.S. election year, there was little chance of the issue remaining dormant for long."[88]

The few positive signals which emanated from some Hong Kong firms late in the summer of 1959 led Assistant Secretary Kearns to predict that Hong Kong would voluntarily restrict its textile exports within two months. Yet not everyone in the Hong Kong textile community agreed. Big firms stood to gain from limiting exports, but the vast majority of small firms were profiting handsomely from the status quo. Orders contracted with small companies had them booked to capacity for over ten months in advance. An export restraint would hurt the small firms, in particular, because they were the newest entrants into the market, and export allocations would be based on historical market shares. In addition, the VER with Britain was not operating as most exporters expected. This experience left many manufacturers in Hong Kong wary of negotiating a similar arrangement with the United States.[89]

Before the second round of negotiations began in November of 1959, both the United States and Hong Kong initiated new policies that would have an important impact on the eventual outcome. First, the Hong Kong Chamber of Commerce decided that it needed more information about American trade politics. Therefore, it established its first *transnational* contacts in Washington; the law firm of Covington & Burling was put on retainer to help Hong Kong avoid import restrictions. The firm was responsible for investigating all problems which might lead to the creation of import barriers and for advising the colony on the proper course of actions.[90]

Second, only one week before Kearns' second visit, President Eisenhower ordered the United States Tariff Commission to investigate the desirability of imposing a penalty fee on cotton textile imports made of American-grown cotton. For several years, the United States had paid an eight cent per pound subsidy to exporters of raw cotton. Domestic textile manufacturers complained bitterly that the United States was subsidizing foreign production. Kearns hoped that the threat of a penalty would enhance his bargaining leverage and put a halt to some of the textile industry's incessant demands.

The Negotiations: Round 2

The American strategy remained more or less the same for the second round of negotiations. Kearns emphasized that Hong Kong did not need to reduce its export levels, but it did need to diversify and have more "orderly marketing."[91] The only difference between the American goals in February and the American objectives in November was that the United States could no longer afford to be as generous or as accommodating. Hong Kong exports had registered sharp gains in 1959; in some categories, such as cotton shirts, Hong Kong accounted for 50 percent of the imports into the United States.[92] Kearns also had no authority to offer guarantees or promises that his government would not impose tariffs, penalty fees on cotton, or other controls after a Hong Kong VER. The United States may have been demanding less of Hong Kong in 1959 than it had of Japan in 1956, but it also had less to give in return. Thus despite America's accommodating strategy, the possibilities of tradeoffs were still minimal.

A critical difference for the second round of negotiations was that Hong Kong's policy coherence totally broke down. A dispute within the ranks of Hong Kong's garment producers broke out on the eve of Kearns' arrival. On the one side, a group of small manufacturers strongly opposed any VER, especially because the distribution of quotas would be based on past performance. On the other side, large manufacturers were in favor of export restraints. The large companies had a small majority in a special subcommittee that handled the quota problem, whereas the small manufacturers controlled the Garment Union as a whole. The issue was who would have the authority to negotiate with Kearns. A tenuous compromise was reached whereby the special subcommittee was given the responsibility to hear the American proposals but was not given the power of decision—the power to negotiate.[93]

Agenda Setting 2. An agenda could not be agreed upon for a second time because no one on the Hong Kong side would negotiate. For three days, various representatives of the Hong Kong textile industry listened to American suggestions. No counteroffers were made and no substantive discussion took place. Finally, the Hong Kong Garment Manufacturers' Union as a whole voted to refuse to consider any voluntary ceilings on the colony's exports. Since Hong Kong's Washington lawyers were counseling that import restrictions were unlikely, the vast majority of small producers in Hong Kong perceived little to be gained by a VER.[94] Their official statement noted that a voluntary ceiling would "merely create a monopoly for a small group of manufacturers who have a record of past performance in the American market while it certainly would create a precedent that . . . will cause total destruction of Hong Kong's industry."[95]

The Union's rejection of negotiations represented the last straw for the industry's larger firms. The day before Kearns' departure, a group of local textile industrialists broke away from the Garment Manufacturers Union and formed a rival body called the Hong Kong Garment Manufacturers (for the U.S.A.) Association. Although the rest of the manufacturing community condemned the split, the new association met with Kearns to exchange views on orderly marketing. The seventeen firms hoped that they could make a suitable arrangement with the United States and eventually bring in other producers. These companies impressed Kearns with their good intentions in order to safeguard their present exports and avoid more restrictive American action. Kearns later said that he had expected an agreement with Hong Kong within a month of his visit, but noted that Hong Kong's government would police a control system only if more than half of the textile firms agreed to the restrictions.

In late December, about five weeks after Kearns' departure, the newly formed Hong Kong Garment Association made the United States its first offer for restricting exports. And despite the opposition of major groups within Hong Kong's manufacturing circles, the Colonial Secretary supported the quota. Within the past year, Hong Kong's exports to the U.S. had jumped to 18 percent of the colony's total trade.[96] The colonial government therefore decided that it was in the long-run interest of Hong Kong to avoid restrictions and appease the American textile industry. The Financial Secretary told the rebellious Garment Union that he would support the rival Garment Association's negotiations with the United States, in addition to helping administer any voluntary undertaking.[97]

Despite these gestures, Hong Kong was still unable to formulate a coherent policy. The Hong Kong Garment Union was not convinced that a VER was in its interest or enforceable. Various manufacturers, weavers, spinners, and finishers were all opposed to the negotiations. Hence, the Garment Union concluded that a voluntary restraint would fail despite government support. Maintaining that the "success of Hong Kong's textile trade with America is based on the close co-operation of a series of vertical productive entities," the Union did not believe that artificial restrictions could work.[98] The Spinners Association also appealed the colonial government's decision to Britain. It was the Spinners Association's understanding that Britain would "vigorously oppose the unilateral imposition of restrictions on imports of Hong Kong goods by other countries."[99]

The Bargaining. The negotiations that followed were very loosely structured. The Garment Association felt that any offer to restrict exports voluntarily was a major concession. Therefore, its proposal was not intended to be an opening position. Even though the offer covered only a minimum number of categories and included very high growth rates, the Garment Association considered it to be a genuinely "generous gesture," without need for bargaining.[100]

The American textile community, however, did not agree. When Kearns asked the American industry to suggest a compromise and provide counterproposals, the textile industry went to the opposite extreme. It demanded overall quota limits, a much greater scope than Hong Kong's offer, and drastic cuts in some categories.[101] During January 1960, a few more counteroffers crossed the Pacific, yet neither side was making a concerted effort to narrow the differences. Although some substantive discussions were held between the American Consulate in Hong Kong and the colonial government, most of the bargaining was taking place in the press. The American textile industry's strategy was to obtain the maximum restrictions, and the Hong Kong Garment Manufacturers Association wanted to settle the issue, but American demands went beyond its willingness to compromise. The gaps were so great that the Association saw no possible tradeoffs.[102] By mid-February it was clear that no agreement was going to be reached, even though the negotiations lingered on for months.

The problem with the negotiations was that neither the American government nor the Hong Kong government took charge and established coherent bargaining policies. In 1956, in the case of Japan, the United States government pursued its own negotiating strategy, which it legitimized to the industry; in 1959, dealing with Hong Kong, Kearns allowed the industry to dictate American terms.[103] Furthermore, by bargaining through the press, the industries in both nations were pressured into taking positions which a Hong Kong official admitted "would be very hard to change."[104]

The United States was not the only party at fault. The Hong Kong government had little control over its own industry, and the majority of the Hong Kong textile manufacturers did not sufficiently appreciate their weak position and their need for negotiation. An editorial in the *Economist* commented that Hong Kong was operating in an "atmosphere of unreality."[105] The editorial went on to suggest that Hong Kong had overcome its past vulnerability by "simply avoiding trouble as far as that ideal is possible." The widespread opposition within the textile community, and the government's inability to remove the debates from a public forum, broke Hong Kong's "unwritten code." The key to Hong Kong's past success was "defense—not defiance," and the article correctly noted that the "price of recalcitrance now may well be tighter restrictions later. Japan appears to have learned the hard lesson from the Washington lobbies."

The Outcome

Hong Kong's transnational contacts were right about restrictions being unlikely. Although some analysts were proclaiming the "political climate . . . ripe for quotas" after Hong Kong's refusal, the international costs of QRs were still too great.[106] This was particularly true for Hong Kong, since the British government came out with a firm statement opposing American quotas on Hong Kong goods.[107]

Nonetheless, Hong Kong's strategy did not have long-run payoffs—in fact, the failure to achieve an agreement had severe political and economic consequences. On the economic front, Hong Kong had experienced some minor difficulties before the VER negotiations. American orders, which had poured into the colony in the wake of the Japanese restraints, were causing the expansion of production capacity to proceed at terrifying speeds. A number of firms accepted orders beyond their ability to deliver. This led to subcontracting part of their sales to smaller firms, which failed to produce uniform quality.

During the fall of 1959, American proposals for quotas on certain types of garments further stimulated demand. A spurt of heavy "anticipatory buying" was initiated by small companies that were anxious to build up impressive records of past performance just in case a VER was implemented.[108] The *failure* to achieve a quota, however, caused serious dislocations: both American importers and Hong Kong exporters found themselves overextended. There was no longer a need to stockpile if there were no limitations on trade. Therefore, by March of 1960, orders began to lag. By summer, the inability of producers to meet delivery dates punctually and the lack of universal quality gave importers an excuse to cancel big orders. Ironically, the Hong Kong textile industry would have been better off had it agreed to the restraints, because importers would have had more of an incentive to abide by their contracts. During the second half of 1960, many factories were closed as orders dropped off. In addition to the problem of surplus capacity, Hong Kong's uneven quality made importers skeptical about the colony's reliability. By 1961, even the small firms recognized the necessity for some centralized control and orderly marketing procedures. Almost everyone in the colony conceded that more emphasis was needed on quality control and diversification rather than on aggregate expansion.

The lack of an agreement on voluntary export restraints allowed Hong Kong to benefit in the short run. With no constraints on textile trade, orders that were booked in 1959 made 1960 look like a good year for sectoral and overall trade (see table 2.4). But in 1961, the repercussions were felt: cotton trade dropped by 25 percent, garment exports fell by 33 percent, and overall earnings from trade with the United States declined by 9 percent (see table 2.5). When bargain hunters came to Hong Kong in late 1960 and early 1961, most surplus merchandise had to be sold off at 30 to 40 percent below initial selling prices. The wave of cancellations and the subsequent disruptions "served as a serious lesson to the [Hong Kong] garment industry."[109]

On the political side, the failure to agree had a twofold negative impact on Hong Kong's bilateral trade regime with the United States. First, American difficulties in bargaining with Hong Kong acted as a catalyst to the creation of a new international regime for the control of cotton textile trade. Hong Kong's defiance reinforced the growing belief in the

United States that ad hoc bilateral arrangements were an inadequate response to domestic trade problems. Therefore, in October 1959, Douglas Dillon, Under Secretary of State for Economic Affairs, suggested that the GATT study means to avoid "market disruptions." The purpose of this suggestion was to initiate a process whereby the GATT would multilateralize and legalize a voluntary export restraint scheme for cotton textiles. Since the United States was disadvantaged by existing GATT regulations, Dillon and others decided that it

Table 2.5 Hong Kong Exports to the United States, 1961 (in $ million)

	1961	Percent Change from 1960
Total exports	$124.0	−9.0
Total textile exports	62.3	−27.0
Cotton textile exports	47.0	−25.0
Garment exports	46.2	−33.0
Cotton as percent of total exports	38.0%	−8.7
Cotton as percent of total textile exports	75.0%	0.0

SOURCES: *Hong Kong Yearbook, 1961*; United Nations, *Yearbook of International Trade Statistics, 1961*; and *Hong Kong Trade Statistics, 1961*.

would be better to change the rules. The United States had several motives for seeking this type of international arrangement, but its central objective was more control over textile policy. Ironically, it was the first aborted attempt at negotiations with Hong Kong that gave rise to the suggestion, and the second failure that added fuel to the fire. The American textile industry and future President John F. Kennedy learned from the Hong Kong experience that more bargaining leverage was needed if an acceptable answer was to be found.

The second political consequence of Hong Kong's failure to negotiate an agreement was that the British colony became the prime target for restrictions under the new international textile regime. The Short-Term Arrangement (STA), which will be discussed in the next chapter, was created in October of 1961 to "facilitate consultation between all contracting parties" and to give the importing countries the power to restrict imports (under certain conditions). Japan, which had played the game with the United States, obtained a few benefits under the STA. But since Hong Kong had refused to go along, it was the first to feel the wrath of America's new-found power.

Conclusion

When confronted with similar protectionist demands from the United States, Hong Kong and Japan pursued different strategies and achieved different results. Japan operated on the principle that long-run political and economic goals were primary. It made short-run sacrifices and diversified its product lines and markets. Through subtle linkages, it also stabilized a troubled bilateral regime. Japan's only failing was that domestic politics and a past reputation for cheating limited its short-run gains within the cotton sector.

Hong Kong, by contrast, took the opposite route and experienced the opposite result. By rejecting American pleas, Hong Kong was following a short-run political and economic strategy. In 1960, its gains from United States trade reached all-time highs, but in 1961 and 1962, Hong Kong paid the price for its intransigence. Domestic constraints, again, played a critical role in policy failure. Although the government eventually became aware of the need for a long-run approach, its inability to take charge of the negotiations and legitimize its policies minimized its chances of success.

In seems somewhat paradoxical that Japan made an advantage out of adversity, while Hong Kong did not. Japan had more at stake in the negotiations; structurally, it was more vulnerable than Hong Kong to United States pressure, and American decision makers convinced the Japanese that some type of trade restraint was necessary. Japan then used the image of an unyielding American pressure to force the necessary compromises on its industry and bureaucratic factions. Japan's perceptions of its own weakness fostered enough policy coherence to pursue long-run goals.

Hong Kong's elite, on the other hand, was not universally convinced that there would be costs to refusing American demands. American commitments to freer world trade reduced the credibility of American threats, while transnational actors correctly forecast that the United States would not act unfavorably in the short run. Therefore, powerful elements within the Hong Kong textile community saw no incentive to capitulate. Yet as I will show in the next two chapters, Hong Kong and Japan reversed roles during the 1960s. Japan's policy of "blaming" the United States ran the risk of building resentment.[110] And indeed, Japan's ability to formulate coherent bargaining strategies declined over time as Japan's industry and certain bureaucratic groups "learned the wrong lesson" from the 1956 experience. Hong Kong, however, slowly realized that it could play by the rules and still prosper. Hong Kong's industry and government learned creatively in response to their adversity.

Chapter 3

Textiles, Round 2:
The STA and LTA,
1961–1969

During the 1960s, American cotton textile policy went through a metamorphosis. In 1961, the Kennedy administration negotiated an international agreement which gave the United States the power to control cotton textile imports, and in 1962, a long-term arrangement was devised which institutionalized this new multilateral protectionist regime. These two agreements fundamentally altered the relative bargaining power between developed and developing nations in this issue-area. On the one hand, the United States was no longer severely constrained from restricting certain imports. By changing the international rules, the United States effectively reduced its global obligations. On the other hand, rapidly developing countries had fewer avenues of recourse in confrontations over protectionism. Rejecting negotiations would merely weaken an exporter's bargaining position.

The outcome was that cotton textile exports from many developing nations suffered. The United States was not always consistent in its bargaining or implementation policy, but much of the time it sought to reduce or minimize the growth of cotton textile imports. Exporters could upgrade their products and occasionally cheat, but no major exporting state, with the unusual exception of Hong Kong, substan tially increased its cotton textiles earnings in the sixties.

Limiting gains in "cotton" textiles, however, did not imply that major loopholes in American protectionism did not exist. The myopic nature of American policy combined with the long-run approach adopted by most of the East Asian states led to far greater gains than anyone in 1961 could have expected.

The Road to Geneva

When the Kennedy administration came into office, it sought to embark on a new trade policy. John F. Kennedy was similar to his predecessors insofar as he supported free trade and opposed protectionism. What made Kennedy different was his desire for a bold initiative that would tear down the barriers restricting international trade. Previous administrations had pursued piecemeal efforts which lacked the bargaining power necessary to break the tariff defenses of Europe. Kennedy's plan was to overcome the incremental methods of the past by establishing broad presidential authority to negotiate sweeping tariff reductions.

In order to achieve this objective, Kennedy had to neutralize the "import-sensitive" industries which had blocked trade legislation in the 1950s. Somehow the administration had to satisfy the demands of protectionists or give them a stake in the passing of a new trade bill. The pivotal interest group in this struggle was the textile industry: breaking its opposition would be the key. The failure to curtail textile imports, particularly the failure with Hong Kong, had strengthened the industry's political position. By 1961, a major trade initiative would never pass Congress without the textile lobby's acquiescence.[1] The question was: How could the President appease the textile industry and at the same time further his principal goal of freer world trade?

Kennedy's answer was a seven-point plan that would provide the textile industry with as much assistance as possible without resorting to quantitative restrictions. Proposals ranged from expanding research and development in textile products to the arrangement of an international conference to discuss "avoiding undue disruption of established industries."[2] Unlike Eisenhower's attempts to mollify the textile industry, Kennedy wanted to go beyond short-run solutions. The battle to reduce global tariffs would be a long-drawn-out process; stopgap measures would not be enough. Kennedy therefore adopted a two-pronged strategy: an international conference to be held in Geneva would deal with the political problems surrounding imports; and domestic intervention measures would help the industry adjust over the long run.

The reason for the international conference was that international constraints still limited the United States' freedom. As long as the GATT constrained American policy, and as long as European countries invoked GATT Article xxxv to keep out Japanese and Hong Kong textiles, the United States would be the only open industrial market without accepted tools for the control of imports. This made a Geneva conference essential in order to liberalize European markets and legitimize voluntary export restraints.

Ironically, Japan had a number of common interests with the United States on this issue, even though it was an exporter. Japanese products were severely restricted in French, British, and Belgian markets. Japanese leaders hoped that the legitimation of VERs would alleviate European fears of Japanese imports and facilitate the withdrawal of Article xii. The Japanese also saw an international textile arrangement as the only way to avoid their continued loss of American market shares. Before the July Geneva conference, Japanese delegates insisted that participating countries not be placed at a disadvantage with respect to other exporters.[3]

The Short-Term Arrangement

The one-year agreement that emerged from Geneva, the Short-Term Arrangement (STA), was a great success for the United States. George Ball, the chief American negotiator, not only established the right of importing nations to act unilaterally; he also achieved an expanded scope of restrictions within the confines of cotton textiles, and a commitment from the participants to a long-term solution before the Reciprocal Trade Agreement Act was due for renewal. Moreover, the Common Market nations accepted the principle of liberalizing import restrictions, even though a specific commitment to take more Asian textiles was dropped. And it was further understood that Hong Kong would be subject to special restrictions by the United States, although, again, specific references were eliminated from the text.[4] The STA had two essential features: first, according to Article 3, an importing nation could request restraint from an exporting nation. If thirty days of consultations did not produce an agreement, the importing nation could unilaterally restrict the incoming goods. Second, according to Article 4, a bilateral arrangement was acceptable as a substitute or as a complement to Article 3 restraints.

The American industry had been skeptical about the prospects of the Geneva conference, but it was cautiously optimistic after the results were announced. The only strong disappointment was that synthetic and wool textiles were not included in the restrictions. The chairman of Burlington Industries, one of the largest textile producers in America, correctly forecast that other fibers would be the greatest threat in the future.[5] The administration, however, wanted to limit only those imports that were a direct and immediate threat. The greatest political capital was to be gained in restricting cotton, the market suffering the most from import competition. Protecting a relatively prosperous domestic market segment, such as synthetic fibers, had few political payoffs. The purpose of the STA was not to establish an ironclad protectionist system. Rather, it was an attempt to provide a political mechanism for assuring the textile industry's support for the new trade bill. The rationale behind the Kennedy plan was to promote freer trade by implementing the minimum number of protectionist policies.

The reactions in Japan to the STA were mixed. During the negotiations, Japan had insisted that restraints be limited to only four general divisions in order to maximize flexibility. When the STA specified *sixty-four* categories of cotton textiles and legitimized the right of the importing countries to erect quantitative restrictions, many Japanese mill owners saw it as a setback.[6] The Japanese government felt that two important factors would nonetheless compensate for these losses: the Americans had assured the Japanese delegates in Geneva that Japan would be rewarded for its support of the STA and the faithful observance of its VER, and that synthetic fibers and wool fabrics would not be included in the arrangements. Since MITI was de-emphasizing cotton on a global scale, this latter provision was critical to Japan's long-run gains from textile trade.

The STA and Hong Kong

George Ball warned Hong Kong as early as May 1961 that restrictions were forthcoming. Even though Hong Kong exports were down in 1961, the colony had become the principal culprit from the United States' point of view. Hong Kong imports equaled 26 percent of total textile imports into the United States—a figure that was unacceptable to the American industry and to the Kennedy administration. Therefore, a few weeks before the Geneva conference, Ball suggested that Hong Kong "voluntarily" cut its exports by 30 percent. The Under Secretary noted that "it would be Hong Kong's advantage if such an offer were made before the Geneva meeting," since a failure to act would lead the United States to ask for even sharper cuts.[7]

Although no early offer was made, the United States and Hong Kong reached a tentative agreement in Geneva, which they finalized several months later. Under Article 3 of the STA, the United States had the right to restrict imports of any exporting country. In addition, import levels under the international arrangement were to be held at the same level as the year ending June 30, 1961. For Hong Kong, this meant that accepting the STA entailed accepting a 30 percent cut from 1960 levels of textile exports to the United States. Not surprisingly, Hong Kong officials were reticent at first—especially since they were unsure how serious the United States and Britain were about implementing unilateral restrictions. By fall, however, there was little doubt in the minds of most Hong Kong business executives that protectionism was forthcoming. During the previous negotiations with the British colony, American policy was constrained by its obligations to the GATT. Unilateral restrictions on Hong Kong exports would have had high political costs. This time around, there were positive inducements for the American administration to follow through with its threats. Kennedy and Ball were committed to cutting imports in 1962 in order to get the textile industry's support for the Reciprocal Trade Agreement Act. Thus colonial officials knew they had little choice but to accept American demands. Hong Kong finally agreed to restrict its exports by approximately 30 percent below the 1960 figure, with additional cuts in a few categories.[8]

In order to prosper within the confines of these restraints, Hong Kong needed to follow the strategy outlined in chapter 1: diversify its product lines and upgrade its existing exports. Hong Kong's government took the first step in this direction by creating a Cotton Advisory Board to unify the industry.[9] Nonetheless, the colony had trouble adapting to the new quotas. During the second half of 1961, American buyers and Hong Kong exporters rushed deliveries of previously ordered goods. There was a fear on both sides of the Pacific that the United States Tariff Commission was going to impose the equalization fee on cotton products suggested by Eisenhower in 1959. Within two months of its agreement, Hong Kong had already overshipped its quotas in several categories.[10]

The events that followed Hong Kong's overshipments had an important impact on American protectionist policy. American decision makers were constantly debating their options and groping for appropriate policies in 1962. There was no clear consensus on policy direction, and ambiguities in the new international textile regime left a great amount of room for interpretation. Hong Kong was a central concern in this confusion because it was the second most important exporter to the American market and was widely viewed as the least responsive actor to United States demands.

The American decision on a proper policy was also complicated because the country was in the midst of negotiating another international agreement to replace the STA—the Long-Term Arrangement Regarding International Trade in Cotton Textiles (LTA). On the one hand, a tough stance could jeopardize support among exporting countries. On the other hand, it was imperative that the STA be regarded as a domestic success. Otherwise, the Kennedy administration would not be able to convince the textile industry that such a multilateral framework could control imports. According to this logic, if Hong Kong was allowed to overship its quotas, then the very efficacy of the STA (and LTA) would be called into question. Hong Kong was jeopardizing Kennedy's efforts to appease the textile industry.

Thus, American officials were in a quandary. Some government bureaucrats wanted an aggressive response to the overshipments, whereas others were more concerned with the international implications of unilateral restraints.[11] A decision was finally taken on February 28, 1962, in favor of the hard-line position, and Hong Kong was officially asked to curb eight categories of cotton textile exports. This unprecedented protectionist move brought applause for Kennedy and trouble to Hong Kong. Yet in light of America's authority under the STA, the Hong Kong government decided on March 2 to suspend all further report licenses in the problem areas.

Hong Kong's Cotton Advisory Board then met to discuss the industry's position on the American request. The Board advised the government that export licenses should be issued for another week to avoid major dislocations. Since thirty days of consultation was permitted under the STA, the government complied. There was also a consensus that the colonial authorities should immediately initiate discussions with the United States. The Board assumed that the matter would be quickly resolved, and shipments could be resumed. Meanwhile, exporters were feverishly reserving space on the remaining ships set to sail to the United States before the new deadline. Before the Hong Kong government stopped licensing at 1 P.M. on March 10, six ships left the docks loaded with textiles.

The American textile industry was outraged by Hong Kong's actions. But only in the most extreme circumstances was the United States legitimately allowed to restrict imports on less than thirty days' notice. Nonetheless, on March 18, the United States banned entry of all eight categories of textiles for which export restraints were requested. In an effort to demonstrate a new, tough policy, the American government clamped an absolute embargo—another unprecedented move—on all eight items shipped after February 28.[12] Since Hong Kong had surpassed its quota on most of the restraint categories before the United States request, the government's Interagency Textile Administrative Committee decided that the colony was in violation of the STA. The Committee argued that allowing the extra shipments to enter would cause serious "market disruptions."[13]

Hong Kong's massive overshipments (as much as 100 percent in a few categories) were poorly timed. The Kennedy administration was intent upon proving the STA workable, but moderate amounts of cheating might have been allowed. The American government was not even united on a particular policy position until Hong Kong politicized the issue by reversing its decision to suspend exports. Hong Kong immediately dispatched two high-level officials to Washington for talks, but the damage was done. The Secretary of Commerce informed the colony's representatives that the embargo would not be lifted.[14] Furthermore, the American government continued to request restraints through October 1. By the end of the STA, thirty items were eventually covered—the most applied to any one country. The United States eased the embargo only once; after several months of pleading, importing groups convinced the Interagency Textile Committee to release some raincoats and a few other items.[15]

The STA and Japan

Japan's long-run strategy paid off in 1961. Whereas all other nations were restricted by the STA, and Hong Kong's quota levels were drastically reduced, Japan was compensated for its previous cooperation. The rewards were modest, but Japan was the *only* country to receive an increased quota under the new international textile regime.

Agenda Setting. American negotiations with Japan were directly linked to its negotiations with Hong Kong. The American strategy was to follow a maximal protectionist policy toward Hong Kong, accommodate Japan, and hold all other nations' exports constant. Since Kennedy planned to reduce 1961–62 imports as much as possible, Japan's compensation would have to be less than the 30 percent cut from Hong Kong. During the earliest quota discussions in May and June of 1961, the Japanese government demanded all of Hong Kong's reductions. But after several sessions that included a summit meeting between Kennedy and Japanese Prime Minister Ikeda, the two sides reached an agreement in principle. According to the American formula, Japan was to receive up to 30 percent in some categories, greater flexibility, and an aggregate hike of only around 5 percent.[16] Substantive discussions, however, were postponed until the Geneva conference. Japanese officials knew that the United States needed Japan's support for the STA.

The Bargaining. During the international conference in July, the United States formally offered Japan concessions in return for its backing of the STA. Yet as noted earlier, Japanese mill owners were so displeased with the outcome in Geneva that they told their government to reject the Short-Term Arrangement and any secret bilateral agreement that might have been negotiated. The vociferous outbursts by some textile producers led the Japanese government to withhold public approval of the STA until there was further consultation with the United States.[17] Japanese negotiators had noted strong reservations at the time the arrangement was drawn up, but the intensity of the domestic reaction reinforced the need for new bilateral talks.

Negotiations between the two sides formally started on August 9 with high level officials in attendance. For its opening position, Japan returned to its earlier demands. But unlike their relatively accommodating strategy in May, Japanese negotiators perceived themselves to be in a more powerful position, having several ways available to exploit their enhanced bargaining leverage. First, a Japanese delegation in Geneva declared that Japan would not sign the STA until a "satisfactory" bilateral quota was worked out with the United States.[18] Both sides knew that without Japanese approval, the STA would be virtually meaningless. Second, negotiations were to be held in Tokyo. This strengthened the influence of the Japanese industry, because holding negotiations in one's own capital allows an interest group to scrutinize more closely its government's behavior. Since Japanese textile producers did not see an overriding need to cooperate, nothing less than a "substantial hike" was going to be acceptable. Finally, the Japanese negotiating team was "unusually solidified." In the past, the Foreign Ministry and MITI had held divergent views; this time, both groups agreed that the United States should make the majority of the concessions.[19]

Confronted with a tough, coherent Japanese strategy, the Americans retreated to their negotiating demands of the previous May. Yet unlike 1956, and unlike the Japanese, the United States delegation was not united. Japan's opening position was clearly unreasonable, but some officials were willing to fight against any increase over 5 percent, while others were willing to be more generous. The Americans also were disadvantaged because, for some unknown reason, they entered the negotiations without adequate statistics on all import categories.[20]

The gap between the opening positions was so wide that it took several days of preliminary discussion before concrete proposals could be advanced and a serious bargaining range created. Although the Japanese had the upper hand, many of their threats, such as discontinuing export restraints, were simply not credible. As one observer noted, the best thing the Japanese could do for the American industry was to end their quotas. Congressional uproar would be so great that the Japanese would clearly lose.[21] Moreover, the American delegation believed that some of the protests from Japanese textile manufacturers were contrived—designed to create as much pressure on their own government as possible. The Americans accurately assessed that Japan would compromise at about 10 percent for aggregate growth accompanied by added flexibility.[22]

By early September, the overriding problem was the intensity of domestic pressures. It was clear that neither Japanese industry nor the American textile community would be satisfied if their respective governments made *any* compromises. Whereas the American team was trying to keep the negotiations secret in order to foster coherent bargaining strategies and a quick end to the negotiations, Japanese officials continually leaked American demands to the Japanese press.[23] Part of the explanation for this was that the Japanese wanted to use the advantage they had gained by hosting the negotiations to build domestic commitments around their bargaining strategy. The rest, however, was bureaucratic politics. As the negotiations wore on, Japan's Foreign Ministry became anxious to compromise even though MITI insisted upon holding firm. Leaks to the press were being used by these ministries to bolster their bureaucratic positions. On a

number of important issues, these tactics worked, and the
Americans clearly perceived the Japanese as being more
strongly motivated than themselves.

Decision Phase and Agreement. Once Japan started to
submit concrete proposals, the remainder of the negotiations
was largely horsetrading. For example, the United States permitted increases of up to 25 percent in specific categories in
exchange for a lower aggregate limit; the Americans also reduced the number of divisions provided by the STA, while
Japan acceded to a more restrictive breakdown than it had
under its previous quotas; and so on. Only domestic factors
impeded the earlier signing of an agreement. The Japanese
textile industry kept pressure on its government until the very
end. Using factional rivalries within the ruling Liberal Democratic Party as a lever, the industry almost sabotaged the
agreement as the talks entered the final stage.

The intense dissatisfaction displayed by the textile industries of both nations is a strong indication of the degree
of mutual compromise. A joint statement issued by several
Japanese textile associations said blatantly, "We are extremely unhappy about the results of the negotiations." At
the same time, one American textile official complained, "We
don't mind them giving away the barn. We just don't like
them giving away the cows, too." [24] In many ways, these negotiations were more of a strain to the industries in both nations than the first VER of 1957.

Obviously, it is hard to specify a winner under these circumstances. Although Japan was given an 11 percent increase over its 1960 quota, this hardly seems magnanimous
compared to Hong Kong's dramatic gains during the years of
Japanese restraint. Nonetheless, the combination of tough
bargaining, American generosity, and a good grasp by the
Japanese of important technical issues provided Japan with a
number of substantial benefits. Even though the aggregate
levels did not meet the Japanese industry's expectations, large
increases in critical categories were designed to make it eas-

ier for Japan to fill its quota in 1962 compared to any previous year. Only 80 to 85 percent of Japan's quota was shipped in 1960—largely because the earlier VER lacked flexibility. Under this new arrangement, Japan could increase its exports by almost 40 percent in some fabrics and almost 30 percent in apparel. In contrast to Hong Kong's 30 percent cut under the STA and America's policy to hold all other nations' exports at the 1960 level, these concessions were certainly favorable. Japan also negotiated for one additional clause in its bilateral agreement which reflected an important lesson learned from its 1956 experience: the United States government agreed that Japan would not be placed in an inequitable position vis-à-vis its competitors.[25]

Implementation and Adjustment Under the STA

October 1961 through September 1962 was a period of trial and error for American decision makers. Despite the hardline United States policy toward Hong Kong imports generally, market penetration actually increased under the STA. Seventy restraint actions and a larger number of requests could not prevent a 64 percent increase in the quantity of cotton imports during 1962.[26] Even Hong Kong, which was subject to the greatest number of restrictions, exported 128 percent of its quota. American officials willingly admitted that they had "things to learn."[27]

In terms of export earnings, Japan made a significant recovery in 1962. Cotton earnings reached an all-time high—44 percent above 1961 and almost 20 percent above 1956 (see table 3.1). At one point, Japan suspended exports of a few cotton garments to avoid the United States' invoking Article 3 of the STA. But by using its increased flexibility and higher import levels under its bilateral agreement, Japan exported 98.3 percent of its quota. While cotton trade prospered, the Japanese also continued diversifying into synthetics. By 1962, the Japanese supplied the U.S. with 51 percent of its synthetic textile imports. The White Paper on Japanese Foreign Trade issued in 1962 noted, "For Japan to cope with . . .

Table 3.1 Japan's Trade with the United States, 1962 (in $ million)

	1962	Percent Change from 1961	Percent Change from 1960
Overall exports	$1,353	+25	+11
Overall textile exports	294.5	+23	+ 5
Cotton exports	100.5	+44	+37
Wool exports	67.5	+17	0
Synthetic exports	35.9	+30	+ 7
Cotton as percent of overall textiles	33%	+ 4	+ 7
Synthetics as percent of overall textiles	12%	+ 1	+ 1

SOURCE: Hunsberger, *Japan and the United States in World Trade*, pp. 244–245, table 8-1.

[these] import restriction moves, it will be necessary not only to maintain order in her export trade, but also to make further efforts to diversify and switch the emphasis of her exports to high-grade products and to strengthen her commodity structure."[28]

Hong Kong increased its gains during 1962 by exploiting loopholes in the STA. Although American restrictions imposed severe costs on selected firms and prevented the colony from reaching its 1960 export levels, garment and textile earnings nonetheless registered a substantial rise (see table 3.2). Hong Kong's flexible industrial structure allowed the colony to stay one step ahead of American embargoes. Also, to avoid future implementation problems, the colony created

Table 3.2 Hong Kong's Trade with the United States, 1962 (in $ million)

	1962	Percent Change from 1961	Percent Change from 1960
Overall exports	$169	+29	+24
Overall textile exports	78	+25	− 8
Garment exports	67.5	+38	− 7
Textile exports	19.1	+ 2	+16

SOURCES: *Hong Kong Trade Statistics, 1962*; United Nations, *Yearbook of International Trade Statistics, 1962*.

an "export authorization system" to control textile shipments. This complex arrangement enabled the Hong Kong government to forecast future export levels for every category and every country up to six months in advance. The colony would then transmit this information to the importing country on the condition that any restraint order would apply only to subsequent shipments.[29] As we will see later, this system not only maintained a relatively free market in Hong Kong but also helped the colony adjust to future restrictions. It organized the industry, reduced the infighting, maintained flexibility, and provided the colonial government with a wealth of information. Hong Kong's government, more than any other government, learned to maximize its cotton export potential by forecasting its industry's capabilities and knowing where to negotiate for its short- and medium-term needs.

The LTA

From the Kennedy administration's perspective, the Short-Term Arrangement was a success. It laid the groundwork for the LTA, which, in turn, produced an American textile industry endorsement of the Trade Expansion Act of 1962. The STA allowed the United States unilateral control over most of its textile imports for the first time since World War II, and the Long-Term Arrangement institutionalized this change. Under the LTA, more flexibility was given to the exporter, the agreement was to last five years, and bilateral agreements that lasted for more than one year had to contain provisions for at least 5 percent annual growth. The LTA was sold to developing countries as a means to expand trade in cotton textiles. The argument was that if exports could be increased in an "orderly" manner, importing nations would not be frightened into closing off their markets. By the same token, the LTA was sold to domestic industries in the United States and Europe as a means to limit import penetration and minimize competition from "cheap" foreign textiles. In general, the LTA had been viewed since its inception as a highly restrictive arrangement. Most critics feared that the LTA would undermine developing countries' dependence on textiles exports—exports that were critical to such nations' economic growth.[30]

After the LTA came into effect on October 1, 1962, American officials reinforced this restrictionist image by foregoing the negotiation of bilateral agreements. In its place, the United States sought to exercise its rights to limit imports under LTA Article 3. This provided an exporting country with the opportunity for consultation, but essentially it was unilateral control. By December 20, 1962, the United States had agreements with eight countries affecting thirty-nine textile categories in seventy-one separate restraint actions. In addition, negotiations were underway with six more countries, involving nineteen more restraint actions. Compared to seventy actions taken during the twelve months of the STA, ninety restraint measures were taken during the first two months of the Long-Term Arrangement.[31]

Many officials in the United States government were intent upon making the new system effective. Despite a general preference for free trade among such officials as Philip Trezise of the State Department, the presence of tenacious protectionists within the bureaucracy limited the extent to which America could follow an accommodating strategy. Stanley Nehmer of the Commerce Department, in particular, consistently fought to limit the growth of imports. Policy during this period was often a compromise between these competing bureaucratic interests, but much of the time the hard-line position would prevail. A structural analysis of the LTA would predict that the United States' global position as a hegemonic power would make it generous and lax in its protectionist policies. But in fact the United States was willing to impose cotton restrictions unilaterally and sometimes arbitrarily. Under these conditions, a textile exporting country had few avenues of recourse, at least with respect to this limited market.

Japan and the LTA

Japanese officials were disturbed by the new American approach, particularly since Japan was to be placed under Article 3 restraints immediately following the expiration of its 1962 bilateral accord.[32] The United States wanted to use its authority under the LTA to devise more specific category breakdowns, eliminate flexibility, and prevent Japan from carrying over unused portions of its quotas to the following year. American officials wanted uniformity in their country's policy toward all exporting countries in order to simplify implementation. In practical terms, however, this would substantially reduce Japanese cotton textile exports.

Agenda Setting. Consultation began on the United States' Article 3 requests on January 9, 1963. The LTA gave Japan sixty days to convince the Americans that their demands were unreasonable, and if the Japanese failed, the United States could act alone. At first, progress was relatively slow. American negotiators did not want to give Japan special treatment, as they had in 1962. Meanwhile, the government of Japan pursued a relatively accommodating strategy in the early stages of the negotiations. Despite pressure from Japan's textile industry, there was a belief in Tokyo that the problems could be resolved in "friendly" discussions. Many believed that the United States would eventually compromise to accommodate at least some of Japan's demands.

But the Japanese partially misread United States strategy. By mid-February, it looked as though the Americans were not going to be flexible. All indications were that the United States was simply stalling in order to impose Article 3 restraints. Therefore, the Japanese government decided to switch strategy. To bolster their bargaining position, the Japanese threatened to terminate the talks in favor of an appeal to the GATT committee on cotton textiles. Even officials in the Foreign Ministry, who had previously taken a more flexible attitude than MITI or the industry, were now openly criticizing the American position.[33] Moreover, the switch in policy was accompanied by a wave of anti-American sentiment in the Japanese press, similar to what had appeared in 1961.[34]

American officials were somewhat startled by the ferocity of the press campaign. But unlike 1961, there was less sympathy with the Japanese position. In addition, there was a shared perception in the American negotiating team that the government of Japan was not being completely candid with its own industry. American negotiators stated that the gap between Japan's bargaining demands and United States proposals involved less than 1 percent of Japanese cotton textile exports. The "Export or Die" slogans that dominated Japan's press were perceived to be a bargaining tactic rather than a major political issue.

Part of the difficulty was that the Americans interpreted the LTA as not obligating importing nations to expand imports during the first two years of the agreement. Japan, on the other hand, said that it accepted the LTA on the assurance that the United States would minimize the use of market disruption clauses. In other words, much of the disagreement was on principle rather than substance. Once the Japanese argument was clearly articulated, most American officials came to the conclusion that many of the issues in contention should be negotiated, rather than proclaimed by fiat.[35]

On the Japanese side, the government remained split. Part of the Japanese bureaucracy agreed with Prime Minister Ikeda and Foreign Minister Ohira that Japan should take a conciliatory attitude. Recognizing the *political value of short-run sacrifices*, some top-level Japanese officials felt that a delay in resolving the textile conflict could hurt other goals. Specifically they were concerned that Washington might *link* textiles to increased pressure for Japan to remove its own import restrictions. In addition, those who favored accommodation argued that a prolonged textile controversy would reduce Japan's chances to push its demands in a number of other important political and trade issues.[36] Opposing the accommodating strategy were the MITI Minister and the textile industry. Since this coalition saw no justification for giving in to American demands, it continued to advocate a tough line.

The Japanese government finally found an internal compromise that it hoped would break the deadlock. Rather than continue discussion on individual questions of market disruptions, Japan proposed that the two countries negotiate a new bilateral agreement. This proposal, which would give Japan more flexibility, was also accompanied by a threat: unless the United States could demonstrate with detailed analysis a case for market disruption, Japan would appeal the whole issue to the GATT. Since the Japanese government was united in opposing unilateral American restraints, the threat to go to Geneva had credibility. This created a dilemma for the United States. It did not want to negotiate a bilateral accord under Japanese pressure, but neither did it want to defend itself to a GATT committee. As a leader of the industrialized world and supposedly the prime mover for freer international trade, the mere filing of a complaint in Geneva would be an embarrassment to the American government. Even though it probably could win its case at the GATT, the United States elected to change its policy and negotiate another bilateral VER with Japan. By the end of March, the bottleneck appeared to be broken as officials on both sides optimistically projected an agreement within three to four weeks.

The Bargaining. Once the format for the negotiations changed, so did the issues. The major question suddenly became how a 1963 bilateral agreement would differ from the 1962 accord. To get some negotiating room, the Japanese opened the bargaining with a request for a 5 percent increase. Privately, however, Japanese industry and government officials indicated that they would settle for a simple extension of their last year's accord.[37] The Americans also put forth a proposal that was close to the existing agreement except for a few areas that were to be more detailed in their restraints. The only substantive disagreements between the two sides were on technical issues. The United States wanted to broaden the scope of the arrangement to include items such as zipper chains and white toy mice, whereas the Japanese were insisting that these products were not cotton textiles; there was also some debate over classification procedures. Both nations were pursuing relatively accommodating strategies. In fact, the disagreement appeared so minor that by late April some officials were expecting a "quick, friendly agreement."[38] The only apparent obstacle to settling the dispute was the "close emotional scrutiny" of the two nations' textile industries.

Neither government, however, could formulate a coherent bargaining strategy. Whenever an agreement seemed near, the textile industries in both nations would step up their pressure. MITI would respond to its industry's request that "some" increase be allowed; and the U.S. Department of Commerce would follow the American industry's position that there be no increase and possible reductions. Meanwhile, the State Department and Japan's Foreign Ministry were both anxious to settle the five-month-old conflict. Convergence toward an acceptable outcome was difficult under these conditions because the divisions within each government reduced the credibility of each other's threats. Although the Japanese again warned that they would go to Geneva, the Americans recognized that this was less likely than it had been in March. Japan's government was now less united. Similarly, the United States said it would act unilaterally without a quick settlement, but Japanese negotiators remained unconvinced. Even though relatively few issues separated the governments, neither Japanese nor American negotiators had garnered enough domestic legitimacy for their policies to make the final, relatively insignificant tradeoffs.

By mid-May, only one major issue was left in contention: the Americans wanted a separate category for corduroy apparel, whereas the Japanese claimed that it was unnecessary. Time, however, was working against Japan. The cost of incoherent policies and continued bargaining was greater uncertainty in the marketplace. As the negotiations dragged on,

American importers were reluctant to place orders for Japanese goods for fear that the eventual quota might prevent delivery. By June, Japanese cotton textile shipments were off 25 percent from the previous year. Nonetheless, domestic resistance to American demands remained strong in Japan. It was hard for many to believe that two nations which traded over three billion dollars a year could jeopardize so much for so little. Top-level diplomats pointed out that the issues in dispute amounted to less trade in hard cash than the sale of one oil tanker by Japan to the United States or of one machinery shipment from the United States to Japan.[39]

The negotiations headed toward a crisis in mid-July when the Japanese flatly rejected an American proposal and hinted that they wanted a postponement. This outraged American negotiators. Since the bargaining was already in its seventh month, even sympathetic State Department officials were growing impatient. In an extraordinary move, Commerce and State jointly agreed that unilateral action would follow if the conflict were not quickly resolved. Under ordinary circumstances, the bargaining could have been completed through "normal horsetrading."[40] But with no end in sight, higher-level officials now seemed needed to break the deadlock. In essence, Japanese intransigence had politicized the issue and united the American government.

The Decision Phase. As in 1956, a miniature crisis helped bring the negotiation to its quick, logical conclusion. The serious threat of American action, accompanied by the subsequent entrance of Under Secretary of State Ball into the negotiations, provided moderates in the Japanese government with a pretext for retreat. To help circumvent domestic pressure in this final stage, the government of Japan gave more authority to its negotiators in Washington to make an agreement without awaiting government instructions.[41] In addition, Ball's presence in the negotiations was fortunate for the Japanese; he reaffirmed American resolve, but he also strengthened the State Department in its battle with Commerce. This meant that there would be a greater willingness on the part of the United States to make some compromises.

Tradeoffs were possible among three issues: (1) the actual level of the corduroy quota; (2) the degree of precedent this quota would create for other fabrics; and (3) the level of flexibility that Japan would have to switch from one category to another. Since the Japanese felt that corduroy apparel was the most important of these issues, the United States finally gave in to Japan's demand for a high corduroy quota in exchange for side letters that left open the possibility of the United States' limiting other apparel items in the future, and a promise by the Japanese not to use their flexibility clauses in excessive amounts.

The Agreement and Evaluation. The irony behind the final settlement was that in over eight months of bargaining very little was achieved. Neither side could claim victory or defeat because both got more or less what they expected. Needless to say, neither industry was happy.

The agreement itself provided a little something for everyone. The aggregate total was increased by 4.5 percent, but this was coupled with a number of detailed restrictions and a change in conversion factors. This meant that the 1962 and 1963 agreements would be virtually identical. While the Japanese won the major battle over corduroy, they lost several other minor battles ranging from sport shirts to zipper tapes. When Japan asserted that the new breakdowns in the categories would reduce the overall export volume, the United States countered that there were still *ample loopholes* in the treaty which could be utilized if the Japanese would show some ingenuity.[42] Finally, Japan agreed to allocate annual shipments evenly by quarters, a practice which further limited flexibility, but this concession was partially offset by a 3 percent overall increase for the 1964 quota and a 5 percent increase for 1965.

The main difference between negotiation of a bilateral

agreement in a multilateral context and negotiations in the 1950s was that the United States had more direct bargaining leverage in the 1960s. Although political obligations still constrained American policy, threats had to be taken more seriously by the Japanese industry and Japanese government. In addition, technical issues and questions of ambiguity and flexibility played a more central role than they had in the 1950s. For example, there was a general recognition of the value of loopholes in these arrangements. This meant that the U.S. endeavored to close some, but Japan made a point of opening others.

For Japan to succeed in the short run, it was critical that it bargain for its needs—make some sacrifices but negotiate for the loopholes and flexibility. It was through the bargaining process that Japan convinced American negotiators to use bilateral rather than the more restrictive unilateral arrangements. Furthermore, Japan's success in 1962, the standoff in 1963, and its failures in the 1950s can be largely attributed to its greater or lesser ability to bargain for these concessions. A complete explanation requires uncovering not only what the Americans were willing to allow but also what the Japanese were able to take.

Perhaps the greatest similarity in all these negotiations was the role of domestic politics and the problems of formulating a coherent policy. Despite the myths surrounding the Japanese policy process, the influence of Japan's textile industry on the negotiations was growing over time. During the 1960s, two reinforcing factors weakened Japan's policy coherence in textiles: first, MITI's control over the industry was diminished due to structural changes in the organization's authority; second, the shared perception of the need for compromise that was so important in the 1950s was no longer as potent. The result was that MITI was becoming increasingly responsive to the textile industry, rather than vice versa. Thus instead of Japan learning how to cope with these negotiations, each new round of bargaining became more acrimonious. The bitter recriminations that dominated Japan's press only further weakened the government's legitimacy in textile policy.

On the American side, policy coherence played an equally central role. Bureaucratic infighting between the Commerce and State Departments was more the rule than the exception. When the two agencies became stalemated, this frequently produced immobility in American policy, making compromise difficult. When there was a consensus on an accommodating strategy, however, Japan and other exporting states found it much easier to exploit American generosity.

Thus the Japanese were most successful in bargaining with the United States when they formulated relatively coherent strategies and when the Americans agreed to be accommodating. Whenever policy coherence broke down—on either side—finding an acceptable outcome became problematic. Both in 1956 and 1963, top leaders had to be brought into the negotiations in order to break the standoff. Only in 1962, when the United States was clearly accommodating, did the Japanese do reasonably well.

Japan's Implementation and Adjustment Under the LTA

The LTA and its subsequent renewals institutionalized protectionism in cotton textiles for eleven years. Japan negotiated several more bilateral agreements with the United States under the LTA, but they varied only slightly from the 1963 accord. Given America's enhanced bargaining leverage under the multilateral arrangement, there was relatively little Japan could do.[43] The importance of the 1963 bilateral accord was that it set the precedent for all subsequent negotiations with Japan and all other exporting countries. VERs, which at least gave developing nations an opportunity to bargain for their short-run needs, became the norm in American cotton textile trade.

Although VERs gave Japan somewhat more freedom than Article 3 restraints, Japan's earnings in cotton textile exports suffered during the 1960s. At first, the 1963 bilateral agreement was the central problem. The combination of less flexibility, fewer advanced bookings due to the protracted nature of the negotiations, and increased competition from Hong Kong contributed to a fall in earnings. The volume and value of Japanese cotton fabric exports to the United States declined in 1963 by 13 percent and 5 percent, respectively.[44]

To overcome the rigidities in the LTA and American policy, Japan had several options. First, to improve cotton textile sales, apart from the minor quota increases it would receive in later years, hypothetically Japan could cheat. American monitoring methods lacked the sophistication to track all imports. Under a system of VERs, transshipments, mislabeling goods, changing classifications, and the like, are virtually impossible to stop. Second, and most important, the LTA based its quotas on *quantities* of *cotton* textiles. An exporting country could increase export *earnings* by upgrading existing product lines and diversifying into synthetics. The irony behind the LTA was that it provided Japan, as well as other exporting nations, with an additional incentive to move into synthetics, which was fast becoming the most lucrative textile market. Just as the Japanese had earlier predicted, world cotton consumption increased by only 1.8 percent a year from 1955 to 1963, while synthetics grew at 22.5 percent a year. And during the remainder of the 1960s, the changes were even more dramatic. In 1966, cotton consumption reached its peak in the United States, then started to decline. Synthetic fiber consumption, on the other hand, more than doubled between 1963 and 1970. Since the LTA covered only "cotton," this meant that yarns, fabrics, or clothing that was more than 50 percent synthetic or wool by weight was unrestricted.[45]

The weaknesses in the LTA, however, did not guarantee that a country would increase its earnings. Unless an exporter recognized the declining market in cotton and understood the importance of diversification and cheating, it could be severely hurt by the cotton restrictions. In fact, many nations, such as India, the Philippines, and Egypt, floundered in their textile trade. What made Japan successful where these

others failed was its *long-run approach*. Since historical sus-
picion politically constrained the Japanese from cheating, it
was critical for Japan to shift into higher-priced goods, synthetics, and wool.

The Japanese government and industry immediately
grasped the necessity of diversification and upgrading. Japan's Minister of International Trade and Industry noted at
the signing of the 1963 bilateral accord that his country had
to "further its attempts to ship better quality and higher priced
products while maintaining orderly ways of marketing." In
addition, efforts to switch into synthetics picked up momentum in the early 1960s in Japan. By 1965, synthetics accounted for over 22 percent of Japanese textile production,
compared to only 2 percent a decade earlier. The movement
was so widespread that even leading cotton spinners in Japan
started to shift into multiline fiber products.

With this fundamental change in Japanese production
patterns and the shift in American and world market demand, almost all the major increases in Japanese textile earnings were being registered in synthetic fibers. On a global
basis, the overall value of Japanese cotton fabric exports declined from 230 million dollars in 1955 to 188 million dollars
in 1970. By comparison, synthetic and other fiber fabric exports increased from 208 million dollars to 940 million dollars during this period—a fourfold increase.[46] In trade with
the United States, the Japanese steadily lost its market share
in cotton (see table 3.3). They could not even fill all of their
cotton quotas in the late 1960s.[47] Yet in synthetic fibers Japan
accounted for more than 50 percent of the rapidly growing
United States synthetic textile imports during much of this
period (see table 3.3). By 1968, 50 percent of Japan's textile
and apparel exports to the United States were classified as
synthetic fibers, and 8 percent were wool. Thus the LTA
seemed to have had the paradoxical effect of accelerating Japan's diversification out of a slow-growth market and into
the most lucrative textile products.

On a political level, the LTA was also relatively successful from Japan's perspective. As Benjamin Bardan noted, "From a pragmatic standpoint, if the LTA has not operated according to the highest canons of liberalism, it has *at least served to curtail protectionism,* and has helped make the world cotton textile trade much less restricted than it would otherwise have been."[48] Most important for Japan was that the LTA helped prevent any spillover of protectionism that might have damaged other aspects of United States–Japanese trade. By institutionalizing restrictions, the LTA made United

Table 3.3 American Imports of Japanese Cotton and Synthetic Textile Products, 1962–70 (in millions of square yard equivalents)

	Cotton	Share of U.S. Imports (percent)	Synthetic	Share of U.S. Imports (percent)
1962	351.2	30	110.6	51
1963	304.8	27	126.3	56
1964	324.2	30	163.8	50
1965	404.2	30	301.0	53
1966	412.0	22	445.0	55
1967	376.7	24	352.1	38
1968	391.6	23	434.9	30
1969	395.7	23	584.9	32
1970	330.6	21	774.4	28

SOURCE: Compiled from U.S. Department of Commerce data.

States–Japanese cotton textile trade a matter of "low politics" for most of the decade of the 1960s. The two top officials in the American Embassy in Tokyo at that time remembered textiles as being politically insignificant.[49] When one considers the vast problems that textiles created in the 1950s and later in the 1970s, this was a major accomplishment.

On the negative side, the LTA's greatest liability for Japan and others was that it created a precedent for the international control of a manufactured product. All during the 1960s, American wool and synthetic fiber producers bitterly complained about growing import competition. Although the State Department periodically promised Japan that cotton textile and apparel restrictions were a "special case," which would not be used in other commodities, the Americans sought to establish other LTA-type arrangements several times—first in wool, then in all textile fibers.[50] The benefits of the LTA, however, outweighed the costs. The LTA was only partially to blame for United States efforts to extend protectionism. Domestic American politics would have produced similar demands, regardless of whether or not the LTA existed.

The LTA and Hong Kong, Taiwan, and Korea

The United States was relatively equitable in its treatment of exporting countries under the LTA. Before the United

Table 3.4 United States Imports of Cotton Textiles: Hong Kong, Taiwan, Korea, 1960–62 (in millions of square yard equivalents)

Country of Origin	1960	1961	1962
Hong Kong	289.7	183.0	269.4
Taiwan	23.4	22.9	84.1
Korea	13.7	5.0	10.8

SOURCE: U.S. Tariff Commission, *Textiles and Apparel*, TC Publication 226, January 1968, p. C-14, table 10.

States–Japan 1963 bilateral agreement, each state was restricted in proportion to its textile trade. The United States applied thirty Article 3 restraints to Hong Kong, twenty-one to Taiwan, and none to Korea (see table 3.4). After the United States–Japan agreement, the Americans sought to negotiate bilateral arrangements with each of these countries. Taiwan and Hong Kong signed VERs in October 1963, and Korea agreed to limit its exports under Article 4 of the LTA in January 1965. Finally, all exporting countries had the same opportunities and operated under the same constraints as Japan; to prosper under the LTA, they had to upgrade, diversify, bargain for their short-run needs, and/or cheat.

Cheating and the LTA. The technical complexity of the textile trade made iron-clad restrictions a virtual impossibility—particularly in the early stages of the LTA. Neither importing nor exporting countries were fully aware of the potential slippage at the time of the negotiations. Although the United States wanted to be generous and give exporters a certain degree of flexibility, and it did not envision or approve of the widespread violations that eventually occurred.

At first, the difficulties were relatively minor. Exporters would delay answering a United States request for consultations concerning market disruptions, and a few countries were not properly certifying shipments.[51] Over time, however, some exporting states found an increasing number of loopholes. In his second annual report to the Cotton Textile Committee of the GATT, United States representative Stanley Nehmer listed violations which ranged from overshipments and misclassifications to transshipments. Countries also found that if they did not eliminate *unnecessary* quotas, they could use their flexibility provisions to increase restrained exports. With the help of a complicated technicality, some states discovered that they could actually benefit by keeping a quota intact, despite American demands for its removal.[52]

The United States generally tried to enforce the LTA in the 1960s. Nehmer, one of the highest-ranking officials to deal with textile issues, always argued for strict implementation. Sometimes there was a consensus to be generous, but most of the time there were stalemates in the bureaucracy. When this occurred, Nehmer would invariably insist upon taking the issue up to the Assistant Secretary or Secretary level.[53] This frequently led to embargoes or the imposition of import control systems to monitor incoming goods. Yet despite such American sanctions, the United States was only occasionally successful in preventing circumvention. The opportunities for small-scale cheating always remained greater than America's ability to stop it.

There was only one major interruption in the United States battle to control circumvention. During the height of the Vietnam War, the American cotton market switched from one of surplus capacity to excess demand. With a high military demand for textiles and apparel, there were burgeoning profits for domestic producers coupled with insufficient quantities to satisfy war needs. To meet this textile shortage, the government frequently allowed overshipments; thus, overall cotton imports rose by 25 percent in 1966. The domestic industry was unhappy with the situation, but it was hardly in a position to complain. Producers recognized that if imports were unavailable to supply the high demand, the whole government program to control imports would collapse.[54]

Hong Kong and the LTA. Countries varied greatly in their ability to capitalize on the weaknesses in the LTA, but few nations played the game as well as Hong Kong. In many ways, the British colony was an anomaly in United States cotton textile trade during the early 1960s. Hong Kong managed to circumvent almost every obstacle placed in its path. To begin with, the colony was extraordinarily successful in bargaining with the United States. With the help of its export authorization system and the Cotton Advisory Board, colonial negotiators became the masters of technical details. They knew precisely the areas to bargain for, where the greatest flexibility could be gained, and what could be given up with little cost.[55] In addition, the adaptability of Hong Kong's industry—its high degree of factor mobility—made it easier for Hong Kong to adjust to restrictions than most other economies.

Hong Kong's unique strategic position also gave it more bargaining freedom than other exporting states. While most textile suppliers had agreements that limited overall yardage exports, Hong Kong stubbornly refused to negotiate a comprehensive treaty with the United States until 1966. Restrictions were limited to selected categories of textiles. As a result, Hong Kong manufacturers could shift into unrestricted market segments when their quotas were filled, without being restrained by an overall ceiling. One common explanation for Hong Kong's success was that Britain shielded its colony (to some degree) from American pressure. A more important reason was that Hong Kong controlled a strategic American asset—a bargaining chip which prevented the United States from restricting the colony as severely as it limited Japan and others. According to a former director of the Commerce Department's Import Program Office, there was a fear of losing Hong Kong as a base for collecting intelligence. Precious information on the People's Republic of China might be lost if the United States pushed Hong Kong to the "breaking point."[56] Since Hong Kong was not as dependent upon the United States as various other American clients, and since textile exports were crucial to the colony's economic well-being, such a threat was credible. It is doubtful that Hong Kong ever made this linkage explicit, but United States negotiators apparently perceived this as limiting their negotiating freedom, at least until 1966.

Hong Kong's bargaining success was accompanied by implementation success. As noted earlier, bureaucratic politics often created loopholes in American policies. One such potential loophole was that the negotiation of a country's quota was based on the level of an exporter's actual shipments from the previous year. Since most states had difficulties filling their quotas, this policy had little advantage to the average developing state. But if a country could overship its quota—as Hong Kong did *every year* from 1961 to 1970—this could strengthen a nation's bargaining position and quota allotment.[57] Despite occasional embargoes, Hong Kong restraint levels actually rose by an average of 10.5 percent a year from 1962 to 1966. Furthermore, between 1963 and 1965 the average annual growth rate of cotton textile imports from all developing nations into the United States was 9 percent; from Hong Kong it was 12 percent.[58] By 1968, Hong Kong surpassed Japan as the largest cotton textile and apparel supplier to the American market (see table 3.5).

Thus the LTA had relatively little impact on Hong Kong's textile exports to the United States. Unlike Japan and many other states, cotton exports were not severely hurt by restrictions. Hong Kong manufacturers usually operated at full capacity throughout the LTA. In 1965, for example, United States orders were greater than Hong Kong's ability to deliver. The combination of shrewd bargaining, Hong Kong's special strategic position, cheating, and a high degree of adaptability allowed the colony to increase its gains in cotton textiles. At the same time, the LTA provided somewhat of an incentive for the colony to upgrade and diversify its product mix, which enhanced overall trade earnings. As one study of the LTA's effect on Hong Kong suggested:

Table 3.5 United States Cotton Textile Imports from Hong Kong, Taiwan, and Korea, 1962–1970 (in millions of square yard equivalents)

	1962	1964	1966	1968	1970
Hong Kong	269.4	264.4[a]	353.4[a]	402.8	376.6
Taiwan	84.1	46.6	61.6	70.8	65.6
Korea	10.8	33.5	24.6	36.6	39.1

SOURCE: U.S. Tariff Commission, *Textiles and Apparels*, TC Publication 226, January 1968, p. C-14, table 10.

[a]These figures are substantially below the Commerce Department's bilateral report for Hong Kong during those years. LTA records were kept from October through September, while these figures come from the annual Customs reports.

The unfavorable impact of the Arrangement on Hong Kong's economic development turned out to be only temporary. . . . The versatile and resourceful entrepreneurs soon found substitutes for cotton textiles in the textile market. . . . As a consequence, in 1963, Hong Kong's economic growth resumed its swift pace.[59]

Hong Kong's total exports to the United States had grown to 990 million dollars in 1971—almost a 500 percent increase over 1962.

An ironic twist in Hong Kong's success was that it did not move into synthetic textile fibers as quickly as Japan, Taiwan, or Korea. Since these other countries found profits in cotton textiles largely reduced by protectionism, they were forced into a long-run strategy early in the game. But Hong Kong's ability to avoid being hurt by cotton restrictions meant that it had less incentive to adjust. Hong Kong therefore deviated to some extent from the strategy I proposed in chapter 1. Even though it generally followed a short-run approach through the mid-1960s, the colony's cotton textile industry remained profitable. Pursuing long-term objectives was not a necessary condition for Hong Kong to increase its export earnings. The only cost to Hong Kong was that it did not realize the maximum gains. Had the colonial manufacturers followed a two-track strategy—emphasizing both synthetics and cotton—Hong Kong would not have been the smallest

Table 3.6 United States Imports of Synthetic Textile Products from Hong Kong, Taiwan, and Korea, 1962–1970

	Hong Kong	Taiwan	Korea
1962	n.a.	n.a.	n.a.
1963	n.a.	n.a.	n.a.
1964	10.9	14.3	2.5
1965	19.2	24.9	17.6
1966	39.3	32.9	27.7
1967	74.6	59.5	64.2
1968	99.3	122.8	136.9
1969	144.8	237.5	212.3
1970	188.0	349.5	254.0

SOURCE: Compiled from U.S. Department of Commerce data.

synthetic fiber supplier of the four East Asian countries in the late 1960s (see tables 3.3 and 3.6).

Taiwan, Korea, and the LTA. The Republic of China (Taiwan) and the Republic of Korea were latecomers in world cotton textile trade. In 1960, when Hong Kong and Japan had already established themselves as the leading textile exporters to the United States, the shipments from Taiwan and Korea combined were less than one-sixth the cotton exports of Hong Kong, half the exports of Portugal and Spain, and lower than shipments of countries such as India and the Philippines.[60] Their prospects for rapid expansion of textile exports certainly seemed slim after the creation of the LTA. Hong Kong and Japan at least had a base on which they could make adjustments; Taiwan and Korea had to build their industrial infrastructure knowing that their principal manufactured export was going to be restricted by American and European protectionism.

Late industrialization, however, has its advantages. A country may face greater constraints than the early industrializer, but at the same time it may have the opportunity to plan for the future with greater certainty. Taiwan, Korea, and other late developers could observe the rise in protectionist sentiment in the United States and elsewhere, before they planned the expansion of their export industries. Consequently, these states could search for alternatives to cotton textile production as well as look for new markets. As early as 1960, Taiwan sought to compensate for possible protectionist problems in the United States by announcing its intention to encourage export diversification to Southeast Asia and to expand synthetics.[61] It required a long-run perspective for a less developed country (LDC) to take such steps; a LDC's short-run comparative advantage was in the simpler manufacturing process of cotton textiles.

Taiwan's strategy under the LTA was identical to the Japanese strategy of 1955. It wanted to maximize its short-term export earnings in cotton textiles while placing its principal emphasis on product diversification. On the domestic level, the Nationalist Chinese government did not seek any expansion of cotton production during the first half of the 1960s. Furthermore, the Chinese Fourth Four-Year Plan envisaged a reduction in cotton spindles starting in 1965. In the meantime, Taiwan directed its efforts at modernizing the textile industry, upgrading existing products, and expanding synthetic production. The government targeted various segments of synthetic textile manufacturing for increases that ranged from 50 to 300 percent.[62] Taiwan's motivation for this long-run strategy in textiles was largely a consequence of the LTA. According to one analyst, "much of this reorganization was forced on the industry by new quality demands brought about by the restrictions imposed by the United States and Canada on textile imports from Taiwan."[63] Although "prophets of doom [had] forecast the industry's collapse" after the United States imposed its first quotas in 1962, Taiwanese officials thought that diversification could enhance their gains. And the Taiwanese government was right, as textile exports rose from 38 million dollars in 1962 to over 200 million dollars in 1969.

Korea's strategy was very similar to Taiwan's. The Korean Five-Year Plan of 1962 called for an emphasis on synthetic production, with no expansion planned for export earnings in cotton textiles.[64] The rationale given for targeting synthetics was to reduce import dependence on raw cotton, which was the central weakness in Korea's textile industry. Although Korean documents did not make an explicit reference to the LTA, Korea would not have pushed as hard in synthetics without a clear perception of the limited market in cotton (compare tables 3.5 and 3.6).

On the international level, Taiwan and Korea followed identical strategies. Both nations employed variants of the "controlled risk" approach to bargaining. They would ask for as much as possible, stall for as long as they could, and try to push the United States to its limit. When the Koreans negotiated their first bilateral accord with the United States, for example, it took nine months. The United States started by insisting on a 17.2 million square yard quota based on Korea's 1961 exports, whereas Korea proposed 39.9 million, based on its 1963 export record. The negotiations broke down several times before the two sides finally agreed on an American compromise of 26 million square yards.

In comparative terms, Korea and Taiwan did no better than average in their quota bargaining. They lacked the security and political advantages of Hong Kong, and they had the liabilities of being dependent clients, like Japan. As a result, there is no evidence that either state received special treatment because they were American allies. Korea's quota remained significantly below many nonallies such as Egypt and Singapore. In fact, Korea did so poorly in 1965 that it had to reduce its dependence on the American market to maintain its short-run cotton earnings. The United States took 70 percent of Korea's cotton textiles in 1963 and only 25 percent by 1967.[65] And Taiwan, while doing better than Korea, had quotas equal to or lower than those of Mexico, India, and Brazil. American negotiators consistently reaffirmed in interviews that they accommodated and restricted all major textile exporting countries equally.[66]

With regard to implementation, however, Taiwan and Korea were somewhat special, because they had well-known reputations as cheaters. Both countries consistently over-shipped individual categories. As part of the United States' strict implementation policy, Taiwanese and Korean exports were placed on an import control system and frequently embargoed. Yet severe sanctions were usually avoided because the Americans did not view cheating by these states as purposeful or malicious. If Japan had cheated on a large scale, it would be assumed that the Japanese were trying to hurt the American industry. In the case of Taiwan and Korea, United States officials believed that these states "could not control their exports."[67] If embargoed quantities were small, contingent arrangements would be made to accommodate importers and exporters.[68] The Americans did not want to crack down too hard on unintentional cheating; they knew that exporting countries would not cooperate with the United States if restrictions were too rigid. At the same time, Taiwan and Korea had few incentives to prevent cheating. The political and economic costs were low, and the profits in most cases were comparatively high.

Conclusion

The 1960s was a period of trial and error for American textile policy. By institutionalizing protectionism, the LTA gave the United States far greater control over outcomes than it had in the 1950s. Bargaining differed under this international regime largely because American threats were more credible. The system, nonetheless, remained permeable. When the United States pursued accommodative strategies, exporters could still bargain for loopholes. The LTA provided only a guideline, one which left room for interpretation. Exporters could capitalize on this ambiguity if they negotiated for flexibility and technical loopholes and then bargained with coherent policies. Short-run profits could also be enhanced by circumvention. Although the Americans were relatively strict in their implementation policy, small-scale cheating and bending of the rules would usually succeed.

Yet for an exporting nation to optimize its trade earnings throughout the 1960s, it had to go several steps further. First, as long as cotton exports were restricted in quantity, industrializing countries needed to upgrade their produce in order to charge the maximum possible price for the limited cotton items. They also had to try to capture any scarcity gains that might be generated by the quotas. Both these tasks required a well-organized industry that could effectively modernize production, keep up with fashion trends, and bargain well with importers. All four East Asian producers coped well in these areas, particularly after the early 1960s.

Second, maximizing cotton textile earnings provided only remedial, short-term profits to an exporter; in most cases, maximum cotton earnings would not substantially increase overall textile earnings. Since cotton sales were ultimately limited by market demand, the key for all exporting states was to focus on long-run gains from trade, by diversifying into the fast-growing market of synthetic textiles (see figures 3.1 and 3.2). Far greater gains were available to those countries which diversified in response to the LTA than those which tried to operate within the restraints. United States imports of unrestricted synthetic fibers increased 1700 percent in value and 1800 percent in quantity during the 1960s, while cotton imports only doubled (see table 3.7).

The LTA provided an opportunity and an incentive for all countries to switch into synthetics, but not all did. A nec-

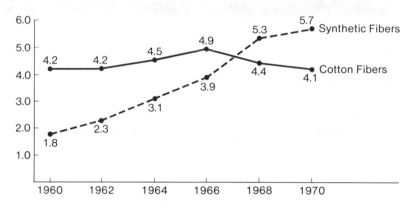

Figure 3.1 Cotton and Synthetic Fibers Consumed in Textiles: Apparent United States Consumption, 1960-70 (in millions of pounds)

Source: U.S. International Trade Commission, *The History and Current Status of the Multifiber Arrangement*, p. C-3, table 2.

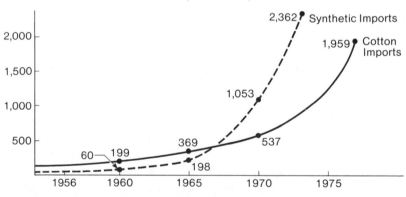

Figure 3.2 Total United States Imports of Synthetic and Cotton Textiles, 1956-75 (in $ millions)

Source: Compiled from U.S. Department of Commerce data.

essary condition was that an LDC possess factor mobility—the capacity to move resources and technology into new, untried areas. The bureaucratic organizations (public and private) that existed in each East Asian state provided one element of this prerequisite. The *sufficient condition* was that the exporting country have a long-run perspective. Hong Kong was the slowest to move into synthetics precisely because its manufacturers generally operated on a short-term basis.

The British colony continued to export cotton textiles for two reasons: first, it had attained a substantial market share before restrictions, a fact which minimized the incentive to adjust; and second, it had unique political and strategic assets. In such a highly competitive market, the colony was especially adept at reacting to short-run demand pressures.

Table 3.7 United States Imports of Apparel and Textiles, 1961–70 (in $ million and square yard equivalents [SYE])

	Cotton		Synthetic Fibers		Wool		Total	
	Dollars	*SYE*	*Dollars*	*SYE*	*Dollars*	*SYE*	*Dollars*	*SYE*
1961	199	720	60	151	200	85	459	956
1962	307	1,165	78	213	272	156	657	1,534
1963	299	1,101	90	221	297	161	686	1,483
1964	310	1,058	129	328	289	138	728	1,524
1965	369	1,312	193	566	357	212	919	2,090
1966	463	1,824	258	797	354	204	1,075	2,826
1967	417	1,485	312	934	327	167	1,056	2,586
1968	477	1,648	499	1,453	410	210	1,386	3,311
1969	527	1,562	695	1,783	410	191	1,632	3,626
1970	537	1,536	1,053	2,760	359	170	1,949	4,466

SOURCE: Compiled from U.S. Department of Commerce data.

Through 1966, Hong Kong industrialists were simply "hesitant about branching out into this new field [of synthetics]."[69] Moreover, Hong Kong was already the second largest textile supplier to the United States when the LTA came into effect. It started off less sensitive than Taiwan or Korea to supply constraints. When one combines these two factors with Hong Kong's unusual political and strategic position and expert bargaining, one can understand why Hong Kong remained in cotton trade and why it prospered where others suffered.

Japan, Korea, and Taiwan differed from Hong Kong because they had more centrally controlled textile sectors as well as industrial plans that were not as responsive to short-run market considerations. All three of these states were also American allies, which in this case carried more burdens than benefits; each country had more to lose than the British colony. Finally, even though Japan had a large market share similar to Hong Kong's, less effective negotiating, increased competition from other suppliers, and a reputational constraint against cheating reduced Japan's ability to remain highly profitable in cotton textile trade.

Yet the long-run strategies pursued by Taiwan, Korea, and Japan more than compensated for most cotton textile losses. Diversification put these three exporters into the forefront of the synthetic fiber industry. At the same time, Hong Kong's success in cotton textile trade turned out to be a mixed victory. Hong Kong's short-run approach may have cost it some profit in its overall textile trade. It was not until around 1967 that colonial manufacturers finally started a vigorous campaign to develop the synthetic market.

By 1970, Japan, Taiwan, Korea, and Hong Kong (in order of descending importance) accounted for 90 percent of the United States' non-European textile imports. Not surprisingly, synthetic textile manufacturers in the United States were disturbed by this huge surge in imports. Fortunately for the exporting countries, these producers had a hard time convincing the American government that imports were actually causing "market disruptions." The expansion in American consumption of synthetic textiles brought prosperity to both the United States domestic industry and the Far Eastern countries. Not only had the Asian "gang of four" adjusted to the changing market conditions, but so had the Americans. Textile manufacturers in the United States experienced record growth during the LTA. Therefore, despite the phenomenal increases in imports, the foreign goods' share of the expanding synthetic fiber market rose from 1.3 percent in 1962 to just 3.6 percent in 1968.[70]

Nonetheless, the American textile and apparel industry perceived the trend in imports as a long-run threat. Beginning around 1967, the textile lobby launched a serious campaign to amass congressional and bureaucratic support for new restrictions. The Johnson administration was not very sympathetic, but Richard Nixon was quite another story. In the next chapter I will investigate the American attempt to broaden protectionism—the one act which the Japanese and other exporters feared most.

Chapter 4

Textiles, Round 3:
The Search for
Comprehensive Protection,
1969–1982

In 1969, President Richard Nixon dispatched Secretary of Commerce Maurice Stans to negotiate a multifiber textile arrangement with the four major exporters of East Asia. Little did the President or his envoy realize that this would be the start of a major crisis in United States trade policy. For the next two and a half years, the Nixon administration would battle with Japan, Hong Kong, Korea, and Taiwan dozens of times without reaching any agreement. It took the near passage of a massive protectionist bill, linkages to the proposed United States reversion of Okinawa to Japan, the imposition of a 10 percent surcharge on imports into the United States, and, finally, a threat to invoke the Trading with the Enemy Act of 1917, before Japan and the others capitulated.

This episode was not only a turning point for American trade relations with East Asia; it was also a critical juncture in the evolution of global protectionism. The multifiber agreements that the United States negotiated in 1971 set the stage for a new and more restrictive international regime that would regulate every aspect of textile trade. By the early 1980s, import restrictions in textiles and apparel would be among the world's most comprehensive and severe.

Prelude to Crisis:
Attempts at Wool Restraints

From the very beginning of the Long-Term Arrangement, the American government had explored the possibility of a multilateral agreement that would cover wool and synthetic textiles. Negotiating multifiber restrictions, however, was not as easy as regulating cotton trade. Britain and Italy were among the United States' most important wool suppliers, and restraining the exports of industrialized allies was more difficult than limiting exports from less developed countries (LDCs). In addition, Article 1 of the Long-Term Arrangement clearly stated that the use of multilateral restraints was not intended for other products. The signators were supposed to "recognize that since these measures are intended to deal with the special problems of cotton textiles, they are not to be considered as lending themselves to application in other fields."[1] Yet none of these considerations satisfied American textile producers. Manufacturers of wool and synthetic fibers wanted restrictions, regardless of American international concerns.

Wool companies were especially vociferous during the 1950s and early 1960s. Moreover, even though they represented a relatively small segment of the American textile industry, they always seemed to have powerful friends in Washington. As early as 1956, President Eisenhower authorized special protection for wool manufacturers, and in 1958, Japan "voluntarily" restricted woolen fabric exports to the United States to avoid further restrictions and to promote "orderly marketing."[2] President Kennedy also sought trade barriers for wool producers. Kennedy felt that he had promised protection to the entire textile industry in 1961, not just cotton manufacturers. At a meeting between the President and his trade advisors, one official informed Kennedy that imports held "only" 16 percent of the wool market. Kennedy thanked the individual for the information but remarked that import penetration made little difference. Regardless of the economic facts, wool textiles were a political problem.[3]

Serious efforts to help the wool industry were nonetheless sporadic. In January 1962, Michael Blumenthal was allegedly sent by the White House to Geneva to ask the GATT Secretariat to put wool on the LTA agenda. Since England, Japan, and others were totally opposed to wool restraints, the proposal made little headway. The next avenue was to ask a heretofore dormant International Wool Study Group to investigate the problem.[4] But here again, as long as the Italians and the British were against restrictions, nothing concrete could be decided. Finally, the American government agreed to support the demands of wool textile manufacturers for a wool version of the LTA.[5] Since no single exporter wanted to restrict its shipments while others would be free to increase their market share, a multilateral agreement appeared to be the only hope for minimizing import growth.

The dilemma the United States faced was where to begin. England and Italy were unlikely to agree to wool restrictions; furthermore, these two countries were the hardest to coerce. This left Japan as the only reasonable target, even though the Japanese were equally determined to fight wool restraints. American officials reasoned that if the relatively weaker Japan could be brought to an international bargaining table, perhaps the Europeans would come as well.

Japan, of course, saw little to be gained by talking with the United States. In 1964, the Japanese firmly rejected American overtures to discuss wool textiles. A year later, however, the Japanese became trapped by diplomatic protocol. During a somewhat mysterious interlude at a summit conference between President Lyndon Johnson and Japanese Prime Minister Sato in 1965, the subject of wool textiles was discussed early in the session. Sometime after the wool question was dropped, the President supposedly remarked to the Prime Minister about how well the two leaders got along in face-to-face discussions.[6] Johnson then allegedly suggested that similar meetings between industries might alleviate trade problems, perhaps even the wool textile issue. Sato agreed "in principle" to the President's statement, at which point the topic was discontinued.

From this rather innocent exchange, momentum started to build for an industry-to-industry meeting. No one was exactly sure what Johnson had said or what Sato had agreed to "in principle," but advocates of protection in the American bureaucracy jumped on this opportunity to get Japan to talk to the United States for the first time about wool restraints. Neither industry wanted such a meeting, but both were presented with a *fait accompli*. Japanese wool producers were totally opposed to any negotiations, but they could not embarrass the Prime Minister by refusing to attend a meeting. At the same time, American wool producers were afraid that the Japanese would agree to restrain their wool exports at a very high level and claim they had cooperated with the United States. Yet American wool manufacturers could not repudiate the President's efforts, lest they weaken their own position and the first concrete United States initiative.

The major problem was determining the precise form of the meeting: should it be industry-to-industry, government-to-government, or include both industries and governments? Johnson seemed to have suggested an industry meeting, without being aware of possible antitrust violations.[7] Therefore, the White House issued a "clarification" stating that the President had proposed government-to-government talks on an international wool agreement, not a meeting of industries.[8] Since Japan had agreed "in principle" only to industry discussions, both sides compromised on a joint business–government conference designed to exchange views. Yet it was no secret that the United States wanted more from this meeting, and that Japan wanted less.

American policy makers, however, were far from united on what to do. Some members of the United States government viewed wool import restraints as imperative, while others were more concerned about diplomacy. As a result, there was no consensus on how far the United States should go to obtain an agreement. The minimum American goal was to get Japan to attend an international wool conference.

The Japanese, on the other hand, expressed their objectives unambiguously: They flatly opposed any multilateral, bilateral, or unilateral restrictions. They did not believe that the United States had any economic justification for restraints, nor did they see any overriding political reason to buckle under to American pressure. There were some Japanese bureaucrats who disagreed with this view, but the majority were resolutely opposed to any compromise. A Foreign Ministry spokesman held a press conference a few days before the wool meeting to emphasize Japan's "unalterable" opposition to an international conference or similar arrangements designed to limit wool exports.[9] Since the Japanese government was "not quite happy" with the LTA, and the Japanese textile industry was "very bitter," the spokesman said that new restraints were virtually out of the question.

To make matters worse, the unique format of the June 7–8, 1965, meeting in Tokyo further dampened the prospects for some kind of an agreement. Previous United States–Japan encounters over textiles were always limited to government-to-government discussions. Industry advisors would be in adjoining rooms, but they never sat at the bargaining table. The very success in reaching accords in previous negotiations could be largely attributed to the fact that each government made concessions which its industries would never have approved. Hence it seemed likely that the mere presence of industry personnel would make convergence toward an acceptable outcome practically impossible. Given the industries' extreme positions, there was no bargaining range from which an agreement could emerge.

During the first day of discussions, each nation presented its views, provided statistics to back its claims, and warned the other about the possible consequences of its action. It was standard operating procedure to employ threats at the start of textile negotiations; bargaining was normally heated, particularly when negotiators discussed the philosophical issue of trade barriers. Nonetheless, most of the Japanese delegation was growing tired and frustrated by American demands. One government official said that Japan "will not go along with setting up another trade barrier, no matter what items are involved." [10] Another MITI bureaucrat told the Americans that the LTA was bad enough, but now the United States was "moving in the direction of a violation of Article 1 of the LTA." [11]

It was not until the second day, however, that the latent tensions in the negotiations finally exploded. Warren Christopher, the chief American negotiator and Secretary of State Dean Rusk's special representative, remarked during the morning session that "if relief from disruptive imports is not forthcoming, Congress may well take matters into its own hands." Although such warnings were not unusual in these situations, the normal amenities of these negotiations suddenly went out the window. Without warning, the Japanese unleashed a fierce (and unprecedented) verbal assault on the American proposals. An infuriated Japanese textile representative exclaimed:

We were shocked by your presentation. We were shocked by your presentation on economic matters. We are confident that if you will get an objective analysis you will support our position that our exports have not injured the U.S. . . . . We could talk all day but not agree . . . furthermore we are shocked by your political presentation. We are the closest friends and allies, therefore, you surprised us by your political threats. So I assure you, we too have a government and legislature and we have leaders who are concerned with our welfare and they will protect us. We too have means for our protection including trade in textiles. Therefore, to avoid an ugly showdown, you should check the real facts and change your position. We are not easily frightened and our relationship will suffer. We do not like political threats. *We are not North Vietnam. We hope you will make distinctions between your friends and your enemies.*[12]

Two other Japanese textile representatives then made equally tough, albeit more polite, speeches. One said: "We have no intention of participating in an international wool conference. It is a domestic problem and must be solved domestically. You should not resort to political pressure." The other noted: "The LTA is a dissatisfaction to me and I am not pleased by it, therefore I oppose an agreement on wool." The chair of the meeting, the textile director of MITI, quickly moved to adjourn for lunch. The Americans agreed but declined an invitation to eat with their Japanese hosts.

During the lunch break, the American negotiators met with the American Ambassador to Japan to discuss their options. Both Warren Christopher and Ambassador Reischauer were angered by the Japanese reference to North Vietnam. Despite the fact that some members of the delegation wanted the talks to go on, the highest-ranking officials decided it would be politically counterproductive.[13] Christopher therefore opened the afternoon session by ruling out the "usefulness of any further discussion." He noted that "many of the factual matters . . . might have been clarified or corrected," but he lamented that it would be impossible after the "atmosphere established [that] morning."

The head of the Japanese delegation apologized for the incident, but both sides were embittered by the exchange. A Japanese Foreign Ministry official later had the meeting reopened to expunge the North Vietnam statement from the record. Yet from the American perspective, the damage was done, and clearing the record would not remove the memory.[14] In the 1950s, it would have been inconceivable for Japan to censure its American patron so explicitly. Moreover, this was the first time that any United States–Japan textile negotiation had ever totally broken down.

Even though the Japanese government and industry were

resolutely opposed to a wool conference, these particular negotiations could have served a more positive function for Japan. Negotiations can communicate differences and educate
opponents, as well as provide an opportunity to bargain for
side payments. Without insulting the United States, Japan
might have exploited the occasion by making a minor short-
run sacrifice, as the American wool producers feared, or Japan could have simply agreed to disagree. Instead, the Japanese succeeded in deterring the Americans from actively
seeking a wool agreement for a few years, but at the cost of
greater American resentment and impatience.[15] Furthermore,
the Japanese government apparently recognized this about six
weeks too late. In mid-July, the Japanese Foreign Ministry
expressed sympathy for United States wool problems. At the
same time, MITI reportedly had a secret meeting with textile
officials to discuss a possible VER.[16] MITI officials noted that
a VER might help increase prices as well as insure orderly
marketing techniques by Japanese producers. If this had been
done in June, not only would a small crisis in United States–
Japan trade relations have been averted, but the Japanese
might have gained some political capital.

This wool episode was a harbinger of things to come.
Throughout the mid-1960s, resentment of the LTA grew in
Japan. Resistance was building within the Japanese bureaucracy against any short-run sacrifices for longer-run gains. In
addition, many in Japan no longer felt obliged to bend to the
will of the United States. Japan had achieved unprecedented
growth during this period; it had gone from a developing
country in the early 1950s to one of the world's largest industrial powers in the late 1960s. Few high-level Japanese
officials, however, clearly understood that Japan's interdependence with the United States was still highly asymmetrical.[17] The Japanese did not seem to realize that an exporting
country's political power does not necessarily increase with
its expanded industrial base. As long as an industrialized importer can allocate or withhold market shares without great
costs to itself, an exporter—even a powerful exporter such as

Japan in the late 1960s—is ultimately vulnerable in a bilateral trading partnership.

The Search for a Multifiber Solution

By the end of the 1960s, policy makers and interest groups in the United States had learned one set of lessons from their years of protectionism, whereas their counterparts in the Far East had learned very different ones. American textile manufacturers and government bureaucrats began to recognize that their textile policy was short-sighted. The LTA had been somewhat effective in moderating imports in the slow-growth cotton market, but its exclusion of synthetic and wool fibers created new competition only six or seven years later.

Under industry pressure, President Johnson had directed the United States Tariff Commission to undertake a thorough investigation of the textile and apparel sector.[18] When no economic damage was found, the President rejected the industry's pleas for protection. Textile producers, however, have never been easily dissuaded by presidential rejections. They persisted in their claims until they found a receptive ear during the 1968 presidential campaign. Richard Nixon needed help in the South, and Southern textile industrialists wanted comprehensive quotas. Under the circumstances, economic justification was unimportant. Nixon wanted textiles' support, so he promised to "take the necessary steps" when elected. As President, Nixon quickly moved to pay off his political debt by sending Secretary of Commerce Stans to Europe and the Far East to arrange a new international conference on multifiber textiles.

Across the Pacific, textile manufacturers and decision makers in Hong Kong, Taiwan, Korea, and Japan had different views on the LTA and comprehensive restraints. Throughout the early 1960s, these Far Eastern countries begrudgingly accepted the LTA as a way to confine broader protectionism.

No one liked the LTA, but at least it quieted the American textile industry and provided the possibility of shifting into synthetics. Multifiber restraints would eliminate the diversification option and defeat the original purpose of the LTA. Industries and policy makers in each of these countries were wondering where restrictions would stop if they acquiesced to the United States now.

The interests of the four East Asian exporters were not identical, however. Korea, Taiwan, and Hong Kong were newcomers in the synthetic market. Each had expanded its exports by almost 100 percent per year since 1966, but their collective share of the United States market was relatively low in 1969 (see table 3.6). Hence any restrictions in synthetic fibers would be disastrous for these three countries. Japan was a different story. In 1969, Japan's first priorities in its relationship with the United States were to bring Okinawa under Japanese sovereignty and deal with American complaints about Japanese trade barriers and an undervalued yen. Moreover, the textile industry was showing signs of decline. Japanese planners recognized as early as 1967 that the country's textile industry was losing its competitiveness to "low-wage" countries. Under these circumstances, the Japanese had little to gain from confrontation. Their best policy would have been to negotiate an agreement with the United States.

Yet countries do not always pursue those policies that appear to be in their logical interests. What followed Maurice Stans' visit to the Far East in 1969 was what some have called a "textile wrangle." [19] The United States tried to negotiate textile restrictions for more than two years without success. Textiles virtually dominated the agenda of economic relations of the five nations during this period, despite other pressing problems. The exporting states eventually capitulated, but not before they helped trigger one of the worst postwar crises in United States—Far East relations.

Round 1: The Stans Trip and United States Goals

In some ways, very little had changed in the thirteen years of American textile protectionism. In 1956, 1961, as well as 1969, it was domestic politics that motivated the administration's desire for trade barriers. He had made electoral promises, and, like his predecessors, Nixon felt that the textile industry had to be appeased. At the same time, Nixon was committed to the Executive tradition of supporting freer world trade. Some form of voluntary restraint was preferable to iron-clad restrictions. Finally, the United States was willing to accommodate Far Eastern exporters, although it was less accommodating in the late 1960s than it had been in the past.

The American strategy in 1969 was to negotiate an LTA-type arrangement for multifiber textiles and apparel. Maurice Stans hoped that the Nixon administration could do for synthetic and wool producers what Kennedy had done for cotton manufacturers. The first step in Stans' grand strategy was to get the Europeans to agree to a Geneva conference; then he would proceed to the Far East for talks with the major exporting nations. Yet from its start, the Stans mission ran into trouble. First, the Europeans told the Americans to go directly to the Far East; the Germans and the French had no interest in a multifiber agreement in 1969. There was no consensus in Europe, nor was there any sympathy for the United States position. Second, when Stans and the American negotiating team arrived in Japan on May 10, 1969, their reception was less than enthusiastic. The Japanese Foreign Minister opened the first meeting in Tokyo by ruling out the discussion of textiles. Other items were on the agenda, but textiles were the most important one to the United States. An infuriated Stans reportedly lashed out at the Japanese, asking how they could refuse to listen to a representative of the American President.[20] The net result was that the United States accomplished virtually nothing in Tokyo before the delegation left for Seoul, Taipei, and Hong Kong.

American difficulties in Japan reflected a twofold problem: (1) the Americans used inappropriate bargaining tactics, and (2) the Japanese had adopted an inappropriate bargaining strategy. Japan's representatives took a maximizing approach, a product of powerful domestic interests rather than of logical analysis. MITI, the Japanese textile industry, and even the Japanese Diet were advocating an absolute rejection of American overtures, regardless of the consequences. In an unusual show of unity, the lower house of the Diet passed an all-party resolution the day before Stans' visit that demanded its government press Washington for no quotas. Some Japanese seemed to hope that firm resistance would lead the United States to drop its protectionist program, just as it had done in 1965 after the aborted wool negotiations. The Japanese strategy was purely short run. According to one MITI official, "The Japanese government at the time was not considering its next step, much less how ultimately to settle the textile question. All we had in mind was to oppose the present demand of the United States." [21]

On the other side of the negotiating table, Stans did not comprehend Japan's domestic problems or the differences between the 1961–62 LTA negotiations and the present discussions.[22] Stans' tactical approach was nothing less than dogmatic; his strategy was to "put down maximum demands and stay in." [23] Yet his maximum demands did not include any meaningful threats. The result was that Stans wanted Japan to sacrifice exports, but he could not provide the Japanese with any inducements. Thus there were no common interests and no bargaining range. In essence, both countries were pursuing policies that responded to their domestic constituencies without in-depth consideration of the foreign policy implications.

United States experience with other Asian exporters was only marginally different from the talks with Japan. In Korea and Taiwan, there was a friendlier exchange of information, but both exporting nations insisted that textiles were simply too important to restrain. The Minister of Economic Affairs in Taiwan explained that the "Republic of China cannot voluntarily curtail its textile exports to the United States. Textile products accounted for 22 percent of total ROC exports in 1968, while exports to the U.S. represented 36.2 percent of ROC textile trade." [24] Both countries nonetheless stated their willingness to continue discussions at a later date. In Hong Kong, the American textile negotiators found the colony "belligerent" and "unresponsive." [25] Colonial representatives lectured the Americans on the principles of free trade, and like the Japanese, they did not want to discuss textiles. In this case, however, textiles were the only item on the United States–Hong Kong agenda. When the Americans returned to Washington, they viewed the Hong Kong visit as the least worthwhile in a generally unproductive trip.

Round 2: The Nixon–Sato Deal

The purpose of the Stans mission was to convince the major exporters of synthetic textiles that there was a high-level interest in the United States for a multilateral, multifiber agreement. The only undisputed accomplishment of the trip was to discover that such a plan was unfeasible—at least temporarily. Stans therefore suggested to the White House two alternatives: legislated quotas or bilateral VERs. Since a multilateral agreement was out of the question and legislated quotas undesirable, Nixon sanctioned the negotiation of a comprehensive bilateral agreement with Japan which would be followed by similar VERs with the other exporters. [26] The only problem was that Nixon refused to give Stans financial or trade leverage for obtaining the accords.

In Japan, high-ranking officials were also reassessing the textile question. At a ministerial meeting in Washington, two months after the Tokyo talks, MITI Minister Ohira agreed to send a "fact-finding" mission to the United States. Although the meeting was to be limited in scope, this represented a major shift from the refusal to discuss textiles the previous May. By the fall, the Japanese even started to express their willingness to discuss the specifics for textile restraints. A preliminary meeting was scheduled for November 17, 1969, in Geneva, where the two countries could exchange detailed proposals for voluntary controls.

The Japanese changed their approach for several reasons. The most important one was a growing concern in Japan for broader problems in United States–Japan relations, and particularly the question of Okinawa's reversion to Japanese sovereignty. During November 1969, President Nixon had scheduled a summit with Prime Minister Sato, at which time Okinawa and possibly textiles were to be discussed. Both Foreign Ministry and MITI officials wanted to avoid a possible United States linkage between textiles and Okinawa at the summit; the Foreign Ministry did not want many years of work on Okinawa complicated by the textile issue; and MITI did not want to be forced into substantive concessions on textiles because of Okinawa. Hence the only way to avoid the linkage, the Japanese thought, was to give the appearance of progress in normal bilateral talks.

The best-laid plans, however, are not always successful. If textiles had been inconsequential to the United States government, then the Japanese strategy might have worked. But textiles were not unimportant to the President. Both Henry Kissinger, Nixon's National Security Adviser, and Richard Nixon viewed the Okinawa talks as an opportunity to solve their domestic textile problem. In fact, Nixon felt the textile negotiations would be easier if he intervened personally. Meanwhile, Sato had staked much of his political reputation on the return of Okinawa to Japanese rule and effecting that return without nuclear weapons being stationed on the island. By comparison, textiles were an insignificant issue to the Japanese Prime Minister.

A bargain should have been easy under these circumstances. Sato could have given ground on textiles in exchange for Nixon's concessions on Okinawa. The only thing stopping such a tradeoff was Japanese domestic politics; for months before the summit, the Japanese bureaucracy, press, Diet, and textile industry had been pressuring the Prime Minister to reject a textile–Okinawa linkage.

The Secret Deal. If Sato had had the same control over textile policy as Nixon, there would have been few problems in the negotiations. But textiles was a highly salient issue in Japan which deeply divided the Japanese bureaucracy. Moreover, there was an upcoming Diet election in December 1969, which limited Sato's flexibility. The question was, How could Japan formulate a coherent, long-run strategy to deal with textiles and broader issues, if Sato could not take control? The answer was a secret plan invented by Henry Kissinger.[27] Before the summit conference, Kissinger and a personal emissary of Sato's worked out a deal whereby the Japanese would agree to voluntary restraints in textiles in exchange for a nuclear-free Okinawa. To help Sato avoid accusations of buckling under to American pressure, an elaborate scenario was devised to cover up the secret accord. According to the Kissinger plan, no announcement about textiles would be necessary after the summit. This would reassure the Japanese public that there was no Okinawa linkage. Then the United States would submit an overly restrictive plan to Japanese textile negotiators in Geneva, *before* the Diet elections, which the Japanese Prime Minister could summarily reject. By standing up to the Americans, Sato would enhance his own legitimacy and secure his party's position in the Diet elections. After the elections, the United States would submit a revised textile proposal in Geneva—the one agreed to at the summit—and the Japanese would accept the American concessions.

In many ways, Kissinger had a brilliant scheme. He recognized the problem as one of policy coherence, and his plan sought to rectify it by bolstering Sato's domestic base. At first, everything proceeded on schedule. During the summit, the Japanese Prime Minister gave Nixon the impression that he would deliver a textile agreement in exchange for American compromise on Okinawa.[28] The Japanese then rejected, as planned, the first American textile proposal in Geneva; a few weeks later, the Japanese public provided Sato's party with eleven new seats in the Diet. At that point, high-ranking American officials had every reason to believe that Sato would fulfill his end of the bargain. A second United States plan was submitted to the Japanese delegation in January 1970, with the assumption that all was well.

Yet all was not well. The Japanese rejected the American textile proposal, much to the surprise of certain United States negotiators. Despite Sato's good intentions, he was not able to deliver on his promise. Sato could not inform key members of the bureaucracy of the deal because he feared repercussions. That meant that the Americans were negotiating with one scenario in mind, while the Japanese were bargaining according to standard operating procedures. The Prime Minister apparently was not fully aware of the restrictive nature of the agreement he had secretly promised in Washington. As a consequence, he could not convince his ministers that they should compromise with the United States. To most of the Japanese bureaucrats and textile producers, the second American plan was not much better than the first. The result was that Sato maneuvered himself into a catch-22: if he informed the bureaucracy of the textile–Okinawa deal, he would undermine his own authority; if he did not, he could not achieve an agreement. By March 1970, the pact had unraveled, and the negotiations were again without an agenda.

Rounds 3–7: The Failures

Between March 1970 and April 1971, negotiations with Japan and the other East Asian exporters went through several rounds, at several levels. Sometimes bargaining took place through official government-to-government channels, including a second Sato–Nixon summit; [29] at other times, there were new attempts at secret transgovernmental alliances; and, finally, there were various efforts made by transnational actors to negotiate independent deals.[30] Despite the variety of styles and formats, the negotiations had one thing in common: they all ended in failure. No government—particularly not the government of Japan—was sufficiently united to narrow the bargaining range. Japan's textile industry applauded every breakdown, and the American textile industry used the failures to push for global quotas. The outcome was growing intransigence on both sides of the Pacific, with no end in sight.

The Costs and Benefits of Failures. The first major consequence of these failures came in mid-1970. For over a year, Congress, especially Congressman Wilbur Mills, had threatened to legislate textile quotas if VERs could not be negotiated. The administration's official position was to oppose quantitative restrictions, but after a "final" breakdown in the bargaining in June 1970, Nixon and Stans reluctantly endorsed protectionist legislation. The massive protectionist program which emerged from the House that summer included a rollback for 1971 textile imports to almost 40 percent below 1969 levels. If this so-called Mills bill passed both houses of Congress, it would represent a major setback to all of the East Asian states and world trade in general. Such restrictive quotas had not been used by the United States for industrial trade since World War II. Although Nixon was not pleased with the legislation, he made no effort to stop it. It turned out to be a close call for Japan and the other textile exporters; the bill passed the House but a filibuster prevented a vote in the Senate.

A more serious cost for Japan was a renewed linkage to Okinawa. Despite Nixon's promises to Sato, reversion of Okinawa required Senate ratification. Okinawa's status was connected to the 1951 peace treaty with Japan, and only the Senate could approve such a change. Under normal circumstances, this would not have been a problem. But after two years of unfinished textile negotiations, textile lobbyists found sympathetic ears in Congress for the idea of holding Okinawa "hostage" until the Japanese agreed to reduce exports. Since it took only thirty-four Senators to block the reversion of Okinawa—a two-thirds majority being needed for approval—this was no idle threat.[31]

The potential costs of the confrontation were therefore mounting for the exporters, and particularly for Japan. The failure to compromise was politicizing the textile issue and creating a crisis in the bilateral trading relationship. For the first time since 1956, there was a serious possibility that textile problems would spill over into more general trade and military–security areas.

While some broad foreign policy objectives were being threatened, specific textile interests in each exporting nation were benefiting from the delays in negotiations. As long as there were no quotas, foreign producers could ship freely to the United States. Furthermore, the threat of protection provided a catalyst for exporters to accelerate shipments. Everyone recognized that the greater the historical exports of firms

Table 4.1 United States Imports of Synthetic Fibers, 1970–71 (in millions of square yard equivalents)

	Japan	Hong Kong	Taiwan	Korea
January–May 1970	288	73	112	95
January–May 1971	522	89	236	169

SOURCE: Data released by U.S. Department of State.

(and nations), the larger their eventual market share under a quota system. Hence during 1970 and the first half of 1971, exporters in Hong Kong, Korea, Taiwan, and Japan were cramming ships with yarn, fabrics, and clothing made of synthetic fibers. In Korea, textiles were given top priority by the Ministry of Commerce. Between January and May 1971, exports of synthetic materials from the Far East were up over 100 percent in some cases from the previous year (see table 4.1).

The acceleration of textile imports into the United States had a twofold negative impact on the negotiations. First, the phenomenal growth in export earnings realized by Far Eastern textile producers made them increasingly reluctant to agree to voluntary restraints. Each country's industry believed that the longer they waited, the better off they would be. And second, the rapid increase in market penetration coincided with the end of the domestic textile industry boom and a decline in American synthetic textile production, employment, and market share. This strengthened the American industry's political position, added to the government's frustration, and heightened the potential for conflict.

Round 8: The Kennedy Negotiations and the "Forced Settlement"

By the spring of 1971, the White House was losing patience with Japan. One of the last straws came in March 1971 when Wilbur Mills, with the help of some transnational actors, negotiated a "voluntary" export restraint directly with the Japanese textile industry.[32] Japan hoped that this VER would appease the Americans and forestall further protectionist activity. But to Nixon and others in the White House, this was too little, too late, and politically inappropriate. Not only was the program itself unsatisfactory, but Nixon viewed Mills's participation as an attempt to undermine the Republican President's authority. Nixon felt that *he* should be the principal sponsor of the industry's protection, *not* a Democratic congressman and meddling international lobbyists.

One outcome of this episode was a feud between Nixon and Mills. A second result was that the White House would no longer accommodate the Japanese. Although the legislative route to quotas was temporarily blocked by the Nixon–Mills feud, this did not stop the President from taking the initiative. Nixon decided to move the negotiations off dead center by appointing a new negotiator with greater authority. He chose Ambassador-at-Large David Kennedy—a man uniquely suited to the task. Kennedy, a former chief executive officer of Continental Bank, had had extensive dealings with the Japanese. Unlike Stans and most of Stans' successors, Kennedy was acutely attuned to the subtleties of negotiations and politics in the Far East. In addition, as a former Secretary of the Treasury, Kennedy's appointment enhanced the status of the negotiating team.

To facilitate the bargaining, Nixon did not dispel the rumors of an Okinawa linkage and allowed the Ambassador to find other usable carrots and sticks. Furthermore, there was to be a change in strategy. Instead of focusing exclusively on the Japanese, the United States would try negotiating VERs with Hong Kong, Taiwan, and Korea, as well as Japan. The hope was that these weaker states might be easier to coerce into an agreement. Once they capitulated, the Japanese would find resistance difficult.

Agenda Setting. For most of the two years of failure after the Nixon–Sato secret deal, American policy lacked coherence. Rampant bureaucratic politics, press leaks, and fighting between Congress and the Executive were more the rule than the exception. With the appointment of David Kennedy, however, the United States entered a new stage in its textile policy. Kennedy accepted the job on the condition that he would be given direct access to the President as well as be free from bureaucratic constraints. Kennedy was allowed to organize his own negotiating staff, which permitted him to exclude those individuals who had complicated the negotiations in the past. This centralization of policy, combined with Nixon's personal endorsement, created the most coherent American bargaining strategy in years. No longer was it possible for bureaucrats or transnational actors to undercut the negotiations; only Kennedy, a tightly knit staff, and the President would be involved.

For his first mission in April 1971, the new American Ambassador-at-Large had several goals. First, Kennedy recognized that it was important for the East Asian governments to establish their own policy coherence. Unless this was done, the textile industries in Taiwan, Korea, and Hong Kong would continue to constrain their governments, just as the textile industry had done in Japan. Therefore, the Ambassador sought a counterpart in each country who would have the authority to negotiate. Second, Kennedy wanted to convince the exporters of the seriousness of the problem. In these types of distributive bargaining situations, it is often critical to impress your opponent with your resolution, before the substantive negotiations begin. Many of the past failures had occurred because there was never a consensus within the exporting countries that the United States would follow through with its threats. Kennedy's goal was to emphasize that this was no longer a realistic basis for policy. Finally, the Ambassador wanted to set up a basic agenda for further negotiations.[33] He sought trust and understanding rather than specific details on export restraints. Greater trust, he believed, would facilitate more honest communication, help each party find the other's resistance points, and lead to mutually satisfactory outcomes.

During his first trip, Kennedy was generally successful in accomplishing each of these goals. Kennedy met with President Park in Korea, who decided to remain personally involved; he met with Chiang Kai-shek in Taiwan, who delegated his son, Chiang Ching-kuo; in Hong Kong, the British were opposed to assigning a newly responsible individual, but another negotiator was eventually appointed. Furthermore, Kennedy agreed that he would not give interviews or get involved with the press. He would allow each government "to handle their own industries," and do whatever was necessary to foster coherence.[34] In addition, Kennedy convinced the Asian governments that he would not quit. He kept hammering at the same points time after time, regardless of the lack of response.

The Bargaining. Substantive discussions did not really begin until Kennedy's second trip to the Far East in late May. His first stop was Taiwan—the most vulnerable exporter and the most likely candidate to reach an agreement. This was a period of crisis and uncertainty in United States–Republic of China relations. A vote was coming up in the United Nations over the status of Taiwan and admission of the communist People's Republic of China. This made the Taiwan government, more than the other governments, desire an accommodating strategy at this stage of the game.

By the same token, Kennedy was willing to be relatively accommodating to the Nationalist Chinese. Appreciating their weak position, he tried to build their confidence. His approach was to discuss a range of issues, such as expanding bilateral trade, then put textiles back into the broader context. Yet three obstacles blocked the negotiations. First, textiles were of critical importance to Taiwanese export trade. Clothing and yarns comprised 29.2 percent of the total value of Taiwanese exports to the United States in 1970, and synthetic textile exports had been expanding by an average of more than 75 percent per year since 1968.[35] Second, Taiwan did not want to be the first to agree. Taiwanese negotiators insisted, and Kennedy concurred, that no agreement would be final until Korea and Hong Kong were also willing to sign, and, if one state bargained for an additional concession, that concession would go to all the countries. Third, Kennedy's most generous bargaining position was severely constrained by the United States textile industry. Since the lobby's influence was close to its height in the spring of 1971, the industry had a virtual veto over most concessions. There was now widespread support for textiles on Capitol Hill, and an important textile executive (Robert Milliken) had direct access to Nixon.

The critical areas of contention in this first round of bargaining were the base period, the flexibility and category breakdown, and annual growth rates. Since exports had been expanding so rapidly, a change of a few months in the base period could make a dramatic difference in Taiwan's quota. In addition, the Taiwanese wanted to avoid some of the rigidities in the LTA by allowing for maximum flexibility and high growth, and they wanted a late starting date to minimize short-run dislocations. Kennedy, for his part, did not want to reduce export levels from Taiwan, Korea, or Hong Kong, but rather wanted to moderate the rate of increase. Japan was the principal target for export reductions. Thus Kennedy was willing to trade off concessions on the base period and flexibility (assuming the industry approved) for lower growth rates. In exchange for a five-year comprehensive agreement and a base period that would be calculated from

April 1970 through March 1971, the United States discussed a compromise of an 11 percent growth rate, which would decrease 1 percent per year.[36]

Although several issues were still unresolved, Taiwan agreed "in principle" to a VER on June 9. The Taiwanese broke the united front against restrictions principally because they did not want to exacerbate bilateral tensions. Furthermore, there may have been some discussion during these meetings about possible compensation for Taiwan in other issue areas. Before leaving for the Far East, the American delegation had put together a package of carrots and sticks for each country. While the sticks were few and far between, the carrots included increased cotton textile quotas and additional military and economic aid for Taiwan and Korea.[37] Exactly how the agenda was structured on this issue and who suggested the linkage remains unclear. The evidence indicates that linkages were discussed.[38]

The next stop was Korea, where the Americans did not find the negotiations as easy. Korean textile workers and industrialists demonstrated during the talks, highlighting the scope of Korean resistance.[39] Korea's dependence on the United States market was obvious; in 1970 it shipped to America 177.34 million dollars in textiles, 97 percent of which were synthetics and wool, amounting to 45 percent of total exports bound for the United States.[40] Since the Koreans felt that any cut would be disastrous, they put forth "outlandish" proposals as part of a maximizing strategy; their minimum position was not even close to the maximum American position. The Koreans also used several unorthodox tactics to avoid concessions. They would stall, try to get opposing negotiators drunk, and attempt to undercut the Kennedy team through transgovernmental channels. For example, when an America negotiator threatened a possible linkage to troop levels and other military questions, Korean officials went to the United States Embassy in Seoul and the National Security Council in Washington in order to contact Kissinger. The Korean objective was to foster incoherent policy in the United

States by lobbying with sympathetic bureaucratic actors. These tactics were rarely successful during the Kennedy negotiations. In this particular case, however, Kissinger cautioned Kennedy about the limits to his authority, as well as assured the Koreans that no such linkage would be made.[41]

Similar to the negotiations with Taiwan, the carrot was a more important negotiating tool for the United States. Agricultural aid under the Public Law (P.L.) 480 program and increases in Korea's cotton quotas were discussed as possible compensation for a VER.[42] The Koreans, however, would not budge. They insisted that they had a "special" relationship with the United States, which demanded American generosity. David Kennedy replied that a special relationship was a two-way street, and at some point the Koreans would have to give as well as take.[43] Otherwise, Kennedy warned, the United States would impose quotas, which would hurt the Koreans more than voluntary restraints. Nonetheless the talks broke down when the Koreans refused to reduce their minimum demands. There was an agreement to continue talking, but few American negotiators were optimistic. The results were the same in Hong Kong. Proclaimed by the press as the "most unwelcomed guests" in the colony, Kennedy and his associates used every argument at their disposal without success.

Lacking an agreement from either Hong Kong or Korea, the Americans postponed talks with the Taiwanese on a final accord.[44] Part of the reason that Hong Kong and Korea continued to resist restrictions was that they were still not convinced the United States would act unilaterally. A number of Washington lobbyists told their clients that American quotas were unlikely.[45] In addition, the American strategy of divide and conquer was frustrated by collaboration between the exporting governments.[46] This forced a change in the United States approach. Although Kennedy's assistants continued the discussions with Taiwan, Korea, and Hong Kong, the Ambassador again turned to Japan as his primary target.

Yet for Kennedy as well as the East Asian exporters, time

was running out. Kennedy tried to convince Nixon that the Japanese would eventually agree to restrictions, if the President would give the Ambassador more time. But after another round of failures in late July and early August 1971, Nixon's patience was exhausted. Kennedy had submitted new proposals to the Japanese and explained the possibility that the Senate would torpedo Okinawa's reversion, but the Japanese showed few signs of compromise. Prime Minister Sato had even created a new Cabinet with a new MITI Minister, Kakuei Tanaka, but this did not have an immediate impact on Japan's intransigence.

It is possible, and indeed likely, that Japan, Taiwan, and the others made a serious tactical miscalculation during this round of negotiations. The terms that Kennedy was offering were better than those eventually agreed upon.[47] By late July, it should have been obvious to all of the exporters that restrictions were imminent and that little was to be gained by stalling.

Crisis and Decision Phase. On July 15, 1971, Nixon made a surprise announcement that he would be the first American President to visit Peking. To Japan, Taiwan, and Korea, this came as a shock; none of the countries was prepared for such a major foreign policy change. Then on August 15, Nixon further astonished the world by bringing the twenty-seven-year-old Bretton Woods system of international monetary regulation to an abrupt end. The President suspended the dollar's convertibility into gold and imposed a temporary 10 percent surcharge on all imports coming into the United States. To most analysts of American foreign relations, August 15 represented a breakpoint in American hegemony and a watershed for the international economic order.[48] No longer was the United States willing to assume the full costs of maintaining the liberal trading system. Nixon's "New Economic Policy" was designed to realign exchange rates and improve the United States balance of payments. The surcharge was also seen as a device to jolt America's trading partners, particularly Japan, and reduce the threat of protectionist legislation in Congress.

Destler and his colleagues have contended that the administration's "obsession with textiles contributed to the neglect of broader trade and monetary issues which helped bring on the international economic crisis of 1971."[49] Although this may be an exaggeration, the textile conflict undoubtedly explains in large part why Nixon did nothing to soften the blow on America's Asian allies. Diplomacy had failed to make the Japanese revalue the yen and limit their textile exports; therefore, a more dramatic display of force seemed necessary. Under other circumstances, the administration might have prepared Japan for what was to come. Yet in the wake of two years of broken deals, no top-level adviser even suggested this course.

The relevance of Nixon's New Economic Policy for textiles went beyond its shock value. Until August 15, the administration had few options for imposing unilateral restraints that did not need the support of Congress. To rectify this situation, the following statement was embedded in the presidential document which proclaimed the import surcharge:

> I hereby declare a national emergency during which I call upon the public and private sectors to make the efforts necessary to strengthen the international economic position of the United States.

In a state of national emergency, the President could impose quotas under the Trading with the Enemy Act passed in 1917. Although Kennedy preferred not to invoke this new authority, he regarded it as an important source of leverage that could finally bring the textile crisis to an end.

During a United States–Japan ministerial conference in late August, Ambassador Kennedy informed MITI Minister Tanaka that a textile accord was urgent. Unless an agreement was forthcoming, Kennedy warned, Nixon would impose the unilateral restraints. Tanaka understood the situation, but he said that he would need time to persuade the Japanese bureaucracy and textile industry. The two men therefore devised a simple scenario which would allow Tanaka to create enough policy coherence to promote acquiescence to American terms. First, the United States would issue a public ultimatum giving Japan and the other exporters until October 15 to sign VERs. Any country that did not agree by that date would be subject to unilateral quotas under the Trading with the Enemy Act. Second, Tanaka, for his part, could exaggerate American demands in the press, advertise last-minute concessions, champion the textile cause—basically do whatever he wanted so long as he agreed to the United States' terms by October 15, 1971. Kennedy made it quite clear to the MITI Minister that there was to be little bargaining over substantive issues. The President planned to satisfy the textile industry, unilaterally if necesssary. The textile proposals discussed in July would be the basis for the agreement(s), whether the Japanese (Koreans, Taiwanese, and those in Hong Kong) liked it or not.

To reinforce the need for technical drafting rather than substantive bargaining, Kennedy dispatched his negotiating staff to the Far East, while Kennedy himself literally went into hiding. The purpose of this tactic was to allow Tony Jurich, the Ambassador's special assistant, to take full charge of the negotiations.[50] Jurich would deliver the ultimatums to the four capitals, and with Kennedy nowhere to be found, it would be impossible for the exporters to circumvent Jurich and the others. Since the American negotiators were charged with very limited instructions that only Kennedy or Nixon could amend, a forced settlement on American terms would be inevitable. Furthermore, Jurich had no power to discuss the 10 percent surcharge on imports, which was of critical importance to each of the exporting nations.

For Hong Kong and Japan, there was little room left to maneuver in these negotiations. The United States had the least sympathy for the two states which had been the most unresponsive and most belligerent during the past two years. Hong Kong tried to implement its own "voluntary" restraint program, like the one Japan announced the previous spring, but such tactics were to no avail.[51] The United States allowed a very narrow bargaining range for these two exporters. Korea and Taiwan, however, were in a somewhat different category. The United States was more concerned about damaging the economies of its dependent clients and disrupting bilateral relations. This opened the door for Taiwan and Korea to seek additional compensation. Both countries grudgingly accepted the fact that this did not preclude the possibility of integrative bargaining and exploration of possible linkages. American negotiators had instructions to give nothing away, but they were told to make additional concessions if there was no other way to obtain an amicable accord.

The last two weeks of bargaining were nonetheless arduous, despite the ultimatums and the possibility of compensation. VERs were no more appealing to the textile industries in the exporting countries in late September than they had been three months or two years earlier. The only difference was that the costs of noncompliance were now higher. The American strategy during this period was to obtain a comprehensive agreement with Japan and a general framework with the other exporters, all by October 15. Since the negotiations were so complex, it was easier to focus on one country and fill in the details for Taiwan, Korea, and Hong Kong at a later date.

Although no agreement was formally announced until October 15, it was Taiwan that became the first to buckle under to American pressure. Taiwan was the earliest to accept restrictions because it hoped that the United States would remember and appreciate its cooperation.[52] Being the first to agree produced no tangible results for Taiwan, but Kennedy did promise the Taiwanese something in the "defense area" in exchange for their agreement.[53] While this was not a major concession on the part of the United States, it was nonetheless an accomplishment for the Nationalist Chinese. If they had not bargained for the linkage, it is unlikely that they would have received any special compensation.

The second country to capitulate was Hong Kong. After fighting every American initiative for over two years, Hong Kong finally became worried that unilateral restrictions might be worse. When a colonial negotiator asked one of Kennedy's assistants what would happen if the colony did not agree, he was told that the base level would be pushed back twelve months and the growth rates limited to a maximum of 4 percent.[54] Even though this threat was exaggerated, Hong Kong officials were sufficiently convinced that they quickly proceeded to draft a VER. The only concession that Kennedy made to the colony was symbolic; he agreed to try to negotiate a multilateral, multifiber agreement—something he had already intended to do.

Finally, the Koreans and the Japanese agreed to restraints around the same time, and both at the last possible moment. For Korea, stalling and resisting until the very end was part of its traditional "controlled risk" bargaining strategy. In this case, the Koreans held out as long as they could to wring every possible concession from the Americans. Although the United States had little room for give and take on the textile issue, Kennedy did use additional P.L. 480 agricultural aid to settle the dispute. In exchange for the textile agreement with some amendment of America's terms, the Koreans extracted 776.3 million dollars' worth of P.L. 480 commitments.[55] Some of this aid, according to Kennedy, was already targeted for Korea. But through tough bargaining, the Koreans managed to increase the amount enough to offset all of the projected costs of the textile restraints.

The rationale behind Japan's stalling was less Machiavellian than Korea's. Internal politics rather than tactical considerations continued to dominate Japan's bargaining strategy for several weeks. Once the reality of the "Nixon shocks" set in, however, the Japanese government finally started moving toward a more coherent policy. By mid-September, MITI Minister Tanaka was able to use the threat of unilateral

American action to centralize decision making. This controlled the rampant bureaucratic politics which had sabotaged previous negotiations. In addition, Tanaka found that the Japanese textile industry suddenly lost much of its broader industrial support after the United States levied its 10 percent surcharge. Government negotiators had more freedom to make difficult concessions once the powerful business leaders known as the *zaikai* became determined to get rid of textiles as a perennial irritant in United States–Japan trade.

Once the negotiations were well under way, Ambassador Kennedy came out of hiding on October 13. Tanaka was insisting on a few major changes which only Kennedy could make. Among other things, the MITI Minister wanted to shorten the length of the agreement from five to three years and push back the starting date and, most important, he wanted the United States to rescind the surcharge on textiles. Since all of these issues were largely symbolic to Kennedy, he readily agreed. A three-year accord would satisfy the short-term demands of the U.S. textile industry; the starting date was not critical; and on what appeared to be the most central issue, Kennedy gladly conceded the removal of the surcharge. For the Japanese (and other exporters), this would allow the government(s) to claim victory. In actuality, it was a minor concession for Kennedy. The purpose of the surcharge was to limit imports into the United States, which implied that it would not be used for goods already subject to quantitative restrictions.

The Agreements. On October 15, 1971, the United States announced new bilateral accords with each of the four Asian exporters and the removal of the 10 percent surcharge on textiles. Similar to all previous VERs, there were pluses and minuses for both sides. All of the exporters complained bitterly that the restrictions would cost them anywhere from 200 million to one billion dollars over the five years of the quota. Likewise, the American industry, especially apparel producers, claimed that the government had given away too much.

For the most part, the October pacts were consistent with America's bargaining position.

The Japanese agreement was basically the same comprehensive quota arrangement that the United States had proposed ten months earlier, in December 1970. The only significant differences were that the agreement was to last only three years; the base period of the quota was higher; and the flexibility was reduced. Although Japan was allowed to borrow from its cotton quotas, the VER was expected to cut Japanese synthetic textile exports in 1972 by 100 million square yards.[56] Overall growth was reduced to 5 percent and the carryover and borrowing provisions were considered tight. This led the Japanese textile leaders to accuse their government of "total surrender." The limited flexibility meant that Japan was unlikely to fill its allotted quota.

The agreements for Hong Kong, Taiwan, and Korea were also relatively restrictive, but somewhat better than Japan's. According to reports in late October, each country would be given 7.5 percent growth, a little greater flexibility than Japan, and a bonus in their cotton textile quotas for signing a five-year agreement instead of a three-year accord.[57] In addition, Korea's intransigence paid off. That country was given a slightly increased quota base and a reduced number of quota categories. These terms, however, were only the outline of the agreements. Since the details still needed to be worked out, Taiwan, Korea, and Hong Kong sent delegations to Washington for "technical" clarifications.

Normally, the original negotiators would have worked with the exporters to fill in the gaps. But for Kennedy and many of his staff October 15 marked the end of their day-to-day involvement in textile problems. Therefore, the task of finishing the negotiations reverted to the textile bureaucracy. Taiwan and Korea used this opportunity to re-exploit bureaucratic differences and practically renegotiate the VERs. In the agreement signed on January 4, 1972, Korea's growth rates had been increased to 9 percent in the first year and 8 percent in the second year, and its aggregate quota for 1972 was hiked

from 332 million square yards of synthetic textile products to
344 million. In Taiwan's treaty, its growth rates were increased even more, to 9.5 and 9.0 percent for the first and
second years, respectively, and its aggregate also rose to 467.5
million square yards from 448.4.[58]

For the American textile industry, this led to nothing but
frustration. The textile issue lost its salience after mid-October, which meant the textile industry lost its clout. Nixon as
well as the Congress felt they had paid their political debt.
Ambassador Kennedy, for example, was so removed from
textile problems that he did not even know any changes were
made after October 15. Taiwan and Korea, on the other hand,
were in a good position to take advantage of the shift in decision-making personnel. Their network of close transgovernmental ties and their allied status helped them to mobilize
support. Hong Kong, by comparison, had few friends in
Washington in the fall of 1971. As a result, the colony's final
agreement was left virtually unchanged after October.

Evaluation

Did these countries act in their best interests by resisting
protectionism for two and a half years? Or were there other
alternatives that might have maximized their export earnings
and eased political frictions? Some American textile critics
charged that the exporters were the real winners in 1971. By
stalling, all of the countries substantially increased their aggregate limits between 100 million and 500 million square
yards. Indeed, for Taiwan, Korea, and Hong Kong a textile
agreement in 1969 or 1970 with low base levels would have
been disastrous. Taiwan and Korea planned to build much of
their industrial expansion during the 1970s on synthetic textile exports. Hong Kong similarly was just beginning to move
into the synthetic fiber field with private plans for rapid
growth. In cases such as this, confrontation was worthwhile
because it preserved vital economic interests. As long as restrictions were not an immediate threat and the brunt of the
economic pressure was being applied against Japan, there was

a great deal to be gained by resistance and no overriding reason to make short-run sacrifices. It was only in the summer of 1971 that these countries seemed to have erred. By that time, restrictions should have seemed inevitable. Slightly better deals might have been available in July compared to the agreements they reached in October and January.

Japan, however, was not as well served by this type of strategy. Japanese synthetic textile exports to the United States represented less than 5 percent of the total value of Japanese exports in 1969.[59] Although the Japanese textile industry had much to lose in the short run, the Japanese economy would have lost relatively little in overall export earnings. Furthermore, the Japanese textile industry would have lost practically nothing in the long run. Just as Japan's economic planners had predicted in 1967, the textile industry was losing its comparative advantage in the late 1960s. The textile industry had good years in 1970 and 1971, but domestic inflation and a revalued currency accelerated sectoral decline. As their prices increased, Japanese textiles were no longer an attractive purchase for American importers. Within two years of signing their VER, the Japanese could not even come close to filling their hard-bargained quotas (see table 4.2).

Hence Japan violated one of the fundamental tenets of the strategy I outlined in chapter 1. It had no long-run future in the sector, yet it promoted confrontation for the sake of short-run gains. What, then, were the costs of this opposition? Japan was fortunate that the worst case analysis did not evolve. Yet the risks of politicizing the textile issue were great indeed. Japan jeopardized the return of Okinawa to Japanese sovereignty, and only narrowly escaped passage in the United States Congress of a highly restrictive trade bill. In addition to these near misses, the textile controversy undoubtedly aggravated United States–Japan relations at a time of great uncertainty. While textiles may not have directly contributed to the Nixon "shocks"—the overtures to China and the monetary declarations—they played a major role in disrupting the alliance. It is no exaggeration to call the autumn of 1971 the

Table 4.2 United States Imports of Japanese Synthetic Textiles, 1968–75 (In millions of square yard equivalents)

	Imports (Calendar Year)	Quota
1968	447.8	—
1969	584.9	—
1970	774.4	—
1971	1,381.6	—
1972	943.0	954.6 [a]
1973	650.3	1,004.1 [a]
1974	690.3	1,056.1 [a]
1975	576.8	— [b]

SOURCE: U.S. International Trade Commission, *The History and Current Status of the Multifiber Arrangement*, p. C-11, table 9.

[a] October 1 to September 30.

[b] It became clear by 1975 that Japan could not meet its quotas. Therefore, the United States eliminated several category limits of synthetic textiles starting on October 1, 1975, and by 1977 all specific limits were eliminated. In 1978 a new bilateral accord was negotiated to prevent sudden surges of Japanese imports.

nadir of postwar United States–Japan relations. The issuance of an ultimatum which threatened to invoke the Trading with the Enemy Act was exemplary of the fact that a once close relationship had reached its lowest point to date.

Lessons of the Textile Wrangle. Beyond demonstrating the overall failings of Japanese policy, the textile wrangle illustrates a number of other important lessons for bilateral trade conflicts. First, in no other case did cross-issue linkages play such a prominent role. The Sato–Nixon deal on Okinawa and the later Senate debates on reversion clearly point to the potential hazards of politicizing an issue. If the Japanese had not rejected the Stans talks in May 1969, they probably could have minimized the involvement of Nixon and Kissinger. Negotiations on Okinawa and textiles might then have proceeded on two separate paths. By politicizing the issue—by forcing the Americans to reassess their options at the presidential level—the Japanese helped create the linkage possibility. Japan exacerbated its weakness by failing to resolve (or failing to pretend to resolve) a highly salient problem, such as textiles, at lower levels of the bureaucracy.

Part of the reason that linkages were so central to this bargaining episode was that changes were taking place in America's global position. When hegemony starts to erode, as it did for the United States in the late 1960s, a hegemonic state calculates the tradeoffs between domestic and international objectives in a different way. Domestic interests tend to be given priority while foreign policy goals are devalued. The United States never employed cross-issue linkages before 1969 precisely because foreign policy concerns were always dominant. But Nixon's willingness to broaden the textile agenda to include Okinawa and his support of the 1970 trade bill suggest that a greater weight was being placed on the domestic side of the equation.

The compensatory linkages employed by Korea and Taiwan were possible for a somewhat different reason. By May 1971, a situation had developed in which the United States and the exporters had reached a deadlock. Neither side wanted a crisis in the overall relationship, but there was no acceptable solution within the existing agenda. Therefore, the parties to the negotiations had to break off the talks or search for an innovative approach. For the United States, side payments were legitimate for weaker countries, and politically easier than concessions within textiles. For Taiwan and Korea, something was better than nothing.[60]

Another lesson of the textile wrangle is that exporters must be able to formulate coherent policies if they hope to avoid breakdowns in negotiations and a crisis. Despite Japan's centralized governmental structure, adaptive economic system, and recognition at the highest levels of government that defending textiles was not in the country's long-run interests, the Japanese nonetheless followed an inconsistent short-run strategy. Had Prime Minister Sato been able to establish legitimacy for his preferred policy, he probably would have overcome the considerable influence of the Japanese textile industry. But Sato could not do it by himself, and the Nixon–Kissinger charade proved insufficient. It took a dramatic American threat to bring Japan's policies into line with that country's top decision makers' goals. This pattern is similar to what Snyder and Diesing have discovered in their work on conflict bargaining: even when the "weaker party knows it must concede . . . [it] needs a little help from the adversary to get itself . . . onto the accommodative track."[61]

In addition to the role of policy coherence, this case illustrates the problems and opportunities created by transnational and transgovernmental politics. Transnational representatives of foreign governments stationed in Washington provided a critical link to the American political process. They usually made accurate predictions about United States policy in the short run; they formed coalitions with domestic actors to fight protection and constrain the Executive; they helped maintain unity among the exporting countries; and they served as negotiators, seeking informal arrangements. Exploiting these transnational and transgovernmental channels was beneficial for the exporters until Japan politicized these linkages with the Mills–Japanese textile industry agreement. After that episode, Nixon took a stronger personal interest in the negotiations—an interest in settling the dispute quickly on American terms. Thus manipulating transnational and transgovernmental ties was helpful only for low-key, behind-the-scene bargaining.

Epilogue: Textiles in the 1970s and 1980s

October 15, 1971, was the climax of the international textile controversy, but it was certainly not the end. Throughout the 1970s and into the 1980s, barriers to textile and apparel trade have grown increasingly restrictive. The myopic nature of this protectionism, however, is not changing very quickly. The combination of accommodative American policies and the sheer technical complexity of textile trade has allowed Hong Kong, Taiwan, and Korea to prosper during most of this period. By moving up markets, by successfully bargaining for loopholes, by cheating, and by exploiting transnational and transgovernmental ties, these countries have continually minimized the dangers of protectionism.

Adjustment to the New Bilateral Accords

Once agreements were signed in 1972, the key for the textile exporters of East Asia was to make adjustments to the new restrictions. The first adjustment made by all of the countries was to raise prices in order to capture scarcity rents and recoup losses from reductions in quantities. The United States General Accounting Office estimated that prices of Taiwanese, Korean, Hong Kong, and Japanese textiles had more than doubled in the year following the bilateral accords. Imports rose from 276 to 632 million dollars, of which 92 to 105 million dollars could be directly attributed to premiums charged by foreign quota holders.[62] Second, each of the industries accelerated the upgrading of existing product lines. Between 1969 and 1971, the exporters shipped as much as possible to raise quotas. Once expansion was limited, exporters turned their attention toward improving the quality of their products (see table 4.3). Within just two years of restraints, Taiwan illustrated how hiking prices and raising quality could increase earnings. From 1971 to 1973, the quantity of Taiwan's synthetic fiber shipments destined for the American market dropped by 26 percent; meanwhile, the overall value of its textile and apparel exports to the United States went from 267 million dollars to 387 million dollars—an increase of 45 percent.

The third adjustment made by the exporters was to find alternative buyers. Through 1971, the United States had dominated their export trade in textiles, sometimes accounting for as much as 50 percent. Yet after the bilateral accords were signed, there was a concerted effort to diversify markets. Ironically, Japan was one of the most important new

Table 4.3 United States Imports of Selected Textile and Apparel Products, 1971–76 (in millions of square yard equivalents [SYE] and $ millions)

	Hong Kong		Korea		Taiwan	
	Synthetic Textiles (SYE)	Clothing (SITC 841)[a] (dollars)	Synthetic Textiles (SYE)	Clothing (SITC 841)[a] (dollars)	Synthetic Textiles (SYE)	Textile Products[b] (dollars)
1971	247.0	$353.8	408.4	$198.1	540.1	$267.0
1972	263.6	376.4	415.6	237.6	465.8	393.7
1973	203.6	427.4	316.9	238.9	397.2	387.0
1974	146.2	461.1	305.7	301.4	403.6	481.6
1976	226.5	n.a.	507.0	n.a.	512.2	835.4

SOURCES: U.S. International Trade Commission, *The History and Current Status of the Multifiber Arrangement*; United Nations, *Foreign Trade Statistics of Asia and the Pacific, 1971, 1972, 1973, 1974,* and *1975.*

[a] Standard International Trade Classification (SITC).

[b] These figures are not comparable with the SITC figures for Korea and Hong Kong. Since the United Nations stopped keeping statistics for the Republic of China in 1971, these figures came from the *Taiwan Statistical Data Book, 1976* (Republic of China, 1976). The label the Taiwanese provided was textile products, which probably includes all textile and apparel exports to the United States.

markets. Not only had Japanese manufacturers lost some of their export competitiveness in the early 1970s; they also found their domestic market suddenly under import pressure. The Koreans, in particular, started exporting large quantities to Japan. By 1977, the Japanese took a full 20 percent of Korea's textiles.[63] Hong Kong followed a similar strategy but put more emphasis on Europe and especially Britain. In 1971, Hong Kong almost doubled its previous year's exports to the British market, and in 1972, the British colony increased textile exports to the European Economic Community by 35.5 percent.[64] Thus, despite the predictions of ruin and immediate export losses, between 1971 and 1973 Korea's global textile and clothing earnings jumped from 486 million dollars to 1.27 billion; Hong Kong's export total rose from 1.13 billion to 1.8 billion; and Taiwan's overall textile and apparel shipments increased from 729.9 million to 1.33 billion.[65]

One implementation problem arose during this transition period when Hong Kong started blatantly cheating in early 1972. In a repeat of the mishap over cotton overshipments during the LTA, Hong Kong exceeded its limit in synthetic fiber knits only four months after it signed its bilateral agreement.[66] When the Commerce Department detected the overshipments in May, it ordered an embargo that was unprecedented for synthetic fibers. Sale of these Hong Kong goods was to be prohibited for five months, and this prohibition covered products already stored in American warehouses. Consultations and British pleas could not stop the embargo until the following September. Some members of the Commerce Department wanted to penalize Hong Kong more severely for what they viewed as a contemptuous act.[67] But after the intervention of Ambassador Kennedy, the Secretary of Commerce, and various other high-level officials, a compromise settlement was eventually reached.[68]

The Multifiber Arrangement and the Oil Crisis

The oil crisis and the negotiation of an international Multifiber Textile Arrangement (MFA) heralded a new era for textile trade in the mid-1970s. The oil crisis affected the textile exports of the industrializing countries in two ways. First, synthetic textiles have a petroleum base. Therefore the increase in oil prices had a direct impact on the price structure of synthetic fibers. Second, the 1974–1975 recession in the United States and Europe, which came in the wake of the quadrupling of oil prices, was accompanied by a slackening in the world demand for textiles. As a result, market conditions rather than restrictions became the major problem for the East Asian textile industries. During 1975, none of the exporters was able to reach its aggregate quota.

Equally significant for the textile producers was the negotiation of a new international agreement in 1974—the Multifiber Textile Arrangement. By the early 1970s, the Long-Term Arrangement had outlived its usefulness. Cotton imports were no longer the primary concern of the United States or the European Community. A new arrangement was therefore required which could legitimate the regulation of synthetic and wool textiles as well as cotton.

Modeled on the LTA, the MFA offered something for

everyone. For the industrial nations, it created a multilateral framework for restricting imports of virtually all textile and apparel products. Bilateral accords could be negotiated, but in case of a "market disruption," unilateral action was permitted. For the developing countries, a standing Textiles Surveillance Body was established to review all actions taken under the MFA and mediate any disputes. This institutional innovation was supposed to guard the developing countries' interests. In addition, the minimum growth rates were increased from 5 to 6 percent.[69]

The MFA had both positive and negative consequences for Taiwan, Korea, and Hong Kong. On the positive side, multilateral restrictions would help guarantee their market shares against uncontrolled competitors. Just as the LTA had locked Hong Kong and Japan into large cotton quotas which could not be challenged by other exporters, the MFA would help assure the market positions of Hong Kong, Taiwan, and Korea in synthetic and wool textiles. In addition, the United States wanted to make all of its bilateral agreements consistent with the MFA to ease implementation. Since the United States needed the support of the Far Eastern countries to make the MFA work (just as Japan's support was necessary for the STA in 1961), Hong Kong, Taiwan, and Korea each received generous bonuses for accepting new VERs in 1975.[70]

On the negative side, the MFA marked the beginning of a highly sophisticated, comprehensive protectionism. Even though the 1974 agreement had a number of safeguards for the exporting countries, the MFA established a precedent for multilateral restrictions that was potentially more harmful than anything that preceded it. For example, the MFA allowed the United States and Europe to close some of the loopholes in the LTA. To prevent an exporter from switching into uncontrolled categories, all import quotas were divided into three types: minimum consultation levels, designated consultation levels, and maximum levels. These divisions created a sophisticated trigger system which minimized flexibility.

The problems of the MFA became obvious when the

agreement came up for renewal in 1977. Once the precedent for comprehensive restraints had been set, it was probably inevitable that efforts would be made to close the remaining loopholes. The Europeans contended that the MFA was inadequate to protect their domestic industries. An EEC commission estimated that a simple extension of the Multifiber Arrangement would cost 1.6 million textile jobs by 1982. Therefore, the European Community stated its readiness to forgo the international regime in favor of more restrictive unilateral policies.[71] Although the United States saved the MFA, it came at a high cost to the major exporters. The compromise reached in Geneva allowed for "reasonable departures" from the arrangement. This safety clause permitted the Europeans as well as the Americans to limit severely annual growth and even reduce export quotas.[72]

The Carter administration used its authority under the safety clause to eliminate export growth for Korea, Taiwan, and Hong Kong during 1977. Then in 1979–1980 the United States renegotiated the bilateral accords to restrict further these nations' flexibility. In exchange for the textile lobby's support of the Multilateral Trade Negotiations, Jimmy Carter promised to "assist the beleaguered textile apparel industry." This involved two major steps: (1) forcing the major exporters to accept a "surge mechanism" that reduced their ability to switch goods from one category to another; and (2) launching a campaign against cheating. According to the Special Trade Representative's Office, the government would make every effort to

improve and make more thorough its monitoring and enforcement efforts, including the use of penalties available under law where appropriate, with respect to improper transshipments, limits, with the objective of preventing evasion of restraint agreements and quantitative limitations.[73]

The Impact of the MFA

On paper, the Multifiber Arrangement and its accompanying bilateral agreements appear to be disastrous for the NICs. As a comprehensive system covering all textiles, the

MFA does not allow exporters to diversify product lines as easily as they could under the LTA. Moreover, the United States has developed a massive bureaucracy devoted exclusively to textiles while the restrictions, themselves, have become increasingly differentiated. These efforts by the United States and Europe to close loopholes, limit growth, and minimize flexibility are indications that the importing governments and their interest groups have learned a great deal about coping with protectionism. The MFA of the mid-1970s is a world apart from the first VER negotiated with Japan in 1956.

In practice, however, the Multifiber Arrangement has not been as restrictive and harmful to the newly industrializing countries as many feared it would.[74] Many of the most important loopholes in modern protectionism have persisted. First, restrictions continue to be based on quantities. This has meant that exporters who focus on long-run gains can still upgrade their quality and increase their earnings. Second, the institutionalization of American textile policy has not improved the quality of implementation. Ironically, the interpretation of textile policy has generally been less strict and more accommodative in the 1970s than it was in the 1960s.[75] Even in the most protectionist government agencies, such as Commerce and Labor, bureaucrats do not see their role as "trying to establish an iron wall of protection."[76] The majority of bureaucrats responsible for textile policy are interested in more limited goals, such as preventing "market disruptions" in particular categories. Finally, the complexity of the textile trade has become so extensive that no matter what the government does, the existence of some technical loophole always seems to endure.

One result of this accommodative policy has been that transnational and transgovernmental coalitions have become more successful in warding off crackdowns. The American Textile Manufacturers Institute, the most prominent textile lobby in Washington, has accused the State Department of notifying Asian governments that their quotas are about to reach their limits. The State Department then supposedly makes an arrangement for these nations to submit requests for quota adjustments that are to be reviewed "favorably."[77]

A more important consequence of the lax implementation and complexity problem is that cheating and circumvention have continued to be widespread. Despite America's sophisticated tracking methods and stiff penalties, evading quotas has remained a multimillion dollar business in the Far East. In what the *Daily News Record* has called the "Asian Export Shell Game," manufacturers in Hong Kong, Taiwan, and Korea are "looking—and finding—many ways to avoid limits on the apparel they can export to the U.S."[78] Within this game, transshipment is still the classic quota dodge. Even though bilateral accords have been extended to include most exporting countries, entrepreneurial cheaters can always find some nonquota country (like Sri Lanka or Indonesia in the 1970s) to repackage or relabel their goods. Transshipping, however, is not the only method of circumvention. Exporters have uncovered every possible angle. For example, if a nonquota country is unavailable, a manufacturer will simply falsify shipping records and certificates of origin. False papers are one-third the cost of legitimate quotas in countries such as Hong Kong. In addition, producers have been known to ship piece goods to Japan for assembly and to misclassify products.[79]

The United States has tried to deter circumvention by raising fines and improving surveillance. Yet this has been ineffective because the government has been unable to prove culpability. When importers claim they did not know their goods were fraudulent, establishing criminal intent becomes practically impossible. Furthermore, the highest fine ever paid as late as 1979 was only $10,000—a relatively trivial sum compared to the profits that can be made. Washington has pressured the exporting countries to police their manufacturers, but when surplus capacity becomes a serious threat to the exporting countries, the NIC governments, particularly Korea and Taiwan, usually look the other way.

Thus despite the restrictive structure of the MFA, limited opportunities were still available for the exporting countries to increase their earnings throughout the 1970s. As long as exporters pursued long-run strategies of moving up markets and supplemented their profits by cheating, they were successful. As table 4.4 illustrates, exporting nations have varied greatly in their degrees of success (or failure). Korea, Taiwan, Singapore, and others have done quite well, while others could not keep up with inflation.

Table 4.4 LDC Exports of Textiles and Apparel Products, 1975–78 (in $ million)

	1975	1976	1977	1978	Annual Compound Growth Rate	Total Percentage Change
Korea	$1,797	$2,799	$3,142	$4,103	31.6	+128
Taiwan[a]	1,617	2,504	2,463	3,195	25.4	+ 97.5
Hong Kong	2,625	3,728	3,810	4,422	18.9	+ 68.5
Philippines	55.5	109.1	147.5	n.a.	63.0	+165 (1975–77)
Singapore	247.1	361.1	403.4	563.6	31.6	+128
India	794.2	1,076	1,222	n.a.	24.0	+ 54 (1975–77)
Brazil	372.9	380.5	483.6	547.3	13.6	+ 47
Pakistan	408.7	480.0	504.2	n.a.	11.0	+ 23 (1975–77)

SOURCE: United Nations, *Yearbook of International Trade Statistics, 1978.*
[a] Since Taiwan is not included in United Nations statistics, these figures were taken from *Taiwan Statistical Data Book, 1979* (Republic of China, June 1979).

The 1980s and Beyond. The growth of import penetration in the United States textile and apparel market has led American producers to lobby intensely for a firmer lid on import growth.[80] In the meantime, the European Economic Community has continued to take an extremely hard line toward increased imports because of the prospect of thousands of lost jobs. The outcome of this strong protectionist pressure has been a third, even more restrictive, Multifiber Arrangement. Signed in December 1981, MFA-3 allowed for further departures from the operating procedures devised in the two previous agreements. In addition to lower growth, MFA-3 gave importers the right to discriminate against exporters with high market shares. Since the "Big Three"—Hong Kong, Taiwan, and Korea—accounted for 62 percent of the volume and 77 percent of the value of the American textile–apparel import market in 1981, it was no surprise that these nations would be singled out as the principal targets for greater restrictions.[81]

This trend toward more comprehensive restrictions, with fewer loopholes and less opportunities for growth and profit, is probably inevitable. In fact, the combination of myopic bilateral protectionism and the successful strategies adopted by the East Asian exporters virtually assured this result. As exporters circumvented the restrictions and moved into higher value-added markets, they increased the competitive pressure on American and European producers. Over time, the manufacturers in these industrial countries learned how their competitors operated as well as how to exert pressure on their governments to prevent further inroads by imports. Slowly these governments have responded by tightening the restrictions. If it were not for a broader American interest in relatively free trade and a strong desire by all industrial nations to avoid a return to the protectionism of the 1930s, the growth in international textile restrictions would undoubtedly have been faster.

The implications of this tighter protectionism for leading countries, such as Taiwan, Korea, and Hong Kong, is that they must de-emphasize textile and apparel exports, shift into higher value-added industries that are not characterized by surplus capacity, and avoid the short-run confrontational approach adopted by Japan in the late 1960s. Future growth in textiles for these NICs is not promising. For other developing nations that export textiles, however, the basic tenets of the strategy I outlined in chapter 1 will continue to be relevant. As long as bilateral protectionism exists, there will be payoffs to a strategy of upgrading, bargaining for loopholes, cheating, and exploiting transnational ties, especially if the latter policies are done on a small scale and without much fanfare. The road will surely be difficult; but in the early 1960s, many proclaimed the death of Japanese textile exports; and in the early 1970s, it would have been unimaginable that Taiwan, Korea, and Hong Kong would come to dominate the American and EEC markets. Barring a complete reversion to the "old-style" protectionism of global quotas, it is not impossible for a new generation of textile exporters to emerge by the 1990s.

Chapter 5

Footwear:
The Spread of Protection,
1977–1981

Throughout most of the 1960s and 1970s, American shoe manufacturers unsuccessfully tried to follow in the footsteps of textile and apparel producers. They made numerous attempts to pressure the government into erecting import barriers, but each time they failed. Finally, on April 1, 1977, the shoe industry got its wish. In response to recommendations from the International Trade Commission, President Jimmy Carter announced the implementation of a "special" footwear program designed to "revitalize" the "non-rubber" shoe industry.[1] Government aid would include funds for technological development and revamping trade-adjustment assistance, but the core of the program was the negotiation of orderly marketing agreements (OMAs) with the principal producers, Taiwan and Korea (see figure 5.1). Since import penetration was approaching 50 percent in 1977, restrictions seemed necessary and appropriate if the government wanted to prevent a precipitous loss in employment and productive capacity.

American shoe producers reacted favorably to the President's proposals. Unlike its previous assistance to the sector,

Figure 5.1 United States Nonrubber Footwear Imports: Top Five Countries, 1968–77

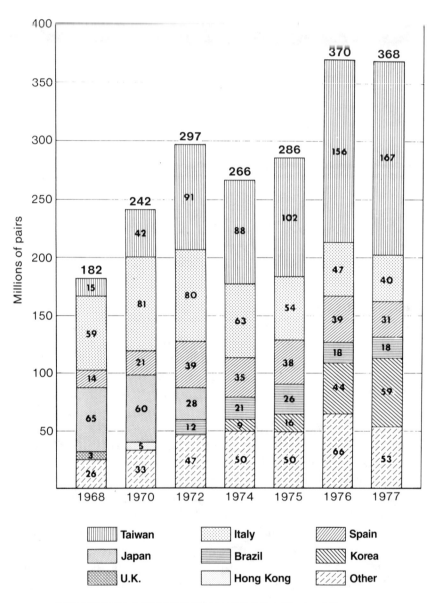

Sources: Department of Commerce; American Footwear Industries Association.

Note: Other includes over fifteen countries in 1968, a recent estimate suggests over seventy countries supply footwear to the United States.

the government now appeared willing to take major steps to reverse ten years of decline.[2] Taiwan and Korea, on the other hand, were less than enthusiastic. Footwear had been a rapidly expanding export for both nations (see table 5.1). The two countries feared that these new restrictions might reduce their export earnings as well as indicate a shift by the United States away from a free-trade orientation. Never before had the Americans used formal VER-type arrangements outside of textiles to restrict developing countries' trade.

Table 5.1 United States Imports from Taiwan and Korea, 1976 (in $ million)

	Taiwan	Korea
Overall imports	$3,038.7	$2,439.9
Nonrubber shoe imports	279.3	165.1
Shoe imports as a percent of total	9%	7%
Percent increase in shoe imports since 1974 (pairs of shoes)	77%	480%

SOURCES: *Industry of Free China*, July 1977; United Nations, *Yearbook of International Trade Statistics, 1976*; U.S. Department of Commerce data.

Hence this footwear episode would raise critical questions about future United States ventures into the new protectionism. Was this the beginning of a new protectionist tide or was it an aberration—a one-time effort to appease domestic pressure? Would there be any similarities between restrictions in textiles and these new restraints in footwear? Had the Americans learned from their many years of textile experience how to make these agreements effective? Or would it still be possible to negotiate for loopholes as exporting nations had done in the early stages of textile protectionism? To the world trading system in general, and to Taiwan and Korea in particular, the answers to these questions could have far-reaching significance.

The Politics and Economics
of the American Footwear Industry

The American government had played a minor role in the footwear industry before Carter's program. Industry associations, labor groups, and Congress had argued for government intervention during the 1970s, but retailers, importers, and most of the government bureaucracy had resisted. The industry had at least four chances to receive protection: in 1970, footwear could have been given quantitative restrictions as part of the 1970 Trade Act; in 1971, the United States Tariff Commission found that the industry had been injured by imports; in the 1974 Trade Act, footwear problems were given extensive treatment, including a promise for protection similar to the Multifiber Textile Arrangement (MFA); and in 1976, the newly named International Trade Commission (ITC) again recommended some form of presidential action on imports. Yet in each of these instances, the Executive refused to provide the shoe industry with substantive support. Unlike textiles, and other industries such as steel, footwear did not have political clout. The shoe industry did not receive substantial aid prior to 1977 for the simple reason that it lacked organization, money, and a broad political base.

Ironically, footwear was in much greater need of government assistance than textiles. In the early 1960s, there were over 700 footwear firms in the United States employing 240,000 workers. During this heyday of the shoe industry, domestic production reached a peak of 600 million pairs, making the United States the largest producer of shoes in the Western world. Since 1966, however, over 350 firms had gone out of business, shutting down almost one-third of the manufacturing capacity. Domestic production fell to 392 million pairs in 1977 and employment dropped by 33 percent to 160,000 workers.[3]

The overall decline of the shoe industry is attributable to three sources. First, American consumption leveled off in the early 1970s and subsequently dropped. Second, footwear

production is a labor-intensive process with low skill requirements. Labor costs account for up to 33 percent of the
price of a pair of shoes. Since no country has a technological
edge in present footwear manufacturing, nations with low labor costs, such as Taiwan and Korea in the 1970s, have a
price advantage in production. And third, footwear is a
fashion-conscious market. Most American firms have not been
flexible in meeting demand, a failing which has allowed Italy, Spain, and Brazil to capture most of the high-priced shoe
market.

Despite the overwhelming evidence of industry decline,
footwear's case for protection has always been relatively weak.
On the economic level, the industry is not universally affected by imports; some firms remained highly profitable by
exploiting economies of scale or using sophisticated marketing techniques. Forward integration into retailing and back-
ward integration into processing raw materials made a core
of twenty-plus firms strongly competitive with imports.
Therefore, the prevalent view within the executive branch was
that the footwear industry should be "capable of responding
to market pressures" without government interference.[4] No
one in the bureaucracy felt the need to aid prosperous
companies.

On the political level, footwear manufacturers were re-
gionally concentrated, which gave them some influence in
Congress. Yet the industry lacked the financial strength and
organization required to be successful. The biggest, most profitable firms did not have the same stake in pushing for protection as the majority of small producers. They were not dis-
interested, but their survival did not depend upon the
government's erecting import barriers. This meant that the
large companies would contribute a much smaller proportion
of their revenues to the industry's lobby—the American
Footwear Industries Association (AFIA). The outcome was
that decision makers viewed footwear as a small political fish
in a big economic sea. Since footwear could not threaten important trade legislation as textiles had done throughout the

postwar period, the government had few incentives to provide the sector with special help.

Why, then, did the United States change course in 1977? In a strange paradox of American politics, the industry's political strength grew out of its economic weakness. Each time the government denied the footwear industry protection in the 1970s, shoe production would fall and import penetration would rise. By 1976, sectoral decline was reaching crisis proportions. In response to an ITC recommendation, President Gerald Ford implemented a "monitoring system" for imports in 1976, in addition to providing some trade-adjustment assistance for individual footwear firms.[5] When it appeared obvious that this program would fail, the President and the Senate Finance Committee requested the ITC to reactivate its footwear investigation. A member of Ford's inner circle felt that the President would have vetoed any protectionist recommendation after the 1976 election, but Ford never had his chance.[6] On January 6, 1977, President-elect Carter was presented with his first major trade challenge: the ITC suggested for the second time in two years that the President protect the shoe industry with tariff rate quotas.[7]

During the ninety days the President had to respond to the ITC, the pressure for import restrictions was immense. The combination of Carter's election commitments to organized labor, greater sympathy in Congress for the plight of the footwear industry, and an all-out effort by AFIA made a decision in favor of free trade extraordinarily difficult. During the first month of the decision-making process, various levels of the bureaucracy debated five policy options: "voluntary" export restraints, tariff rate quotas, orderly marketing agreements, quantitative import restrictions, and domestic adjustment assistance.[8] By the time the issue reached the President, the alternatives had narrowed to two international options. Everyone favored additional trade-adjustment assistance, but State, Treasury, the Council of Economic Advisers, and Housing and Urban Development wanted no import relief granted, whereas Labor, Office of Management and Budget, Commerce, and Agriculture favored the ITC recommendation for tariff rate quotas. Interestingly enough, the orderly marketing agreement option was not even mentioned as an alternative.

The administration quickly agreed upon a domestic policy, then proceeded to discuss imports.[9] The principal constraint against implementing protection was the global position of the United States. Although American leaders were not as strongly committed to the GATT and free trade as they had been in the 1950s and 1960s, there was a desire to avoid protectionism and complete the then-stalled Multilateral Trade Negotiations. America no longer wanted to carry all the burdens of hegemonic responsibility, but neither was it willing to jeopardize freer world trade for the footwear industry. Therefore, balancing the domestic demands of Congress against international trading obligations was still a complicated task.

When the high-level Economic Policy Group convened to deal with these problems, it started to move toward a "no relief" position. At that point, a Carter aide suggested that an OMA might serve as a compromise. Not only would OMAs avoid a conflict with Congress; they could also be targeted to individual producers without disrupting the entire trading system. Attracted by the idea, Carter dismissed the other options, for all practical purposes, and instructed the new head of the Special Trade Representative's Office (STR), Robert Strauss, to prepare a memo on OMAs.

During the next two days, a flurry of memos bombarded Carter for and against the OMA option. No one except STR and the President's staff approved of the policy. State suggested that voluntary restraints (VERs) were less restrictive and more acceptable for foreign policy purposes, but Labor argued that neither VERs nor OMAs would be effective. When the footwear industry was consulted, it said that OMAs were not optimal, but they would be acceptable if "fully implemented."[10] With no unanimous agreement in sight and time running short, Carter opted for OMAs.

Thus American motivation for pursuing protection via orderly marketing agreements in 1977 was almost identical to the rationale for a voluntary export restraint in 1956. Like his predecessors, Carter preferred free trade, but congressional pressure and electoral promises created a perceived need for some kind of import barrier. Without restraints, Congress might have implemented quotas. This would have been worse for Taiwan and Korea, and it would have had negative implications for the Tokyo Round of GATT talks. Carter elected OMAs for the same reason Eisenhower chose VERs: the choice was a political compromise that circumvented international trading regulations. Furthermore, rampant bureaucratic politics left the President with little choice. According to an Executive commission that studied the shoe decision, the President encouraged competing departments and agencies to lobby for their own bureaucratic interests when he did not consider all the alternatives at the highest levels.[11] An orderly marketing arrangement was the only policy that appealed to the middle ground.

The administration sold its program to Congress and the footwear industry with great political finesse. Robert Strauss, a genius at political maneuvering, reassured members of the House, senators, and industry representatives that the OMAs would roll back Taiwanese and Korean imports. Then, to prevent other countries from filling in the void, as Hong Kong and others had done in textiles in the wake of Japanese restraints in 1957, Strauss allegedly promised that imports of nonrestricted countries would be "capped."[12] Other footwear suppliers were supposed to receive cables telling them to hold their present export levels constant. Because the industry and its consultants were content with the OMAs and Strauss' promise, they did not ask for the commitment in writing.

The footwear industry had learned very little from textiles' twenty years of experience with export restraints. By its own admission, it was a "naive" group in 1977.[13] In the first place, there was sufficient information available to suggest that OMAs had a low probability of success in the short run or the long run. Until 1977, Taiwan and Korea were largely producing very cheap shoes, whereas the American domestic industry's only strong market hold was in middle-priced shoes. The worst possible outcome for American footwear manufacturers was to pressure two dynamic producers, such as Taiwan and Korea, to upgrade their product lines. Moreover, Strauss' promise to "cap" other imports was a political fantasy. He did not have the power to make or enforce such a policy. Strauss later told industry representatives that he had had no authority to make the promise. He admitted that he "may have made the statement," but he said it was "unrealistic" for them to expect it.[14]

The government also learned very little from its many years of textile protectionism. One might have expected American decision makers to remember that the early voluntary restraints in textiles did not help the industry adjust. Instead, the VER with Japan merely postponed the political problem for a short period of time. As Hong Kong and other nations increased their exports, and Japan upgraded and diversified, the American cotton textile industry continued its decline. The pressure for protectionism increased rather than decreased only a few years after 1957. There was no reason to believe that the same pattern would not occur in footwear, yet no one in the government seriously discussed the connection.

There were several reasons for this inability to learn from others' experience. First, the industry itself did not recognize the problem. The textile lobby learned from its own mistakes, but footwear had no previous experience with the "new protectionism." Second, textile policy had become a major operation in the 1960s and 1970s, which required a separate bureaucracy and staff. As a result, the formulation of textile policy was usually isolated from general trade discussions, as well as treated in more long-run terms. Bureaucrats did not expect the political or economic problems of the textile industry to disappear. For other sectors, however, the government had no interest in creating a comprehensive protectionist regime as it had in textiles. Since a free-trade ideology remained in the Executive branch, most decision makers *purposely avoided* all comparisons to the Multifiber Arrangement; protectionist issues in other sectors were to be treated exclusively on a short-term basis.[15] Finally, the lack of a permanent civil service impeded institutional learning. Textile trade is a highly technical field. Bureaucrats who handle textiles rarely deal with other trade issues, and vice versa.

When it came time to implement Carter's decision, the lack of widespread legitimacy for the OMAs and the bureaucracy's limited time horizon played a major role in shaping the American bargaining position. The footwear lobby (AFIA) insisted that the United States reduce Taiwanese and Korean total exports as well as create categories of footwear based on price, age group, sex, and material characteristics. The industry wanted to prevent Taiwan and Korea from upgrading or shifting product lines into dynamic markets. Conflicts between government departments, however, seriously watered down the negotiating goals. The State Department and Treasury tried to minimize the restrictions as much as possible. Thus, in order to achieve an internal agreement, the bureaucracy had to settle on a loosely devised position.

Robert Strauss assured the industry that imports would be cut back, but he also said that there was "no way" their category demands would be met. *Before* the negotiators left for the Far East, Strauss told the AFIA that the best the United States could do was negotiate for categories of protection by materials—leather, plastic, vinyl, and others.[16] In terms of bargaining strategy, the United States had high resistance points on the visible issues, such as aggregate import levels, but on most other dimensions there was a willingness to accommodate. The American delegation's negotiating instructions called for five-year treaties, Korea and Taiwan to rollback their exports between 25 and 30 percent from 1976 levels, divisions by material categories, and minimum growth provisions.[17]

One serious problem that arose before the negotiations

began highlighted the weakness of the footwear industry's organization. Since the early 1960s, the sector had been divided into two groups: rubber and nonrubber. Rubber footwear manufacturers maintained separate lobbies because they had a history of special protection from the government. Under an arrangement known as the American Selling Price system (ASP), particular types of rubber shoes could be registered with the Customs Bureau, and then taxed at a special rate. Since ASP afforded American rubber shoe producers greater confidence in their market position, the AFIA was unable to mobilize the rubber segment of the industry to join forces when it filed its petition with the Trade Commission. As a consequence, the negotiating team's legal authority was limited to nonrubber footwear. In the 1960s, this would not have been an issue, but by the 1970s, rubber had become a misnomer. The tariff classification listed as "rubber" various materials, including canvas and rope-covered shoes that were in vogue in the late 1970s. In addition, to be classified as rubber, a shoe has to be only 50 percent rubber by weight. This left an obvious loophole in the American negotiating position—a loophole that was almost identical to the problem of "cotton" and "synthetic" textiles of the 1950s and 1960s.

Taiwan, Korea, and the OMA Decision

Taiwan and Korea reacted swiftly to the ITC's recommendation for tariff rate quotas. Both countries' policy makers were aware that regardless of the form of American protection, they were the most likely targets for restrictions. The Koreans were concerned because they had planned a 20 percent expansion of their shoe exports to the United States in 1977; and Taiwanese footwear manufacturers felt that they would be especially hurt, since over 70 percent of their shoe exports went to the United States.[18] As an initial response, the two nations launched a coordinated diplomatic offensive, seeking to form coalitions with each other as well as with Spain, Brazil, and Italy to fight the possibility of a quota.[19] At the same time, private organizations in Korea and Taiwan dispatched missions to the United States to mobilize support among importers and consumer groups.

Although such transnational efforts were part of the reason that Ford rejected import barriers in 1976, Taiwanese and Korean officials were less sanguine this time around. They recognized that the pressure on Carter for protection was simply too great. Therefore, in anticipation of imminent restrictions, both exporting countries adopted strategies that looked practically identical to the strategy discussed in chapter 1. First, Taiwan increased its shipments of nonrubber footwear to the United States by 8 percent in the first half of 1977, while Korea exported 60 percent more shoes than it had a year earlier.[20] Second, both governments encouraged producers to increase prices. Prices would soon start rising in the United States if retailers anticipated a shortage of low-priced shoes. By hiking the price tags themselves on existing product lines, Korea and Taiwan could absorb most of the potential scarcity rents. The Koreans even set up an "export price formula" to insure a minimum price on all shoes exported to the United States.[21] Finally, the two countries encouraged their exporters to accelerate the upgrading process in their footwear production. Even though both states were heading in this direction, their principal emphasis was still on aggregate expansion. With the prospect of restrictions, only higher-priced exports could maintain or increase foreign earnings over time. It was for this reason that the Korean government instituted an "incentive system" that gave preferential tax treatment to high-priced footwear manufacturers.[22]

The active, anticipatory roles assumed by the Korean and Taiwanese governments in their respective industries was only one element of the strategy that gave these nations an advanced start in adapting to protection. To preserve long-run interests, neither state wanted a confrontation with the

United States. Korean officials stressed that their producers understood the inevitability of protectionism and that they would "adjust and accommodate to this ever-changing international economic situation"; similarly, Taiwanese officials refused to fight the United States. The Taiwan government told its industry that it would "do its best to negotiate with the United States authorities on this matter."[23] To minimize short-run dislocations, the two countries collaborated before the United States talks to establish a baseline position. Both intended to push the Americans as far as possible without rupturing the negotiations. Finally, Korea exploited all its transgovernmental ties. Korean representatives visited various members of the American negotiating team in an effort to discover what information they could send back to their government.[24]

Korean and Taiwanese negotiators had several advantages over their American counterparts. First, they were part of a permanent civil service that negotiated textiles, footwear, and all major trade agreements. Both exporting countries had experience in dealing with protectionism in other sectors, and both knew what to avoid. While the American bureaucracy was shunning comparisons to textiles, Korean and Taiwanese negotiators were insisting that equity and market-share clauses from their textile treaties be transplanted intact to the footwear accords. In addition, they were highly sensitive to questions of flexibility and loopholes.

A second advantage favoring the exporters was their underlying motivations toward the upcoming negotiations. Korea and Taiwan had a narrow set of interests: they wanted higher trade earnings and amicable relations with the United States. Their goals were clear, and their methods relatively straightforward. The United States, on the other hand, had a number of competing objectives to balance. Only one thing was certain: the American delegation needed an agreement which would satisfy the minimal demands of Congress and the footwear industry. Given the low level of sophistication of the footwear lobby and most members of Congress about

the highly technical problems associated with export restraints, the potential for creating loopholes was enormous.
Albert Hirschman's suggestion that "there is no substitute for
the 'wise and salutory neglect' " of great powers was especially appropriate for this situation.[25]

Finally, there were differences between Taiwan and Korea. Korean footwear production was highly concentrated in
a small number of firms and organized by Korea's powerful
trading companies. This gave the Korean government almost
total control over its manufacturers. Korea was also relatively
secure in its relationship with the United States, despite a
threat by President Carter to pull out troops. Unlike Taiwan,
Korean officials faced nothing comparable to the dangers of
"derecognition" or being "abandoned." Taiwan had a great
deal to fear in its relationship with the United States. As the
1970s wore on, there was a growing likelihood that the
Americans would recognize the Communist regime in Peking
and abrogate its defense treaty with the Nationalists. Moreover, Taiwan had greater domestic constraints than Korea. The
Kuomintang's domestic political control was not as absolute
as the control of Korean President Park Chung-Hee. In addition, the Taiwanese footwear industry was decentralized with
hundreds of small shoemakers. Such sectoral fragmentation
would make adjustment more difficult for Taiwan, especially
since its shoes were generally of low quality. The combination of these factors meant that Taiwan faced greater uncertainty than Korea. The Koreans, therefore, were willing to
push a little harder than the Taiwanese, even though Korean
footwear exports were relatively less important to their economy.

The Negotiations

Publicly, Taiwan and Korea pronounced their opposition to
the OMAs, but privately they admitted their relief when Carter

rejected the ITC recommendation. Under the Trade Commission's plan, Korean shoe exports might have been cut by 75 percent, and Taiwan's exports might have been reduced by 44 percent.

To set the stage for upcoming negotiations, Robert Strauss met with a number of high-ranking Korean and Taiwanese officials, including their ambassadors to Washington. In each meeting, Strauss discussed general issues, and one can speculate that he reminded them that the ITC alternative was still open to the administration. The Korean Minister of Industry, in turn, reminded Strauss that Korea was in the process of opening its markets to the United States. A Korean purchasing mission was in the United States at that time, expecting to buy 200 million dollars' worth of goods. Strauss nonetheless remained confident that agreements would be reached.

The chief negotiator for the footwear OMAs, Stephen Lande of the Special Trade Representative's Office (STR), was apparently not as confident about the bargaining prospects. According to STR's deputy general counsel and Lande's fellow negotiator, Thomas Graham, Lande leaked United States negotiating instructions to the American Importers Association before the delegation left for the Far East. Lande apparently wanted this transnational group to inform the Koreans and Taiwanese exactly how high the Americans would go. Lande hoped this would expedite the negotiations by reducing uncertainty.[26] The result, however, was exactly the opposite: the American maximum resistance points suddenly became Korea's and Taiwan's minimum bargaining objectives.

Setting the Agenda

The Republic of Korea was the first stop for the American delegation, on May 2, 1977. The Koreans opened the negotiations by talking about numbers. They suggested that since their overall export capacity for 1977 was sixty million pairs of shoes, this would serve as a reasonable upper limit. To accompany this quota, Korea wanted only a single category breakdown.[27] Lande, however, preferred to brush aside discussion of export figures until a formula and procedures were worked out. He thought that a referent was needed before details could be decided.[28] Yet Lande felt that the Korean position was so outlandish that he responded with an equally outlandish and absurdly low figure of sixteen million pairs—twenty-eight million less than Korea's 1976 exports. Lande also proposed thirty-two category divisions, based on price, materials, and age group. At that point, the discussion of details temporarily ended.

With the preliminaries out of the way, the rest of the day was devoted to laying out the variables and raising general issues. The Koreans insisted that the first item on the agenda deal with the question of implementation. They wanted to administer the agreement in order to capture any scarcity rent. Other issues, such as the length of an agreement, spacing, starting dates, flexibility, and guaranteed market shares, were also raised. Although their positions were far apart on almost every point, they successfully created an agenda by the end of the session. Since this accomplished the Americans' objective for the first trip, they were optimistic when they left for Taiwan a day later. The strategy was to make incremental agreements with each country that would strengthen America's bargaining leverage. The problem was that neither exporter wanted to be the first to make concessions.

The opening Taiwanese position was almost identical to the Koreans'. Taiwan talked about numbers, whereas Lande sought an agenda. The Taiwanese, like the Koreans, asked for a single category breakdown, an export limit based on 1976 figures (which were 25 percent higher than United States statistics), a late starting date, guaranteed market shares, and so on. The Americans countered with their maximum demands, and by the finish of the meetings, a framework was established.

The only significant difference between the Korean and Taiwanese negotiations was the role taken by each nation's press. In Seoul, reporting was minimal and generally factual.

In Taipei, newspapers made a big issue of American threats and the extent of the disagreement. The American negotiators thought that the Taiwanese government was using selected press leaks to (1) pressure the United States, and (2) build domestic legitimacy for future concessions.[29]

The Bargaining and Decision Phases

The second round of negotiations began on May 10 in Korea. The United States immediately agreed to the Korean request for an equity clause similar to one in their textile treaties (Korea would not be placed at a disadvantage with respect to other exporters) and agreed to make the restraints based on export control versus import control. To appease the American footwear industry advisers, the wording of the latter provision was amended to say the United States would "assist" in implementation. The principal areas of contention, however, remained the actual numbers: What would be the aggregate limit? How many categories would there be with what flexibility? How long would the agreement last? And when would the agreement start?

During two days of bargaining, neither delegation made anything more than marginal concessions. The Koreans confided to the Americans that they were under tremendous pressure from President Park himself to get high numbers. But at the same time they were told to appease the United States. The Americans conveyed their sympathies to the Koreans but insisted throughout the negotiations that they needed a rollback to satisfy their own domestic pressures. The AFIA was trailing them around the Far East, and daily reports were being sent back to Washington. To the House representatives, senators, and various bureaucrats overseeing the negotiations, the single most important item was a low aggregate total.

Before Lande broke off the talks to return to Taiwan, some minor progress was made. The Koreans gradually lowered their position on the ceiling figure from the sixty million suggested earlier. At one point, they demanded that their final offer begin with a "four"—at least forty million pairs. The Koreans knew that Washington's instructions called for an aggregate of around 35 million, but they still hoped that they could push the United States into additional concessions. The two sides also approached a compromise on the starting date. Korea and Taiwan had proposed August 1; they both insisted that organizing for export restraints would take time, and they knew that every added day of free trade would reduce short-run costs. The Americans wanted May 1; the sooner the restrictions began, the more likely imports would drop during 1977. Although its negotiating instructions allowed the American delegation to fall back to a June 1 date, the bargaining was heading toward a July 1 compromise. On this issue, it appears the Koreans (and the Taiwanese) persuaded the Americans that they had the stronger motivation.

When the American team finally left Seoul, the negotiators were reasonably confident that their differences with the Koreans were manageable. Yet the gap on most of the remaining questions was so great that there was some lingering doubt.[30] In Taiwan's case, however, there was little question about the prospects of an accord. The Taiwanese were tough, insistent bargainers, but they also did not want to jeopardize their relationship with the United States. The only obstacles for Taiwan were industry pressures and a desire for parity with Korea's eventual agreement. Without the latter, Taiwan's footwear manufacturers would "roast" their negotiators.[31]

Just as they had done in Korea, the Americans stressed their overarching need for a low aggregate limit. Taiwan would compromise on the ceiling, but only if the United States would make a number of other concessions on critical issues. Taiwan wanted the OMA to last less than five years, a high degree of flexibility, and some way to avoid the possible short-run dislocations that would result from the sudden imposition of an export quota. The Taiwanese knew that some of these demands were outside the American negotiating team's instructions, but they threatened to break off the talks unless these desiderata were met.

The American negotiating team was now confronted with a choice: either terminate the discussion with little hope of extracting an agreement from Korea, or find an innovative way to accommodate Taiwan's demands. The breakthrough in the bargaining came when someone in the American delegation suggested a "pipeline" clause—an arrangement which would allow passage for a certain percentage of Taiwanese footwear to enter the United States after the agreement date without being counted against the quota. If Taiwan would scale down the aggregate ceiling, the United States would reduce the span of the OMA to four years, provide significant flexibility, and give Taiwan an additional *thirty-three million pairs* of shoes under the pipeline clause.

When Lande telegraphed this outline back to Washington, some STR officials screamed. They said that this amounted to a gift of thirty-three million pairs for Taiwan— an added 25 percent of the first year's quota—and complained that it was not in the instructions. STR's chief textile negotiator then intervened by suggesting that it could be sold domestically. He argued that if the starting date was in late June or early July, the government could claim that the exports had been shipped before the agreement started and thus were not formally covered in the quota. Even though the pipeline was in actuality nothing more than a thirty-three-million-pair gift, this rationale made it "optically more satisfactory." [32] The American footwear advisers were very upset by this concession, but they nonetheless gave their consent. The negotiators convinced the AFIA that without this compromise, an agreement would not be reached.

The remainder of the bargaining with Taiwan was largely horsetrading and hairsplitting. To expedite the process, the negotiations dealt only with the core issues. A meeting was set up later in the month in Washington for ironing out some of the technical questions. For the aggregate limit, a Taiwanese footwear official had previously suggested that a "figure reflecting the average volume exported to the U.S. over the past two years would be much more reasonable than the present demands."[33] This was precisely the result: the ceiling was figured on the basis of a four-year average—an average slightly less than Taiwan's mean exports during 1975 and 1976. The Taiwanese were told that they could space the shipments however they wanted over the four-year period, which avoided arguments about growth rates. Thus the outcome on paper was exactly what the Americans said they wanted: Taiwan would cut its nonrubber shoe exports during

Table 5.2 Comparison of 1976 Footwear Exports with OMA Ceilings (in millions of pairs)

	Exports 1976	OMA Limit	Percentage Change
Taiwan	156	122	−22
Korea	44	33	−25

SOURCE: U.S. Department of Commerce, *Footwear Industry Revitalization Program: First Annual Progress Report* (1978), pp. 27, 31.

the first year of the OMA by 22 percent. To Congress and the American footwear industry, this alone made the accord a great success (see table 5.2).

On other major issues, Taiwan acceded to three category divisions (leather, plastic, and other), but it still insisted on various flexibility clauses that had generous percentages ranging from 6 to 15 percent (see table 5.3). The starting date was also moved two days earlier because the administration was required to implement its policy within ninety days of the President's April 1 announcement. June 28 was the last possible day. Lastly, the AFIA insisted that some provision restrain the exporters from upgrading and shifting into rubber shoes. The American negotiators recognized the problem, but they did not consider it critical. Furthermore, the Taiwanese would not bargain over these issues. They knew that the Americans had no legal authority to include rubber. In addition, the Taiwanese government and industry had stated

Table 5.3 Summary of Principal Provisions of the Footwear OMAs

A. *Product Coverage*—All nonrubber footwear except zoris, disposable paper footwear, and wool felt footwear.

B. *Duration*—Four years and three days, starting June 28, 1977.

C. *Restraint Levels* (millions of pairs exported).

	Taiwan	Korea
First year	122	33.0
Second year	125	36.5
Third year	128	37.5
Fourth year	131	38.0

D. *Categories*

Taiwan—a) Leather	8% of total
b) Plastic	86% of total
c) Other	6% of total

Swings among categories are allowed up to 10 percent of the receiving category in the case of shifts into leather and plastic footwear and up to 15 percent for other footwear. (The United States, at its discretion, may permit shifts into the category "other" greater than 15 percent—up to a total of 50 percent.)

Korea—a) Leather, except athletic footwear	34.9%
b) All other, including leather athletic footwear	65.1%

Swings among categories are allowed up to 10 percent of the receiving category in the case of shifts into leather footwear and up to 15 percent for other footwear.

E. *Carry-over*—If exports are below the ceiling levels, the shortfall can be carried over to the following year, but the amount carried over into individual categories may not exceed 11 percent of the ceiling for those categories.

F. *Carry-forward*—Exports in excess of ceilings will be allowed to enter up to a maximum of 6 percent in any category. Reductions equal to such overceiling entries will be made in the entries allowed in the following year.

G. *Import Spacing*—Taiwan and Korea will employ their best efforts to maintain an even distribution of imports throughout the year, taking into account seasonal factors.

H. *Equity*—In the event of large increases in U.S. imports from other countries, Taiwan or Korea may initiate consultations with the United States. If mutually agreed, the United States will take appropriate remedial action.

I. *Pipeline*—Footwear exported prior to June 28, 1977, will be allowed to enter the United States. However, such exports entering after June 1 will be counted and any excess above 33 million pairs for Taiwan will be charged against the ceilings for the first year. For Korea, any excess above 9 million pairs will be charged against the ceilings for the first year.

SOURCE: U.S. Department of Commerce, *Footwear Industry Revitalization Program: First Annual Progress Report* (1978), p. 32.

throughout the negotiations that they planned to upgrade in order to avoid damage from the restraints. Yet to appease the Americans, Taiwan let it be stated in the "Agreed Minutes" that there would be "no major shifts away from the normal pattern of exports to the United States in nonrubber footwear by type, material, or price range."[34] Both sides knew at the time that this was ambiguous and unenforceable. The AFIA nonetheless acquiesced because Lande allegedly promised that the agreement would be "faithfully" implemented.[35]

With the outline of an agreement in hand, Lande and the American delegation returned to Seoul on May 15 for their final round of bargaining. But despite the American accord with Taiwan, the Koreans were still not ready to compromise. They demanded that there be only two material divisions versus Taiwan's three, that the vast majority of their quota be placed in the "other" category to maximize flexibility, and that there be an aggregate total above forty million pairs. They also had a few special requests for their industry's particular needs. The Americans, however, would not concede on the overall limit. Without a significant reduction from Korea's forty-four million pairs of shoe exports in 1976, the OMA would be politically useless. Therefore, the negotiations broke down, and the American team headed for home with the intention of unilaterally restricting Korea's footwear exports.

While waiting for a plane at Seoul's Kimpo Airport, Lande received a call from Korea's chief negotiator expressing his willingness to capitulate. Rather than risk a crisis, the Koreans accepted an average ceiling of thirty-seven and one-half million pairs over the four years of an OMA in exchange for the two category divisions. In the end, both sides felt that they had come out ahead. Despite the fact that the Korean aggregate was at the top of Washington's instructions, the Americans considered their mission successful. Korean footwear exports during the first year of the OMA would be cut by 25 percent (see table 5.2), which would please Congress as well as the shoe industry. The Koreans could be satisfied because they were given all of the advantages won by Taiwan, plus a few of their own. By pushing the negotiations to the crisis point, the Koreans extracted the final two-category concession from the United States. In addition, Korean exporters could use a pipeline that amounted to nine million pairs, or 27 percent of their first year's quota; they were provided with flexibility provisions similar to Taiwan's, and identical ambiguous clauses about upgrading and shifting product lines (see table 5.3).

Taiwan, Korea, and the United States worked out the technical details and resolved last-minute problems between mid-May and June 28. Taiwan, of course, was displeased that Korea was given greater flexibility. Two categories would make it easier for an exporter to meet shifting market demand. Since the Americans wanted the Taiwanese to feel that they were treated equitably, the following clause was inserted into the Republic of China's bilateral accord: "It is understood that the Government of the United States of America may, at its discretion, permit shifts into the Category 'Other' . . . up to 50 percent."[36] If the Americans were to allow the full 50 percent, Taiwan and Korea's flexibility would be virtually identical.

Evaluation

One of the American negotiators accurately noted that the United States could have been much "more brutal" in the bargaining. They had the authority and capability to impose their will, even though this was not the intention.[37] The United States wanted minimal trade restrictions that would have maximum political results. In essence, the Americans would accommodate Taiwan and Korea as much as they could without jeopardizing domestic support for the OMAs. Since the footwear industry's approval was a "necessary condition" for the agreement to get past Congress, the extent of American generosity was limited. Nevertheless, the American bargaining strategy was to employ the strongest forms of accommodation.

The outcome of the negotiations, however, was by no means predetermined. Taiwan and Korea made skillful use of their information and limited bargaining leverage to extract the maximum possible concessions. On the one hand, a maximizing strategy on their part would have sabotaged the negotiations and led to more restrictive American action. This reaction almost occurred in the Korean case. On the other hand, a more accommodating strategy would probably *not* have resulted in the pipeline clauses, the high degree of flexibility, late starting dates, reduced time spans, and so on. Each of these provisions went beyond the Americans' initial resistance points. Also, had the American footwear industry or the American bureaucracy learned more from the United States' textile experience, it is doubtful that as many loopholes would have appeared. Taiwan and Korea carefully insured the easiest possible implementation. They bargained for both loopholes and flexibility during the negotiations. The American negotiators and the industry advisers, by comparison, were too concerned with the politically salient issues to worry about implementation. Standard features in textile accords that protect the importer, such as an article that states the illegality of transshipments, were nowhere to be found in the footwear OMAs.

The other notable feature of this bargaining episode concerns the role played by transnational actors. By providing the American Importers Association with Washington's negotiating instructions, Lande established a tacit alliance between the Korean and Taiwanese governments and the American Executive. Armed with this information, Taiwanese and Korean interests were served because they could bargain with the United States on a more equal footing. Yet the American negotiating team also benefited because it helped build domestic legitimacy for concessions. Congress, the AFIA, and various bureaucrats were consulted every day on the progress and obstacles confronting the negotiators. Therefore, everyone in Washington as well as in the Far East could observe the intensity of Korean and Taiwanese negotiating strategies and understand the necessity of compromise.[38] Textile bargaining episodes sometimes lasted for several years because the exporting countries were uncertain about the intentions of the United States, or American interest groups were unconvinced that their government had done its best. This footwear bargaining episode lasted only two weeks because effective communications and the ITC deadline reduced uncertainty between governments as well as within the nations.

Implementation

The Americans thought that despite their relatively accommodating strategy, they would succeed in reducing imports by the end of 1977. After all, *on paper*, the United States had cut Korean and Taiwanese exports significantly. Yet no one in the government fully understood the potential for slippage in these arrangements. Furthermore, within two years of the restrictions, both exporting nations accelerated their footwear earnings by upgrading their product lines into middle-priced shoes.

Preparing for the OMAs

Once the agreements were signed, Taiwan and Korea faced similar short-run constraints, but slightly different long-run problems. Neither country was particularly concerned about short-run costs affecting employment or export earnings. Since there were no unrestrained producers which could immediately fill a void in low-cost shoes, both exporting nations could raise their prices on existing product lines. Moreover, the flexibility in the Taiwanese and Korean agreements, in addition to their pipeline clauses, would minimize any losses in production in 1977. The major questions concerned what would happen in 1978 and beyond.

The Koreans had a clearly defined long-run strategy that recognized the need for upgrading their products and diversifying buyers. The government plan called for the production of quality footwear in the $6.00 to $8.00 range. As the Ministry of Commerce noted, "The voluntary quota system is set to operate on a quantitative basis; [therefore] Korean exporters can offset their losses caused by the restraint formula by increasing shipments in quality shoes." [39]

Taiwanese officials also told their local footwear producers that they should manufacture higher-priced shoes, but their industry's structure was not as easily manipulated as Korea's. [40] A majority of Taiwan's manufacturers produced vinyl footwear, such as sandals and slippers. As a result, it was not entirely obvious where the upgrading would go. Yet despite this uncertainty, the Taiwanese found one saving grace in the OMAs: the restrictions would help guarantee Taiwan's market shares in the face of growing competition from Korea. Taiwan's production was close to its peak in 1976. Even with the threat of upcoming restrictions, Taiwan could not increase shipments to the United States more than 8.4 percent in the first quarter of 1977. Korean manufacturers, on the other hand, were still in the process of rapid expansion; their exports to the United States increased almost 90 percent in the same three-month period.

Once the orderly marketing agreements became effective on June 28, 1977, Taiwan and Korea capitalized immediately on their treaties' vagueness. The first problem was that there was no definition in the accords of what constituted date of export. Through June 27, Korean and Taiwanese manufacturers loaded every available shoe on vessels bound for the United States. A few of the ships, however, did not sail until after the deadline. The Americans insisted that these goods should be considered part of the quota, but the Taiwanese and Koreans argued that they were "exported" as part of the pipeline. Since some of the ships were ready to unload by the time the problem was discovered, American importers were exerting pressure on the bureaucracy to allow the goods quota-free entry. The best the United States government could do under the circumstances was to add side letters to both

OMAs which specified the American definition of an exporting date for future reference.[41] Yet the damage was done: Taiwan shipped over forty-three million pairs in the pipeline and Korea exported over fifteen million—33 and 74 percent over their respective limits.

The second implementation problem was the lack of reference to sanctions concerning transshipments. Taiwanese producers quickly learned from their countrymen who were textile exporters that OMAs did not constitute an impenetrable barrier. On the contrary, Taiwanese footwear manufacturers found that they could avoid underutilized capacity and their quotas by shipping shoe parts to third countries, which would assemble and export the finished product to the United States. In other words, the classic quota dodge in textiles became an equally profitable quota dodge in footwear. In the first twelve months of the OMA, Taiwan allegedly exported large quantities of shoe parts to Hong Kong and the Philippines. These two countries were singled out because both wanted to enter the low-cost American shoe markets as Taiwan and Korea raised their prices. By mid-1978, Hong Kong's footwear exports to the United States jumped 225 percent, and shipments from the Philippines rose from less than one million pairs in 1977 to nearly eight million pairs in 1978— an increase of 800 percent. Particularly in the early stages of these export surges, the evidence clearly pointed to transshipments.[42]

By the end of 1977, both Taiwan and Korea had successfully circumvented all the short-run burdens that normally accompany the sudden imposition of export restraints. Korean and Taiwanese exports were up in quantity as well as value in 1977 (see table 5.4). In fact, the export goal of sixty million pairs of shoes, which the Korean government had set six months *before* restrictions, was almost met.

Adjusting to the OMAs

By overshipping their pipeline allocations and using their maximum flexibility provisions in 1977, Taiwan and Korea were obligated to reduce their exports of "nonrubber" footwear in 1978. Therefore, it was necessary for both countries to make adjustments if they wanted to compensate for the restrictions. Two avenues were available: first, maintain their export volume by cheating and/or diversifying markets and, second, increase the value of their footwear shipments by upgrading.

The first option turned out to be relatively easy. Most footwear can be made to look similar or identical by using different substances. Since "rubber" footwear was excluded

Table 5.4 United States Imports of Nonrubber Footwear from Taiwan and Korea, 1976–77[a] (in millions of pairs and $ million)

	1976		1977		Percent Change	
	Volume	Value	Volume	Value	Volume	Value
Taiwan	156.7	$279.3	166.4	$346.6	+6.9	+24.1
Korea	44.04	$165.2	58.6	$229.3	+33.1	+38.9

SOURCE: Brimmer and Company, *Trends in the Demand for and the Supply of Nonrubber Footwear*, June 27, 1979.

[a] These figures do not include transshipments.

from the OMAs, the Koreans and Taiwanese discovered that traditionally defined "nonrubber" footwear could be reclassified as "rubber" by simply adding rubber to the sole or making other minor alterations. Furthermore, these "rubber" imports initially entered the United States under the normal tariff rates. The special protection of the American Selling Price system did not automatically apply.[43]

Both nations promised that they would "not circumvent the agreement by disruptively shifting into lines of footwear that technically are not covered by the OMA, but in fact compete." Yet starting in the first half of 1978, rubber exports from Taiwan surged ahead 55 percent from 1977 and Korean rubber exports rose by 146 percent. When American producers realized what was happening, they had much of the imported footwear reclassified under the ASP tariff. However, this did not remove the incentive for circumventing the quota. By the first quarter of 1979, the Koreans were exporting three times more rubber footwear than nonrubber footwear, as compared to only one-half as much rubber versus nonrubber in the first quarter on 1977.[44] This huge "rubber" loophole allowed Korea to increase by 8 percent the total number of pairs it exported to the United States in 1978, while Taiwan's total shipments dropped only slightly (see table 5.5). Thus in the short run, the OMAs barely restrained the quantities of exports from either country.[45]

The two nations simultaneously pursued their long-run strategies of altering the composition and value of their exports. Although Taiwan did not adapt as well as Korea, both upgraded their product lines and increased prices on their older production.[46] For example, footwear which was valued up to $1.25 comprised 40 percent of Taiwan's shipments in the first month of the OMA. By December 1978, this price bracket represented less than one percent of Taiwanese exports. If one looks at the entire OMA period, the results were even more dramatic. The average unit value of Korean nonrubber footwear increased from $3.91 in 1977 to $7.09 in 1980, and Taiwanese shoes jumped from $2.08 to $4.31. While the average price of a pair of imported shoes (no matter what the country of origin) rose by only 45 percent during this time, the two restricted nations raised their prices between 81 percent and 107 percent (see table 5.6). Thus these foreign producers successfully increased their trade earnings by shifting their production into middle-priced footwear—the traditional mainstay of the American shoe industry. Even the slow market conditions in 1979 and 1980, which forced cutbacks in shipments (see table 5.5), could not prevent these exporting nations from increasing their export earnings. From 1977 through 1980, Taiwan and Korea pushed their export receipts higher by 85 percent and 53 percent respectively (see table 5.7).

Taiwan's and Korea's move into the more expensive product lines was triggered and accelerated by the orderly marketing agreements. Yet establishing causality could be problematic because wage rates were on the rise and the price

Table 5.5 Volume of United States Rubber and Nonrubber Footwear Imports Under the OMA, 1977–80 (in millions of pairs)

	Taiwan [a]				Korea			
	Total	Nonrubber	Rubber	OMA Limit [b]	Total	Nonrubber	Rubber	OMA Limit [b]
Year ending June 1977	227.9	162.1	65.8		91.0	55.2	35.8	
Year ending June 1978	217.8	135.3	82.5	122	86.0	43.1	43.8	33
January–December 1977	227.6	166.5	61.1		83.5	58.7	24.8	
January–December 1978	212.0	117.2	94.8	125	90.1	30.6	59.9	
January–December 1979	178.6	124.8	53.8	125	66.1	24.3	41.8	36.5
January–December 1980	202.9	144.0	58.9	131	79.7	37.1	42.5	37.5

SOURCE: U.S. International Trade Commission, *Nonrubber Footwear*, USITC Publication 1139, April 1981, table 1.

[a] Excludes transshipped parts.

[b] OMA quotas extended from June to June, not calendar years.

Table 5.6 Average Unit Value of United States Nonrubber Imports, 1977–80 (in dollars)

Source	1977	1978	1979	1980	Percent Change 1977–80
Taiwan	$2.08	$3.30	$3.49	$4.31	107
Korea	3.91	5.60	6.83	7.09	81
World average	4.34	5.51	6.00	6.28	45

SOURCE: U.S. International Trade Commission, *Nonrubber Footwear*, USITC Publication 1139, April 1981, table 3.

of raw materials was also soaring. Regardless of the OMAs, both countries would have upgraded within two or three years to maintain a competitive position. But wholesale prices in Korea, for instance, did not increase at an annual rate above 18 percent between 1976 and 1979, nor was the Korean won revalued. Furthermore, the average import price of footwear coming into the United States rose far less than prices for Korean and Taiwanese shoes. Therefore, one doubts that the Koreans (or the Taiwanese) would have pushed as hard or as fast in this direction if it were not for the restrictions. It was only after the OMA that the Korean bureaucracy started to push up the floor prices on its exports every three months.[47]

The big loser in the implementation of the orderly marketing agreements was the American footwear industry. Not only were Taiwan and Korea circumventing the restrictions, but unrestrained countries were also re-entering the American market. Strauss' supposed promise to cap other imports

Table 5.7 Value of United States Rubber and Nonrubber Footwear Imports, 1977–80 (in $ million)

	Taiwan	Korea
January–December 1977	$443.9	$289.0
January–December 1978	575.9	365.3
January–December 1979	567.3	332.6
January–December 1980	823.6	442.6
Percentage change, 1977–80	85.5%	53.1%

SOURCE: U.S. International Trade Commission, *Nonrubber Footwear*, USITC Publication 1139, April 1981, tables 3 and 6.

was ignored, as expected. This meant that nothing prevented Italy, Brazil, Spain, and others from expanding their market shares. As when the United States negotiated the voluntary export restraint with Japan in 1956–57, import penetration actually increased rather than decreased in response to selective protection. As nonrubber footwear imports from uncontrolled sources rose by 60 percent in 1978, the American manufacturers' share of the domestic footwear supply dropped from 51 percent in 1977 to 47 percent.[48]

The officials of the American Footwear Industries Association felt betrayed by Strauss and the Special Trade Representative's Office for not adhering to the letter of the OMAs and allowing imports from other countries to be unrestrained. Furthermore, the surge in imports was endangering the Commerce Department's special domestic program for revitalizing the industry. As production of domestic firms hit record lows—390 million pairs in 1979—the only real victory the Commerce Department could claim for its efforts was a reduction in the rate of industrial decline.[49] The net result was that protectionist pressures were growing.

To alleviate some of this pressure, the government proposed new restrictions for Hong Kong. American decision makers thought that an orderly marketing agreement with the British colony would kill two birds with one stone: it would stop the transshipment from Taiwan and limit the expanding exports of the largest new entrant into the United States market. The American bureaucracy, however, was far from united on a bargaining strategy. The internal dissent was so great that the negotiating instructions were not finalized until the delegation was on the plane to the Far East.[50]

Strongly reminiscent of the American attempt to get Hong Kong to agree to voluntary textile restraints in 1959–60, the American footwear negotiators could not even create an agenda (see chapter 2). Washington had finally authorized its team to negotiate, but it did not provide them with any leverage. Since there was no credibility behind American threats, Hong Kong simply refused to discuss an OMA on any level.

As a compromise, Lande suggested that Hong Kong implement a "certificate of origin." Such documents, which were frequently used in textiles, specified the source of the exported good. If Hong Kong agreed, this could cut down on transshipments and, it was hoped, decrease exports. In fact, the idea for a certificate of origin had been previously discussed in Geneva between Lande and Hong Kong's chief negotiator. It was therefore no surprise when Hong Kong agreed—especially since Lande had been suggesting all along that this be the American fallback position.[51]

The certificate of origin ended up having relatively little impact on the colony's exports. By the time of this certificate, production was almost fully standardized in Hong Kong. This made it relatively easy for Hong Kong's manufacturers to substitute domestically produced parts for transshipped parts and maintain their high level of footwear shipments.

Despite the similarities to the textile negotiations in the late 1950s, Hong Kong's rejection did not have the same adverse effects. In 1960 American negotiators were intent upon restricting the second largest exporters of textiles, but in 1980 the colony's footwear exports were significantly smaller than countries such as Spain, Italy, and Taiwan, and the United States was not as committed to footwear protectionism. Moreover, unlike the period from 1956 to 1960, Hong Kong was not the only country in the late 1970s that rejected footwear restrictions. The Philippines was also approached by the United States, and it also refused to sign an OMA. For Hong Kong, this helped spread the burden of American government failures to several states.

The Decline
of Footwear Protection

There was a vigorous debate in the American government over the future of footwear restrictions following the failure of the Hong Kong talks. In February 1980 proposals for a comprehensive quota system circulated around the Executive branch, and in April 1981 the International Trade Commission recommended a limited extension of the orderly marketing agreements.[52] But despite the ineffectiveness of the OMAs and the continued poor performance of American shoe companies, the footwear lobby could not persuade either the Carter administration or the Reagan administration to grant meaningful protection.[53] President Carter preferred to postpone a decision until the last possible moment, and President Reagan had more important items on his agenda. In early May 1981, Reagan had negotiated a voluntary restraint with Japan in automobiles (which I will discuss in the next chapter). Rejecting protectionism for the footwear industry would publicly demonstrate Reagan's free-trade ideology.[54]

Yet much to the surprise of the American government and the American footwear industry, as soon as the orderly marketing agreements expired, Taiwan and Korea proclaimed their own voluntary restraints on footwear exports to the United States. For one additional year, both national governments decided to exploit the advantages of protectionism without protection. The Koreans thought that restricting shipments could head off excessive investment in athletic footwear—their largest shoe export. The Taiwanese saw a voluntary restraint as a way to continue engineering their footwear industry in addition to minimizing future political problems with the United States. As the Taiwan Board of Foreign Trade put it, the VER was "for the purpose of maintaining orderly exports of nonrubber footwear to the U.S. and encouraging a higher quality product and price structure."[55] The American government and American importers protested the Taiwanese and Korean decisions, but to no avail.

There are at least three lessons that one can draw from Korea's and Taiwan's experience with the OMAs in footwear. The first is that modern protectionism can still be a "paper tiger." Although textile restraints became sophisticated and restrictive in the late 1970s, the low degree of institutional learning in the United States has meant that the loopholes in modern protectionism can persist. This suggests that an exporting nation can avert the dangers associated with VERs and OMAs in new sectors if it pursues the policies I outlined in chapter 1. The very structure of these agreements in labor-intensive manufacturing sectors and the political motivation which underlies them create opportunities for any newly industrializing country.

A second lesson of this footwear episode is that if the new protectionism did not exist, the newly industrializing countries might have had to create it. Conventional wisdom would have suggested that Taiwan and Korea should rejoice upon the lifting of protectionism in 1981. The fact that both nations instituted their own versions of VERs is powerful proof that dynamic exporting countries view these arrangements as potentially profitable for political as well as economic purposes.

The third conclusion from the study of footwear protectionism is not as positive as the first two. The extension of import restrictions into another sector outside of textiles and apparel signals a partial decline in America's commitment to free trade. The singling out of Taiwan and Korea among the many exporters of shoes also illustrates the discriminatory potential in this new trend. As I will show in chapter 6, protectionism continues to spread in the 1980s with potentially insidious results.

Chapter 6

The Pattern of Protectionism:
Color Televisions,
Automobiles, and the Future

Protectionism threatens to become a problem of global proportions. Persistently high unemployment and slow economic growth in the United States and Europe have combined to intensify protectionist pressures and to weaken free-trade norms. Trade frictions have multiplied between nations and across sectors as the expansion of world trade has come to a halt in the early 1980s.

This outbreak of protectionism has taken a variety of forms, many of them reminiscent of the 1930s. Prominent features of trade during the Great Depression—competitive subsidies, barter trade, and an emphasis on bilateralism—are now prominent features of international commerce in the 1980s. The potential dangers of this "new" protectionism are apparent to any student of the 1930s. The total collapse of world trade after 1928 exacerbated macroeconomic problems and inhibited recovery for more than a decade. Although we have not reached this abyss in the early 1980s, a better understanding of the effects of voluntary export restraints (VERs), orderly marketing agreements (OMAs), and other protectionist tools is a matter of utmost importance.

Summarizing the Findings

The results of my study shed light on a large part of this new protectionism and its impact on importers and exporters, as well as the entire trading system. I started this book with the argument that OMAs, VERs, and their equivalents are fundamentally flawed instruments of commercial policy. Industrial countries, and particularly the United States, have employed VERs and OMAs as short-run political tools. The American government designed these barriers to appease domestic industries that clamored for protection rather than to provide domestic firms with iron-clad restrictions. The myopia underlying this protectionism, I said, could provide opportunities for exporters. As long as a newly industrializing country (NIC) was politically adept and had an industrial structure that could adapt to changing market trends, then a NIC could improve its trade earnings in the face of restrictions.

To achieve increased export earnings without disrupting the trade regime, a NIC had to follow a particular strategy. First, it had to pursue what I called long-run gains from trade, minimizing long-run political tensions by agreeing to a VER or an OMA, and maximizing long-run trade earnings by diversifying its product mix and moving up the scale on quality and price in its existing export lines. Second, it had to bargain with the importer for loopholes in the protectionist arrangement in order to protect its short-run trading interests. And third, a NIC had to supplement its profits whenever possible through linkage policies, cheating, and mobilizing transnational and transgovernmental allies.

NIC Gains

The case studies I presented in chapters 2 through 5 suggest that such a strategy could indeed exploit the weaknesses in modern protectionism. When Japan, Hong Kong, Korea, and Taiwan followed the minimum elements of my overall strategy—pursuing long-run gains and bargaining for loop-holes—they managed to increase their trade earnings and maintain a stable bilateral trade regime with the United States. Despite voluntary export restraints, orderly marketing agreements, and elaborate market-sharing arrangements such as the Long-Term Arrangement Regarding International Trade in Cotton Textiles, these relatively weak, rapidly industrializing countries prospered in their textile, apparel, and footwear trades. From 1962 through 1976, Korea expanded its textile and apparel exports to the United States from approximately 15 million square-yard equivalents (SYEs) to 610 million SYEs; Taiwan went from a little over 100 million SYEs to around 640 million SYEs; and Hong Kong started at a very high level of close to 300 million SYEs and had grown to over 900 million SYEs by 1976. Similarly, Japan's total textile exports to the United States in 1956 were around 250 million SYEs; by 1971, these exports reached about 1.7 billion SYEs.

In dollar terms, the improvement in trade earnings appears to be even more dramatic. For example, Hong Kong exported less than a million dollars' worth of textiles to the United States in 1956, while Korean and Taiwanese shipments were not worth measuring. By 1979, these three nations accounted for 77 percent of the 5.2 billion dollars' worth of American textile imports from developing nations.[1]

In footwear trade, the results were equally impressive. During the first three years of the orderly marketing agreements, Taiwan and Korea increased their dollar export earnings to the United States at compound annual growth rates of 22.9 percent and 15.3 percent respectively. Quota cuts of up to 25 percent in the volume of their exports did not stop these countries from upgrading, bargaining, and cheating their way to several profitable years. Furthermore, Taiwan and Korea found export restrictions so helpful to their trade earnings and internal industrial policies that they implemented their own unilateral VERs after the United States formally discontinued the bilateral orderly marketing agreements.

NIC Problems

Yet the gains reaped by these countries were neither easy nor continuous. The path to huge export earnings was not as smooth as these aggregate statistics would suggest. Each country had its share of lean years as well as rough political periods interspersed throughout the profitable times. In chapters 2 and 3, for instance, I showed that Japan's export earnings in cotton textiles were stagnant during the late 1950s; during most of the 1960s, Korea and Taiwan were both severely restricted by major cuts in their cotton export quotas under the auspices of the Long-Term Arrangement. Furthermore, a small crisis between the United States and Hong Kong in the last days of the Eisenhower administration temporarily damaged Hong Kong's trade regime with the United States and contributed to a dramatic decline in the British colony's cotton textile shipments in 1961. And in chapter 4, I demonstrated that Japanese resistance to multifiber restrictions cost them dearly in their trade regime with the United States. United States–Japan trade relations hit a low point in 1970 and 1971, when the American Congress nearly passed a highly protectionist trade bill, and the American President threatened to link the reversion of Okinawa and invoke the 1917 Trading with the Enemy Act unless Japan agreed to a multifiber VER. Only the footwear episode I discussed in chapter 5 seemed to have escaped serious vicissitudes in political and economic relations.

American Accommodation

The major reasons for this variability in American–East Asian trade relations were (1) that the United States would not always accommodate exporters' interests, and (2) that the exporters were not always willing or able to implement the prescribed strategy in a coherent fashion. I suggested the importance of an accommodating American policy in chapter 1, and the case studies clearly demonstrated that whenever the United States wanted to restrict an exporter, it could. Indeed, every time the American government adopted a relatively coherent protectionist strategy, such as the American decisions to limit Hong Kong's exporters in 1961–1962, Korea's cotton textiles in 1965, or Japan's multifiber shipments in the fall of 1971, the industrializing country had very little room to maneuver. It was only when the United States was relatively accommodating that exporters could avoid setbacks within a particular sector.

Such protectionist strategies were infrequent, however, because American leadership objectives and broad foreign policy concerns continually limited protectionist options. The principal reason that voluntary restraints became the dominant tool of modern protectionism was that the goals of American hegemony were inconsistent with quotas and prohibitive tariffs. Policies more restrictive than VERs would have run counter to the United States' obligation to the GATT as well as to its leadership position in world trade. The United States did not become overly protectionist even when the Short-Term Arrangement and the Long-Term Arrangement legitimized trade restraints in cotton textiles. Other American interests, such as an intelligence post in Hong Kong and the Kennedy Round of trade negotiations, favored an accommodative approach.

Furthermore, the cases illustrated that the fragmented structure of the American political system and increased international interdependence made it difficult for the United States to adopt consistent protectionist policies. As the American economy became more deeply involved in international trade, the cost of trade barriers rose. In addition, free traders in the State Department, the Department of the Treasury, and the Special Trade Representative's Office usually counterbalanced protectionists in the Departments of Commerce and Labor. Although interest group pressures and bureaucratic inertia led to the tightening of restrictions over time in textiles and apparel, the fragmentation of American trade policy always made an agreement on tough restraints unlikely. This did not mean, of course, that a consensus for restrictive trade barriers was impossible. During the 1971 Kennedy negotiations that I discussed in chapter 4, the Americans pursued very coherent protectionist strategies. When the members of the United States executive leadership and bureaucracy have felt provoked by exporters, they have had an easier time agreeing on restrictive policies. Nevertheless, in the day-to-day operation of trade policy, bureaucratic differences continued to be crucial. Since organizational infighting was the rule, strict protectionist implementation was the exception.

NIC Coherence

Lack of an accommodating American trade policy was not the only cause of a given NIC's exporting problems. For an exporter to exploit fully the structural weaknesses in VERs and OMAs, it had to coordinate in a consistent and coherent way its political policies with its foreign-trade policies and its domestic industrial policies. When government officials in different bureaucracies failed to cooperate or failed to get the cooperation of domestic and multinational firms, the exporting country invariably endangered its trade regime and/or its export earnings.

The importance of a coherent policy was clear from the first textile negotiations with Japan in 1956. The Japanese textile industry insisted that its government push for high quotas rather than flexibility and ambiguity in the cotton VER. As a result, Japan's cotton textile exports were unnecessarily reduced. Then in 1958 and 1959, Hong Kong's government failed to take charge of negotiations, which led to a total breakdown in the bargaining and ultimately to more restrictive action by the United States. Finally, Japan's problems with the 1963 textile negotiations with the United States and the "textile wrangle" of 1969–71 can also be attributed to its fragmented decision-making process. Policy was so disjointed in the latter episode that even the Japanese Prime Minister, to his public embarrassment, was incapable of settling the dispute.

Yet here again, policy incoherence was not the rule for the NICs of East Asia. With the exception of Hong Kong, each government had a highly centralized bureaucracy with political power concentrated at the top. Moreover, most of the NICs had a very narrow range of interests to protect. The United States, for its part, is involved in so many issue-areas that it must always make complex tradeoffs. Every time a major decision is made about import barriers in textiles or footwear, the value of protecting these sectors has to be weighed against foreign-policy considerations, the impact of protectionism on the world economy, domestic inflation, and so on. By contrast, countries such as Taiwan, Hong Kong, and Korea had relatively few vital concerns. Calculating tradeoffs and making decisions are usually easier under these conditions. This partially explains why Taiwan, Korea, and Hong Kong generally had fewer problems than Japan (particularly in the later 1960s) in identifying their best negotiating strategies. While Japan had to deal with problems ranging from the reversion of Okinawa to American pressure to revalue the yen, these other countries could focus more narrowly on their interests in textiles and footwear.

Perhaps a critical factor underlying the policy coherence of the NICs was the role of leadership and political legitimacy. One of the reasons that Japanese decision makers had so much trouble unifying their bureaucracy in the later 1960s was that there was no longer a domestic consensus on vital national issues. In the earlier years of Japanese foreign economic policy, there was a shared belief among bureaucrats, business executives, and the public that government leaders were on the right path to economic development, and that they knew how to accomplish their goals. This predominant conception of national interest allowed Japanese policy makers to integrate textiles into a larger policy framework.[2] Although the textile industry inhibited the government from the most effective response, bureaucratic politics did not dominate the process until 1969. It took an American ultimatum in 1971, and the reestablishment of policy legitimacy by MITI Minister Tanaka, before the Japanese could formulate a coherent bargaining strategy.

Strong leaders who have gained legitimacy for their policies can overcome many of the structural weaknesses that are inherent in their political systems. By the same token, weak leadership without policy legitimacy can undermine the coherence of a nation's actions even if authority and decision making are centralized. The role reversal of the United States and Japan in the late 1960s and early 1970s is striking in this regard. While the "weak" American government pursued a very coherent strategy with its secret deal in 1969 and the Kennedy negotiations in 1971, the "strong" Japanese state was captive to its domestic textile industry and political infighting. President Nixon, Secretary of State Kissinger, and Ambassador Kennedy formulated and implemented their policies clearly and consistently; Prime Minister Sato could do no better than try to influence Japanese bureaucratic politics.

Achieving policy coherence, however, did not guarantee that the most appropriate decisions would be made. In 1965, for instance, the Japanese were united against any restrictions in wool when a strategy of compromise would have been more effective; and Korea and Hong Kong consistently resisted VERs in the summer of 1971, even when the best policy would have been to capitulate. Policy coherence was a necessary condition for effectively responding, but it was not sufficient. It is entirely possible for national decision makers to agree on a response, but the wrong one.

Generalizing the Findings

The export achievements of the newly industrializing countries of East Asia might not guarantee that other nations could accomplish the same results in the future or that the experience of textiles, apparel, and footwear could be duplicated in other industries. Indeed, one might argue that Japan, Hong Kong, Taiwan, and Korea are unique countries that had unique political and economic advantages in the 1950s, 1960s, and 1970s. Located in the same area of the globe, this "gang of four" would appear to have a common cultural heritage as well as unusually strong ties with the United States.[3] In addition, VERs and OMAs in textiles, apparel, and footwear might be special examples of the new protectionism which are not comparable to high-technology or heavy-industry sectors.

There is some degree of truth to these statements. The astonishing accomplishments of these four countries in the three sectors I studied are without parallel. Each East Asian NIC, for example, exported more manufactured goods and more clothing than *all* of Latin America combined (see table 6.1). Yet the explanation for their phenomenal success had little to do with these nations' inherent uniqueness. Research on Latin America has suggested that the East Asian experience could be repeated elsewhere.[4] David Morawetz's study, *Why the Emperor's New Clothes Are Not Made in Colombia*, has demonstrated that East Asian nations had no special advantages over their counterparts in Latin America. Labor and transportation costs were comparable; moreover, there was no evidence that the United States gave Taiwan, Korea, or Hong Kong preferential treatment. On the contrary, Morawetz and others have found that it was the flexibility of East Asian producers—their readiness to adapt and innovate quickly and their emphasis on quality control and punctual delivery—that gave these countries their initial edge. Protectionism rarely affected the garment industries in Latin America. While VERs and OMAs restricted the volume of exports from East Asia, it was poor pricing decisions, poor labor productivity, and poor quality control that hurt Colombia, Brazil, and others.[5] Latin American countries were not inherently uncompetitive with Taiwan, Korea, and Hong Kong; rather, they lacked an appropriate set of policies and political institutions that would capitalize on their strengths.[6]

Table 6.1 Comparisons Between East Asian and Latin American Economies, 1976

Area	Population (millions) (1)	GNP Per Capita (dollars) (2)	Exports of all Manufactured Goods (3)	Exports of Clothing (4)
			(in $ million)	
East Asia				
Hong Kong	4	$2,230	$6,480	$2,907
Korea	36	700	6,675	1,846
Taiwan	16	1,050	6,921	1,322
Total	56	909[a]	20,076	6,075
Latin America				
Argentina	26	1,580	972	38
Brazil	110	1,300	2,332	99
Chile	10	1,050	109[b]	—
Colombia	24	650	659[c]	40
Mexico	62	1,060	2,327[d]	174[de]
Venezuela	12	2,540	115[e]	—
Total	244	1,256[a]	6,161	351

SOURCE: Morawetz, *Why the Emperor's New Clothes Are Not Made in Colombia.* Cols. (1) and (2) originally appeared in World Bank, *Atlas,* 1978; col. (3) in Hollis Chenery and Donald Keesing. "The Changing Composition of Developing Country Exports," table 8; col. (4) in United Nations, *Yearbook of International Trade Statistics,* 1977, and Donald Keesing, "Developing Countries' Exports of Textiles and Clothing," table 10.
    —Negligible.
    [a] Weighted average.
    [b] Estimated, including border zone, with help of U.S. as well as Mexican data.
    [c] 1975.
    [d] Phi Anh Plesch, "Statistical Trends in Developing Countries' Exports and Imports of Manufactures," table B.10, which gives this figure as 384.
    [e] 1974.

The explanation for the advances of East Asian NICs under protectionism lies not in their uniqueness, but in the political economy of international trade. As long as the United States is accommodating, any exporter with factor mobility and a coherent policy should be able to avoid the damaging effects of modern trade barriers. Long-run adjustment policies combined with "controlled risk" bargaining tactics should undermine the effectiveness of OMAs and VERs. To illustrate this point, I will show that most of the patterns that developed in footwear and textile trade have continued to emerge in newly protected sectors.

The New Protectionism in Color Televisions and Automobiles

NICs in East Asia and elsewhere are increasingly diversifying their exports out of labor-intensive products. A critical question presents itself to these countries in the 1980s. Would VERs and OMAs in these new product lines stifle their export earnings? If modern protectionism extends to new sectors, will the same weaknesses in OMAs and VERs persist? And if so, will the same strategy work?

OMAs on Color Televisions. Outside of footwear and textiles, color television was the first large NIC industry that the United States protected with orderly marketing arrangements. After Japan signed an OMA for color televisions in 1977, Taiwan and Korea agreed to limit their exports in this sector in 1979. By the end of 1981, most of the patterns that developed in textiles, apparel, and footwear were being repeated. Opportunities seemed to abound for Japan, Taiwan, and Korea to minimize the damaging effects of restrictions.

Pressure on the American government to restrict imports on color televisions had a long history that began in the late 1960s. Under the leadership of John Nevin, president of Zenith Corporation, the color television industry waged a political war on Japan. Nevin fervently believed that the Japanese were flagrantly violating international law in their quest for a larger share of the American color television market.[7] To prevent Japanese manufacturers from increasing their television shipments, Nevin tried every conceivable avenue of attack. He filed suits alleging that Japan was dumping (selling for less than "fair value") color televisions in the United States, using fraudulent means to evade dumping charges, subsidizing exports, and conspiring to restrain trade, thereby violating American antitrust laws.[8] Although a decade of legal battles produced very little for Nevin, the color television industry finally did receive some help in 1977. Several labor unions, a number of suppliers to the domestic color television industry, and a few companies had applied to the International Trade Commission (ITC) for import relief. Since imports were gathering over 35 percent of the American market, the ITC recommended that duties be raised on color televisions to prevent further injury to the domestic industry. Higher tariffs, however, have never been very attractive to American presidents—and Jimmy Carter was no exception. Therefore, President Carter opted to follow the same route of his predecessors by negotiating an orderly marketing agreement. Since Japan was the dominant foreign supplier of color televisions in 1977, it was the obvious target for restraint.

Several weeks of tough bargaining produced an apparently restrictive OMA. Japan's exports were cut to 60 percent of its all-time high, 1976 shipments.[9] Yet like the first voluntary restraints in textiles, this OMA came with a price; and like the first OMAs in footwear, this selective restriction had some very wide loopholes. First, in exchange for this huge cut in export levels, Japan linked acceptance of the OMA to favorable settlements of the antidumping, fraud, and countervailing duties suits filed by Zenith.[10] If the lawsuits had been settled in Zenith's favor, Japanese manufacturers would have been liable for hundreds of millions of dollars in penalties. In addition, the tremendous uncertainty created by these lawsuits was inhibiting the marketing of Japanese televisions. As a quid pro quo to the OMA, Special Trade Representative Robert Strauss apparently promised the Japanese that he would support the Department of the Treasury's efforts to have the antidumping actions discontinued and the other measures dropped or weakened. The day the OMA was signed, Strauss sent a letter to Japan's Ambassador in Washington providing such assurances.[11] When all the lawsuits were finally settled in April 1980, Japanese manufacturers had to pay seventy million dollars, which the Commerce Department said was 50 cents on the dollar.[12] According to Nevin and Zenith Corporation, the settlement was only 10 percent of what the Japanese should have paid.

The second problem with the orderly marketing agreement was that Japanese companies had several options for circumventing the restrictions. During the first year of the OMA, for example, Japanese firms simply overshipped their quota on complete televisions by 40,000 sets.[13] By far the most important loophole in the arrangement, however, was that it did not cover the export of "subassemblies." Color televisions are generally divided into three categories: complete sets, incomplete sets, and subassemblies. By excluding subassemblies from the restrictions, Japanese companies were able to maintain their market share by setting up assembly plants in the United States and in countries such as Taiwan and Korea. Although the extent of transshipments is not precisely known, we do know that Japan tripled its subassembly shipments to the United States after the OMA was signed. Five Japanese firms built assembly plants in the United States as Japan's subassembly exports increased from 74 million dollars in 1976 to 215 million dollars in 1979.[14] Thus despite the huge quota reductions, the OMA had a very small impact on Japanese short-run export earnings (see figure 6.1) and virtually no effect on the market share of Japanese firms.

A further drawback of the OMA was that restrictions on Japan provided an incentive for Taiwan, Korea, Mexico, and others to enter the American television market. Taiwan, as the world's top exporter of black and white televisions, saw American restrictions on Japan as an opportunity for export expansion.[15] Similarly, Korea wanted to exploit this new opening in the American market, even though its export capacity was not as large as Taiwan's.[16] Both countries therefore started shipping as many color sets as possible to the United States in the wake of Japan's OMA. This led to a 7 percent increase in foreign penetration of the American market in 1978, with the Taiwanese and Koreans accounting for the lion's share of the new imports. In one year, Taiwan's unit exports doubled from 318,000 sets to 624,000, and Ko-

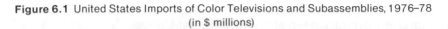

Figure 6.1 United States Imports of Color Televisions and Subassemblies, 1976–78 (in $ millions)

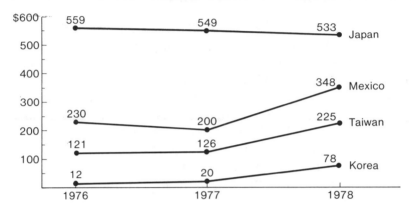

Source: U.S. International Trade Commission, *Color Television Receivers and Subassemblies Thereof,* USITC Publication 1068, May 1980, p. D-2.

rea's shipments quadrupled to about 437,000.[17] Both countries dollar earnings showed similarly impressive gains (see figure 6.1).

The ineffectiveness of the orderly marketing agreement renewed protectionist pressures on the American government. Ironically, this time the Japanese were working alongside American unions to push for trade barriers. Under the provisions of the OMA, Japan had the right to initiate consultations with the United States if it was being placed in an inequitable position vis-à-vis third countries. Since Taiwan, Korea, and Mexico were starting to make inroads into Japan's market share, the Japanese government requested that this equity clause be implemented.[18] Many American multinationals producing in the United States were in favor of the OMAs.[19] Since RCA and Zenith, the two largest American television manufacturers, had moved some of their production offshore to Taiwan, Korea, or Mexico, they were concerned that new restrictions would hamper their new operations.

Despite the substantial involvement of American companies in the Far East, officials in the United States government felt obligated to extend the OMA coverage to Taiwan and Korea.[20] The Americans, however, assumed a relatively accommodating stance during the negotiations. Both exporters stalled the talks for almost a year, as the United States patiently allowed them to increase their shipments to record highs. Both countries also borrowed a few lessons from their experiences in textiles and footwear. When they agreed to restrict their exports at the end of 1979, they did so to prevent political problems with the United States. But neither country capitulated without significant concessions. Taiwan negotiated very high levels for incomplete televisions in exchange for a reduction in complete television exports. Both countries also insured that subassemblies were excluded from the agreements. According to one observer, the two countries coherently bargained for the best possible deals.[21]

To minimize short-run dislocations, Taiwan and Korea followed strategies very similar to Japan's. In their first quota period both exporters overshipped their quota allotments.[22] Taiwan and Korea also followed the Japanese strategy of direct foreign investment in the United States. Tatung Company, Taiwan's largest television manufacturer, started construction of an assembly facility in Los Angeles immediately after the OMA was signed.[23] And in 1981, Gold Star, Korea's largest manufacturer of color television, announced that it would build a plant in Huntsville, Alabama.[24]

For the longer run, each of the exporters followed a variant of the strategy that I outlined in chapter 1. Since color televisions are part of the larger consumer electronics industry, upgrading and diversifying had a slightly different meaning from what they had in textiles and footwear. Japanese firms, for example, responded to the OMA by pushing forward into a higher-technology and higher-value product line—the video recorder. Japanese firms had long viewed the video recorder as the next step in the color television market, whereas American manufacturers continued to concentrate on the lower-profit television receiver market.[25] Once the OMA was signed, Japanese firms accelerated their production and marketing of video recorders to maximize their long-run gains. By 1981 the Japanese had shifted a substantial portion of their color television production to the production of video recorders, and by mid-1982 Japanese firms were exporting over a billion dollars a year in video recorders—doubling their highest earnings from color televisions.[26]

The Korean and Taiwanese strategies were somewhat different. Lacking the technology to upgrade like the Japanese, both countries had limited options. Yet the Koreans as well as the Taiwanese seem to have taken a long-run approach to this problem from the outset of their decisions to move into the American color television market. As soon as the United States announced that it was negotiating an OMA with Japan, the Koreans assumed that they would be a target in the future.[27] They therefore adopted a twofold contingency plan that would offset future restrictions. First, they could shift into radio exports and black and white televisions, and, second, the government would introduce color televisions into the domestic market.[28] Although the OMA did curtail the growth of Korean color television exports to the United States, the Koreans adjusted well by filling underutilized capacity with domestic sales and increasing their global exports of all televisions and radios by 300 percent between 1977 and 1980.[29]

The Taiwanese strategy was similar to that of the Koreans. According to Y. T. Wong, Taiwan's negotiator for color televisions, Taiwan stopped its expansion plans in this market segment before the OMA in 1978.[30] Taiwanese firms were operating on the assumption that world markets for their color televisions would be limited by protectionism. Virtually all their future growth was therefore targeted for the domestic market, which was expected to expand at a rate of 10 to 15 percent a year. Wong expected that domestic demand would require more than 50 percent of total production by the early 1980s, compared to the 35 percent of production that was consumed domestically at the time of the OMA.

The final chapter on the OMAs on color televisions was written on July 1, 1980. Following an ITC recommendation,

Figure 6.2 United States Color Television Imports from Taiwan and Korea, 1978-81 (in $ millions)

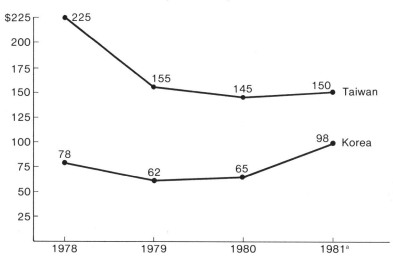

^aEstimated annualized imports as of October 1981.

Source: U.S. International Trade Commission, *Color Televisions Receivers and Subassemblies Thereof,* USITC Publication 1068, May 1980; Department of Commerce, *U.S. General Imports,* October 1981.

President Carter extended the OMAs with Taiwan and Korea until June 30, 1982, and he allowed the Japanese agreement to expire. During the negotiations on the OMA extensions, Taiwan and Korea bargained for highly favorable accords. Partially assembled sets and smaller color televisions were excluded from the restrictions, while the aggregate limits were substantially increased. Since both countries had other plans for their color television industries, however, the better agreements did not affect their export earnings greatly (see figure 6.2). Recession in the United States, lagging demand, and competition from a somewhat revitalized American industry were more serious problems than protectionism for the Koreans and Taiwanese.[31]

The VER in Automobiles. On May 1, 1981, Japan's Minister of International Trade and Industry, Rokusuke Tanaka, announced that his country would "voluntarily" limit its car exports to the United States. From April 1981 to March 1982, Japan would ship only 1.68 million automobiles bound for American shores—a cutback of 7.7 percent. And for the following year, April 1982 to March 1983, Japanese auto exports would increase by only 16.5 percent of any rise in 1981 American car sales. On the same day as Tanaka's announcement, Senator John Danforth, a conservative Republican from Missouri, stated publicly that he was withdrawing his bill that would have restricted Japanese auto imports to 1.6 million cars for three years. Thus a familiar pattern was being repeated, albeit this time in a major, heavy-industry sector. Once again, domestic political pressure had forced a major exporter to accept a VER in exchange for reducing the fires of American protectionism. Yet like every orderly marketing arrangement which preceded it, this VER in automobiles was most likely doomed to ineffectiveness. The inevitable combination of myopic decision making in the United States and creative adaptation by Japanese car producers allowed Japan to offset the potentially damaging effects of American protectionism.

The background to the VER in automobiles differed slightly from that in the other industries I have studied in this book. Unlike the lobbies for textiles, apparel, footwear, and color televisions, automotive firms and unions did not have a long history of pressing for import barriers.[32] In fact, throughout the postwar period, the automobile industry was among the most ardent defenders of free trade. Ford Motor and General Motors had extensive operations in other countries. Import barriers for the American car market could have hurt these firms' international strategies. In addition, American manufacturers never felt threatened by foreign automobile producers until the end of the 1970s. Even though car imports more than doubled, from 980 thousand in 1969 to 2.43 million in 1979, foreign cars were almost exclusively in the small end of the market. Chrysler, Ford, and GM made most of the money from the sale of large cars at home and repatriated earnings from abroad. The only actor to express concern about auto imports was the United Auto Workers

(UAW). But even the UAW did not actively promote protectionism. As Japanese cars tripled their share of the American market during the 1970s, the UAW limited its efforts to persuading Japanese firms to open plants in the United States.

It was not until the doubling of oil prices in the wake of the Iranian revolution that the automobile industry perceived itself in a crisis. The compounding effects of long gasoline lines, recession in the United States, and high interest rates threw the American car market into a tailspin. Not only did car consumption drop by 20 percent in one year, but people who had always owned American cars suddenly turned toward the small, more fuel-efficient automobiles being offered by the Japanese. Unprepared to meet this dramatic shift in consumer preferences, American firms suffered staggering losses. The number-three car maker, Chrysler, survived only by the grace of a government-backed loan guarantee. With as many as 650,000 workers out of jobs in auto-related industries in late 1979, it came as no surprise to officials in Washington or Tokyo that Detroit would start pleading for protectionism.

UAW president Douglas Fraser opened the campaign for trade restrictions during a well-publicized trip to Tokyo in February 1980. Reminding the Japanese that "Americans tend to become emotional in an election year," Fraser insisted that Japan curb its exports to the United States.[33] With President Jimmy Carter in a fight for his political life, the American government took Fraser's election theme very seriously. Yet despite Carter's urgent need for UAW support, the President refused to advocate trade barriers. Fraser therefore sought to force the President into action by petitioning the International Trade Commission (ITC). Joined in the petition by Ford Motor, the UAW claimed that a surge in imports of cars and light trucks was causing serious injury to the domestic automobile industry. Ford and the UAW hoped that a positive finding by the Trade Commission would lead the President to erect a quota or, at a minimum, negotiate an OMA with Japan.

On November 10, 1980, three days after the election, the

ITC rejected the UAW–Ford petition by a three-to-two vote.[34] The majority of the commissioners concluded that imports were not a "substantial cause" of injury to the domestic industry. High interest rates, recession, and the shift in consumer demand to small cars, said the ITC, were the most important reasons for the industry's trouble.

This negative decision deprived President Carter of the legal means to act against Japanese imports, but it did not prevent the UAW or the car companies from pressing forward. Conditions in the auto industry had continued to deteriorate. As a result, Chrysler actively joined the UAW and Ford in calling for import restraints, while General Motors reluctantly endorsed a Japanese voluntary restraint.[35] In January 1981, two ranking members of the Senate trade subcommittee, John Danforth and Lloyd Bentsen, responded to industry pleas by introducing a quota bill. Danforth and Bentsen promised to push the bill till its enactment unless the Japanese agreed to limit their car exports to the United States.

Growing support in Congress for the Danforth bill confronted the new administration with its first major trade challenge. President Ronald Reagan, ostensibly a free-trader and committed to the free market, had promised during his campaign "to try to convince the Japanese that . . . the deluge of their cars into the United States must be slowed."[36] Although Reagan did not take an active role in the decision-making process, he made it clear to all those involved that he wanted to do "something" to the Japanese.[37] Members of the Cabinet, however, had a hard time agreeing on what that should be. The Secretaries of Transportation and Commerce favored trade restrictions, while Treasury, the Council of Economic Advisers, and the Office of Management and Budget strongly opposed import barriers of any type. Under these circumstances, a compromise was obviously necessary, and a voluntary restraint was the obvious choice.

The final rationale for negotiating a voluntary restraint with Japan was indistinguishable from the motivation underlying every decision to negotiate a new VER or OMA in the previous twenty-five years. The President did not want to abandon his free-trade philosophy, nor did he want to neglect the automobile industry and his campaign promise. If the Japanese "voluntarily" chose to restrict their car exports, the supporters of the auto industry would be satisfied, the opponents of protectionism could argue that they had minimized the damage, and the President could save face by claiming that he had successfully avoided import quotas. Reagan therefore dispatched Special Trade Representative Bill Brock to "discuss"—not negotiate—a VER with Japan. Yet if the Japanese resisted or asked for too much, Brock could remind them about the Danforth bill.[38] Under the circumstances, however, Brock had to be relatively *accommodating*.

From the Japanese government's point of view, this was the opportunity it was waiting for. As early as February 1980, MITI had encouraged Japan's largest car producers, Toyota and Nissan, to restrict their exports to the United States. MITI officials believed that such a move would promote more "orderly" marketing and reduce political tensions.[39] At the time, however, MITI lacked the political clout to enforce its will on car manufacturers.[40] Yet once the Danforth bill was introduced and the Reagan administration could promise its defeat if a VER was announced, the Japanese government could create a *coherent* policy to overcome the opposition of its own auto producers and other domestic interest groups.

Angered automobile executives in Japan nonetheless attacked the VER. Eiji Toyoda, president of Toyota, said the agreement was made "with undue haste and insufficient appreciation of the real situation."[41] A prominent Japanese economist similarly complained that the VER would "benefit only a handful of politicians, some lazy managers, and certain irresponsible trade officials."[42] In response to these and other domestic attacks, Vice Minister of MITI, Naohiro Amaya, defended the Japanese government's decision as "inevitable if we are to avoid such open attacks on the free trade system as the Danforth bill."[43] Amaya asserted that a short-run sacrifice along the lines I described in chapter 1 was necessary to maintain Japan's trade regime with the United States. "Preserving the fundamental rules of free trade," he said, "requires that we resign ourselves to some temporary, localized adjustments."[44]

Despite their anger and fears of lost revenue, Japan's car manufacturers had ample opportunities to maintain their export earnings. The Japanese government had supplemented its long-run approach by coherently negotiating a minimally restrictive accord. If Japanese exporters under MITI's administrative guidance were to continue to follow the strategy I described in chapter 1, one could have safely predicted in May of 1981 that Japan would not suffer as a result of this VER.[45]

To begin with, it seemed unlikely at the time of this VER that Detroit's competition would be reduced in the short run. Wide loopholes in the voluntary restraint would make circumvention relatively easy. For example, the agreement excluded four hundred thousand Japanese cars already in inventory in the United States, and it restricted only "cars" rather than all motor vehicles and partially assembled autos. Moreover, unrestrained exporters, such as Renault and Volvo, were in a position to fill gaps in demand caused by any fall in Japanese shipments.

A second predictable problem was that prices of Japanese cars would probably increase under the VER. Even though Bill Brock claimed that the restrictions were "not severe enough to affect price," past experience would suggest that exporters would raise their prices in anticipation of shortages.[46] Finally, if the history of VERs was any guide, one could have expected Japanese car manufacturers to diversify their product lines in response to the restrictions as well as upgrade their exports into more profitable market segments. Just as the new protectionism in cotton textile and apparel spurred Asian nations to become leaders in synthetic fibers, just as the OMAs with Taiwan and Korea in footwear provided a catalyst for these countries to challenge American supremacy in middle-priced shoes, and just as OMAs on color televisions accelerated Japanese marketing of videorecorders, so too could the VER in autos give Japan an incentive to cut back on low-cost economy cars and introduce more fuel-efficient products in the $8,000–$12,000 bracket. If cars in this middle-priced range proved to be the growing segment of the American market, the result would be greater pressure to extend restrictions.[47]

Fifteen months after the VER was announced, virtually all these predictions had been realized. Most Japanese exporters, especially the larger companies, had been trying to maximize volume throughout the 1970s and into the 1980s. Since the automobile market continued to suffer a severe recession in 1981 and 1982, it is highly probable that these manufacturers would have tried to cut prices and move inventories in the absence of trade restraints.[48] But according to one analyst, the Japanese "revised their formula for success" in the middle of 1981, once the VER was in place. Writing in WARD'S Auto World, James Bush said that "their new strategy calls for greater emphasis on sales of compact pickups, which aren't restrained by quotas; higher than usual automobile price boosts in a market where demand seems certain to outstrip supply; and addition of a smattering of all-new or nearly all-new autos that upscale product mixes."[49]

Each of these strategic changes was a logical outcome of the voluntary restraints. To minimize short-run losses, Japanese companies capitalized on the perception of a restricted supply to reduce dealer discounts. This made Japanese cars very difficult to buy below the suggested retail price.[50] In addition, since "cars" were restricted, exporters naturally looked for related products that were unrestricted. Toyota, for example, increased its production and advertising of pickup trucks and predicted that sales would increase 20 percent in 1982—3 to 4 percent above 1981 growth.[51] And Honda Motors, which did not have the capability to circumvent the VER by substituting trucks for cars, decided to push ahead with plans for direct investment in the United States. Reminiscent of Japanese, Korean, and Taiwanese strategies in color televisions, Honda was planning to boost its exports of incomplete cars known as "automobile kits," once its assembly plant in Marysville, Ohio, came on line.[52] Finally, in another move that was consistent with the strategy in chapter 1, Japan diversified its markets. Global exports of Japanese cars, trucks, and buses reached record highs in 1981 as Japan found new customers in the third world.[53]

To maximize long-run profits under the voluntary restraint, Japanese car manufacturers started to upgrade their exports. Japanese shipments of "large" cars bound for the United States were up 17.6 percent in 1981, while "small"-

Table 6.2 Toyota Sales of New Cars in the United States, 1981–1982. By Retail Price Group (units in thousands)

Price Group	1981 Jan.–June [a]	Percent of Sales	1982 Jan.–June [a]	Percent of Sales
$ 4,500–6,000	118	36.5	61	24
6,001–7,500	151	47	105	40
7,501–9,000	33	10	56	21.5
9,001–12,000	19	6	7	2.5
12,001–	2	0.5	31	12
Total	323	100	260	100

SOURCE: *WARD's Automotive Report*, July 26, 1982.
   [a] Rounded to nearest thousand.

car shipments declined by 6.9 percent.[54] Calling this a "new trend," observers of the auto industry noted that Japan had exported more than three-quarters of its highest-quality vehicles to the United States after the VER was announced.[55] Toyota was exemplary of this new trend. The vast majority of Toyota's sales in the first six months of 1981 were of units that sold for under $7,500 (see table 6.2). But between January and June 1982, only 65 percent were in this range, and for the first time ever Toyota had significant sales in the over-$12,000 category. Toyota, moreover, was by no means alone in the upgrading game. Honda revamped and upgraded its major models for 1982, and Nissan introduced two new cars which covered the entire price spectrum.

As of this writing, these changes in strategy appear to have been successful. Despite the collapse of the American auto market in 1981 and the first half of 1982, Japanese-brand cars continued to increase their share of the United States market.[56] Although the recession caused Japanese unit sales to decline, they dropped less than the sales of American cars (see table 6.3). The three highest months of import penetration in United States automotive history occurred during the first thirteen months of the VER. In December 1981 and in January and June 1982, imports took more than 30 percent of the American market.

Under these conditions, pleas for protectionism would not die. Chrysler, Ford, and General Motors had all recovered somewhat by the second quarter of 1982. Yet the productivity gains which helped these American companies regain profitability did little to help the mass of unemployed auto workers. Without an expansion in production, workers could not be rehired. The American government therefore tried to prevail on Japan to reduce its exports in 1982–83.[57] Since the Japanese still wanted to minimize political tensions, they were willing to accommodate the United States—within bounds. Japan would not go along with the American request for a reduction, but the Japanese government did agree to hold exports to 1.68 million units for another year.

No one can be totally certain that the Japanese will continue to turn events in the automobile industry to their advantage. Nonetheless, the accommodating position assumed by the United States and the coherent long-run policies adopted by the Japanese did produce a familiar result, one that we have seen in industry after industry for more than twenty-five years. The re-emergence of the same protectionist pattern and the same type of successful exporter response, even in a heavy-industry sector, adds another piece of evidence in corroboration of my hypotheses about the political and economic logic underlying the new protectionism.

Table 6.3 United States Auto Imports, 1980–1982 (units in millions)

	1980		1981		Percent Change		Jan.–June 1982		Percent Change [a]	
	Units	Market Share	Units	Market Share	Units	Market Share	Units	Market Share	Units	Market Share
All Imports	2.4	26.7	2.3	27.3	−3.0	+0.6	1.1	27.2	−3	−0.6
Japanese imports	1.9	21.2	1.86	21.8	−3.0	+0.6	0.89	21.9	−2	0.0
Selected non-Japanese imports										
Volvo	.056	0.6	.064	.7	+14	+0.1	.041	1.0	+0	+0.1
Renault	.027	0.3	.030	.35	+9	+0.05	.20	0.5	+9	+0.14

SOURCES: WARD's Automotive Report, January 11, 1982, and July 12, 1982.

[a] Compared with January–June 1981.

Will the Pattern Persist?

Most analysts agree that the pressures for protectionism are unlikely to abate in the 1980s. Yet there is little consensus on how the international trade system will evolve in five or ten years. In the section below, I will briefly discuss three very different scenarios for the future of world trade. Two of these scenarios, which I have called *slippery slope* and *declining hegemony*, assert that the outlook for international commerce is dim in the 1980s. For varying reasons, both of these scenarios forecast a total breakdown in international trading rules. The third scenario, which I have labeled the *maturing of modern protectionism*, assumes that the present pattern of ad hoc trade restrictions will largely persist. Although VERs, OMAs, and other discriminatory tools of the new protectionism will spread, the international trade regime will adapt.

The *slippery slope* scenario holds that the growth of trade barriers could lead the world down toward a serious global trade war. According to this view, increasing protectionism is a product of inadequate structural adjustment in the global economy.[58] As the number of industries suffering from surplus capacity multiplies, so does the demand on governments to erect trade restraints.[59] The danger of this trend is that restrictions in one industry could serve as a precedent to restrict others. The resulting spread of the new protectionism across sectors would inevitably heighten uncertainty and raise international tensions. Countries that were the targets of these restrictions might be provoked into raising their own trade barriers. Under these circumstances, there could be a downward spiral of retaliation similar to the 1930s.[60]

The second, equally pessimistic approach looks at the changing distribution of international power rather than the growing incidence of protectionism. It is the *decline in American hegemony*, according to this school of thought, that has weakened the structure of world trade.[61] Stephen Krasner, Charles Kindleberger, and others have argued that a leader is necessary to stabilize international trade in times of crisis. The United States, however, may no longer be willing to assume the role of leader and to absorb the cost of maintaining an open trading environment. During the 1950s and 1960s, the American government had a commitment to free world trade and the power to encourage. Yet in the 1970s and 1980s, the United States has lost both its ability to buffer the capitalist world from external shocks and its drive to resist protectionist pressure. Therefore, if a crisis should develop, the system could be prone to collapse.

The third approach to the future structure of protectionism takes a slightly more optimistic track. While it is true that restrictions have spread into new areas and the decline in American hegemony has weakened free-trade norms, it does not necessarily follow that the world is on the verge of an unyielding trade battle. Although the slippery slope thesis sounds plausible, it rests on the assumption that countries will link together trade barriers in different industries. Yet I have shown in this chapter and in chapters 2 through 5 that the United States rarely makes connections between protection in diverse sectors.[62] Through the early 1980s, each industry has been protected in isolation from the others. A retaliatory spiral of bartering one sector for another would therefore seem improbable under such a makeshift protectionist system. In addition, the countries which are the most frequent targets of these restrictions—Japan and the newly industrializing countries—are relatively weak actors who are the least likely to precipitate a trade war.

One could be equally questioning of the declining hegemony school. Proponents of the declining hegemony scenario have generalized their argument on the basis of one historical case—that of the decline of British hegemony in the late nineteenth and early twentieth centuries. Yet if the analogy was appropriate and a leader was a truly necessary condition for the stability of the trading system, one might have expected a collapse in the aftermath of the 1973 oil price shock or the 1979 price shock. Advocates of the declining hegemony hypothesis must resort to residual factors such as lags in order to explain the continued resilience of relatively free trade norms.[63]

An alternative scenario to both slippery slope and declining hegemony is that there will be a slow *maturing of modern protectionism* similar to the pattern I have described in this book. This would mean that for the foreseeable future orderly marketing arrangements would continue to be introduced into new sectors, but mainly in ad hoc ways. The accommodating policies pursued by the United States through 1982 would also persist in most situations. The only time that barriers to trade would become restrictive is within individual industries that get repeated protection. The evolution of the regime in textiles and apparel would be one such model of more systematic restraints.

The logic of this approach is that past patterns of collaboration provide an institutional inertia which would carry the trading system, virtually intact, into the future. Despite the decline in American hegemony and growing problems associated with international competitiveness in industrial countries, previous collaboration has created a bond that might bend, but will not break.[64] The outgrowth of this commitment to general international trading rules would be a continued reluctance to employ tariffs and quotas. The international trade regime would nonetheless adapt to the growth in VERs and OMAs, perhaps by institutionalizing orderly marketing arrangements as part of the General Agreement on Tariffs and Trade.[65]

A further reason to expect the persistence of ad hoc protectionism is the pervasiveness of transgovernmental and bureaucratic politics. VERs serve as one of the best possible political compromises between advocates of trade barriers and advocates of free trade. Barring an implausible revolution in American policy formulation, the government is unlikely to pursue more-restrictive bargaining or implementation strategies, particularly the first time a VER is introduced into a sector.[66] The exception to this rule, as noted above, will occur as interest groups learn about the deficiencies in modern protectionism. If an industry can convince the government to renew restrictions, that particular sector is likely to achieve tighter restraints.[67]

For exporting nations, the implications of this scenario are mixed. On the negative side, the proliferation of VERs and OMAs across sectors would place added burdens on exporters. Until the mid-1970s, the number of restrictions against important industries was limited. This minimized administrative costs as well as demands on NIC governments. Yet the growing magnitude of NIC exports (see figure A in Introduction), especially to the United States, ensures that the newly industrializing countries will increasingly be targets of political attack in importing nations. To cope with this tenser political environment, it would be critical for exporters to avoid politicized battles over trade issues and excessive circumvention of restraints. Policies that promote confrontation and enhanced surveillance of NIC trade will be more dangerous under this scenario than they were in the past.[68]

On the positive side, exporters would be better off if the present pattern persists than if the world were falling down a slippery slope of protection or on the verge of collapse because of the decline in American hegemony. Everyone loses if there is a total breakdown of trading rules. While a maturing of modern protectionism would be no panacea, at least orderly marketing arrangements could continue to be useful vehicles for NIC industrial policies. By reducing uncertainty in politically troubled regimes and by providing an external stimulus to domestic economic change, OMAs and VERs would remain better than the alternatives.[69] As long as the American government continued to be generally accommodating and as long as NICs could coherently pursue long-run-oriented, loophole-seeking strategies, the new protectionism would be a paper tiger. Orderly marketing agreements and voluntary export restraints should not severely damage the

future export earnings of the next generation of newly industrializing nations. On the contrary, the political economy of
international trade would continue to afford these countries
with an opportunity to turn adversity into advantage.

Notes

Introduction

1. Thucydides, *The Peloponnesian War*, book V, ch. xvii (Melian Dialogues), p. 331.

2. Annette Baker Fox, *The Power of Small States*.

3. W. Howard Wriggins, "Up for Auction: Malta Bargains with Great Britain, 1971," in I. W. Zartman, ed., *The 50% Solution*, pp. 208–234.

4. I. W. Zartman, *The Politics of Trade Negotiations Between Africa and the EEC*.

5. Robert O. Keohane, "The Big Influence of Small Allies."

6. See, for example, Susan Strange, "What Is Economic Power and Who Has It?" p. 219; Klaus Knorr, *The Power of Nations* (New York: Basic Books, 1975); Albert Hirschman, *National Power and the Structure of Foreign Trade;* and James A. Caporaso, ed., "Dependence and Dependency in the Global System," special issue of *International Organization* (Winter 1978), vol. 32.

7. Only when there is a scarcity or restricted supply of a needed good will exporters command oligopolistic powers and bargain on a relatively equal level. See Susan Strange, "The Management of Surplus Capacity"; Gerald Helleiner, "The New Industrial Protectionism and the Developing Countries," *Trade & Development* (Spring 1979); and Bela Balassa, "The 'New Protectionism' and the International Economy."

8. United Nations Conference on Trade and Development, *Growing Protectionism and the Standstill on Trade Barriers*, p. 19.

9. See Albert Fishlow, Jean Carriere, and Sueo Sekiguchi, *Trade in Manufactured Products with Developing Countries*.

10. Albert Hirschman, "Beyond Asymmetry."

11. C. Fred Bergsten, "On the Non-Equivalence of Import Quotas and 'Voluntary' Export Restraints," p. 239.

12. OMAs and VERs have also been called bilateral quotas and voluntary re-

straint arrangements (VRAs). The only difference between these agreements is that OMAs and bilateral quotas are normally formal government-to-government treaties, while VERs and VRAs are informal, tacit arrangements that may be between two governments, a government and a foreign industry, or two national industries. See Malcolm Smith, "Voluntary Export Quotas and U.S. Trade Policy."

13. Heinrich Heuser, *Control of International Trade*, ch. 9, pp. 111–122.

14. Stanley Metzger, "Injury and Market Disruption from Imports."

15. In the 1950s and early 1960s, the U.S. government subsidized cotton exports. This meant American manufacturers paid more for American cotton than foreign producers. See Benjamin Bardan, "The Cotton Textile Agreement, 1962–72," p. 10.

16. Leon Hollerman, "Foreign Trade in Japan's Economic Transition."

17. A host of minor industries have been protected via VERs. These ranged from umbrellas to wood screws. See Jagdish Bhagwati, "Market Disruption, Export Disruption, Compensation, and GATT Reform," in J. Bhagwati, ed., *The New International Economic Order: The North-South Debate*, pp. 166–168 (Cambridge: MIT Press, 1977).

18. United Nations Conference on Trade and Development, *Growing Protectionism and the Standstill on Trade Barriers*, p. 10.

19. *Ibid.*, p. iii.

20. Organization of Economic Cooperation and Development, *The Impact of the Newly Industrializing Countries*, pp. 5–19.

21. For a review of the varying performances of these countries under textile protectionism, see United States International Trade Commission, *The History and Current Status of the Multifiber Arrangement*.

1. Politics as an Instrument of Foreign Trade

1. This is Harold D. Lasswell's definition of politics in his classic work, *Politics: Who Gets What, When, How*.

2. On the concept of regime, see Robert O. Keohane and Joseph Nye, *Power and Interdependence*; Oran Young, "International Regimes: Problems of Concept Formation," *World Politics* (April 1980), 32:331–356; Ernst Haas, "Why Collaborate?" and Stephen Krasner, ed., "International Regimes," special issue of *International Organization* (Spring 1982) 36:2. The notion of a bilateral regime has been discussed in Paul Johnson's "Washington and Bonn."

3. Secretary of State James Byrnes quoted in Joyce and Gabriel Kolko, *The Limits of Power* (New York: Harper & Row, 1972), p. 12.

4. Charles Kindleberger, *Power and Money*, p. 127.

5. Raymond A. Bauer, Ithiel de Sola Pool, and Lewis Dexter, *American Business and Public Policy*, p. 1.

6. Flexibility is emphasized by almost all theorists of weak-state behavior. See especially Annette Baker Fox, *The Power of Small States*, and Robert O. Keohane, "The Big Influence of Small Allies."

7. Albert Hirschman, *National Power and the Structure of Foreign Trade*, p. 28.

8. Albert Hirschman, *The Strategy of Economic Development*, p. 5.

9. Richard Blackhurst, Nicholas Marion, and Jan Tumlir, Trade Liberalization, Protectionism, and Interdependence.

10. Richard Blackhurst, Nicholas Marion, and Jan Tumlir, Adjustment, Trade, and Growth in Developed and Developing Countries, p. 1.

11. Kathryn Morton and Peter Tulloch, Trade and Developing Countries, p. 182.

12. In his classic work National Power and the Structure of Foreign Trade, Albert Hirschman demonstrated this paradoxical relationship between adjustment and trading gains. Hirschman showed that powerful states could limit the growth of developing countries if they could prevent adjustments and provide incentives for the exporting nations to focus on "urgent demand" and short-term gains from trade. The logic of Hirschman's argument is identical to the argument being made here; that is, the country—importer or exporter—that makes adjustments to the market is ultimately the greatest winner.

13. See Oran Young, ed., Bargaining: Formal Theories of Negotiations (Urbana: University of Illinois Press, 1975); Anatol Rapoport, Fights, Games, and Debates; Anatol Rapoport, Strategy and Conscience (New York: Schocken Books, 1964); R. Luce and H. Raiffa, Games and Decisions (New York: Wiley, 1957); Glenn Snyder and Paul Diesing, Conflict Among Nations; and Thomas Schelling, The Strategy of Conflict.

14. Sidney Verba, "Sequences and Development," in Leonard Binder et al., Crises and Sequences in Political Development, p. 302 (Princeton: Princeton University Press, 1971).

15. Albert Hirschman, "Beyond Asymmetry"; see also Annette Baker Fox, The Power of Small States.

16. Robert O. Keohane and Joseph Nye, "World Politics and the International Economic System," p. 117.

17. John Odell, "Latin American Trade Negotiations."

18. Although it is obviously a simplification, I am postulating that exporters can use three generic bargaining strategies: accommodation, controlled risk, and maximizing. An accommodating strategy aims at appeasing the importer; a controlled risk approach seeks to push the opponent as far as possible while minimizing the risk of breakdown; and maximizing refers to a "win" strategy. These three generic strategies were derived from Jack Sawyer and Harold Guetzkow, "Bargaining and Negotiations in International Relations"; Daniel Druckman, Human Factors in International Negotiations; Daniel Druckman, ed., Negotiations: Social-Psychological Perspectives; Fred Iklé, "Negotiation"; Fred Iklé, How Nations Negotiate; I. W. Zartman, "The Political Analysis of Negotiations," World Politics (April 1974), vol. 26; and Michael Blaker, "Probe, Push, and Panic."

19. There is a third element of the bargaining strategy which is technical and relates specifically to OMAs and VERs. Through the bargaining process an exporting country can try to assure that it captures any scarcity gains that might be generated by protection. Under an export restraint arrangement and other quantitative restrictions, prices usually increase because of forced or anticipated reductions in supply. Unlike the situations under a tariff, windfall profits are not automatically absorbed by the importing government. Who captures the scarcity gains will partly depend upon the relative concentration of market power between exporters and importers, partly upon the market-sharing arrangements the exporting nation can bargain for, and partly upon any abnormal shifts in supply and demand that may occur.

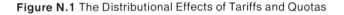

Figure N.1 The Distributional Effects of Tariffs and Quotas

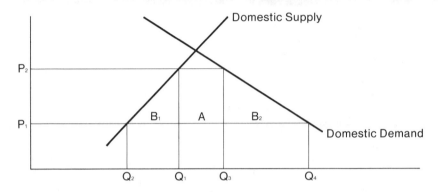

$Q_1 Q_3$ = Imports after quotas; $Q_2 Q_4$ = Imports before quotas;
P_1 = Price of imports before quotas; P_2 = Price of imports after quotas;
A = Scarcity rent as a result of quotas (or tariff of $P_2 P_1$); B_1, B_2 = Deadweight losses.

Source: C. Fred Bergsten, *Towards a New World Trade Policy.*

Figure N. 1 depicts the situation in formal terms in partial equilibrium. A tariff of $(P^2 - P^1)$ would produce a net transfer equal to area A to the importing government. A quota of Q^1Q^3 will, given the domestic supply and demand curves, have the same effect on the price of the goods, but the scarcity rent, A, will not accrue to the government. If the foreign producers do not fear a loss of market shares from other suppliers, they can be expected to raise prices to absorb the rent for themselves. If exporters fear such a loss from other foreign suppliers, and the United States importers are relatively concentrated, the importers will absorb the rent. Finally, if both foreign producers and importers are worried about a loss of market share from the possible entry of domestic firms, prices would remain low. In this case, the supply curve would shift downward and to the right. If a government such as Taiwan or Korea takes an active role in fostering exporters' concentration or bargaining with importers, this will tend to transfer more of the windfall gains to the exporters, even in a market characterized by a high degree of importers' concentration. See William Cline, *Imports and Consumer Prices;* C. Fred Bergsten, "On the Non-Equivalence of Import Quotas and 'Voluntary' Export Restraints"; and Brian Hindley, "Voluntary Export Restraints and the GATT's Main Escape Clause."

20. Jeffrey Pressman and Aaron Wildavsky, *Implementation;* and Eugene Bardach, *The Implementation Game: What Happens After a Bill Becomes a Law* (Cambridge: MIT Press, 1977).

21. Hirschman, *National Power and the Structure of Foreign Trade.*

22. Keohane and Nye, *Power and Interdependence.*

23. Stephen Krasner, "State Power and the Structure of International Trade" and "The Tokyo Round"; Charles Kindleberger, *The World in Depression: 1929–39.*

24. Richard Walton and Robert McKersie, *A Behavioral Theory of Labor Negotiations*, and John Cross, "Negotiations as a Learning Process," in I. W. Zartman, ed., *The Negotiation Process*.

25. Niccolò Machiavelli, *The Prince and the Discourses*, 2:319. The only extended discussion of cheating as a political art took place in sixteenth- and seventeenth-century France in the context of *raison d'état*. Philosophers such as Montaigne and Justus Lipsius defended the principles of prudence and deceit as appropriate for statesmanship. For an excellent summary of these views, see Nannerl O. Keohane, *Philosophy and the State in France*.

26. Heinrich Heuser, *Control of International Trade*.

27. Bart Fisher, "Enforcing Export Quota Commodity Agreements."

28. *Ibid.*, p. 433.

29. Quoted in Bart Fisher, *The International Coffee Agreement*, p. 36.

30. Fisher, "Enforcing Export Quota Commodity Agreements," p. 415.

31. Quoted in Nannerl O. Keohane, *Philosophy and the State in France*, p. 110.

32. For a discussion of transgovernmental coalition-building, see Robert O. Keohane and Joseph S. Nye, "Transgovernmental Relations and International Organizations."

33. Although this strategy implicitly assumes rationality, I will not ignore the role of domestic politics. The coherence of national policies can be an important factor in the negotiations and in the ability of a country to respond to protectionism. See I. M. Destler, *Presidents, Bureaucrats, and Foreign Policy* (Princeton: Princeton University Press, 1972); Gilbert Winham, "Practitioners' Views of International Negotiations," *World Politics* (October 1979), vol. 32; Peter Katzenstein, "International Relations and Domestic Structures"; Stephen Krasner, *Defending the National Interest*; and Peter Katzenstein, ed., *Between Power and Plenty*.

34. Two examples are Donald S. Keesing and Martin Wolf, *Textile Quotas Against Developing Countries*, and Ilse Mintz, *U.S. Import Quotas*.

35. P. Terrence Hopmann and I. W. Zartman have studied asymmetrical bargaining. But neither Hopmann's "Asymmetrical Bargaining in the Conference on Security and Cooperation in Europe" nor Zartman's *The Politics of Trade Negotiations* and *The 50% Solution* contribute to a theory that would help us understand the dilemma facing NICs. John Odell's "Latin American Trade Negotiations" is one of the few works specifically on this subject.

36. Sidney Verba, "Some Dilemmas in Comparative Research," *World Politics* (October 1967), vol. 20; Harry Eckstein, "Case Study and Theory in Political Science"; Arend Lijphart, "Comparative Politics"; and Gabriel Almond, Scott Flanagan, and Richard Mundt, *Crisis, Choice, and Change* (Boston: Little, Brown, 1973).

37. Alexander George, in "Case Studies and Theory Development," recommends the use of standardized questions to structure data collection and to make the cases comparable. To test my hypothetical strategy, I will ask: (1) What is the initial state of trade and bilateral relations before protectionism? (2) Why does the importing state seek protection? (3) What are the goals and strategies of the negotiating parties? Do accommodative, controlled risk, or maximizing strategies affect bargaining outcomes? (4) To what extent do "structural" variables, such as an American hegemony or domestic political structure, constrain the negotiation and implementation of protection? (5) What is the outcome of the bargaining and implemen-

tation? (6) How does the outcome of one protectionist episode feed back into future negotiations? Is there learning and/or innovation over time?

38. Overseas Development Institute, "Protectionism in the West," p. 5.

39. Warren Hunsberger, *Japan and the United States*, and Gardner Patterson, *Discrimination in International Trade*.

40. Since no study of modern protectionism can avoid looking at Japan in the 1970s, the concluding chapter will include analysis of Japanese responses to recent restrictions.

41. See Department of State, *United States Treaties and Other International Acts, 1961–79*; and for 1956 to 1961, see Hunsberger, *Japan and the United States*.

42. Textiles and apparel have somewhat different production patterns and should be treated separately for domestic sectoral analysis. Internationally, however, these two industries have been linked from the first protectionist arrangements. Therefore, textiles and apparel will be treated as the same industry, except when otherwise noted. For characteristics of the textile and apparel sectors, see *Textile Industry*, United Nations Monograph no. 7, based on the *Proceedings of the International Symposium on Industrial Development*, November–December 1967.

43. *World Bank Report* (Washington, D.C.: World Bank, 1978), p. 18.

44. United Nations Conference on Trade and Development, *International Trade in Textiles*, TD/B/C.2/174, May 12, 1977.

45. *United States accommodation* was scored high if the initial U.S. objectives in the bargaining were minimally restrictive; moderate if the U.S. sought to help the exporter in general, but to restrict the country on particular bargaining issues; and low if the American position was to insist on a strongly protectionist position. *Factor mobility* was difficult to determine a priori. Since neither economists nor political analysts can predict a country's adaptability, this variable was scored with the benefit of hindsight. (*Protected*) *sectoral earnings* and *overall sectoral earnings* were scored high if a country managed to increase those earnings by more than 10 percent following a VER or OMA; moderate if the earnings grew between 5 and 10 percent; and low if less than 5 percent. *Bilateral trade regime* was scored according to the actors' perceptions of norms. High meant the bargaining episode had no impact on a highly favorable regime; moderate was used when the bargaining or implementation led exporters to believe that the U.S. was becoming less generous or accommodating; and a low value was assigned only if the rules in the bilateral trade relationship were changed to the detriment of the exporter.

2. Textiles, Round 1:
The Move Toward Protection, 1955–1961

1. Warren Hunsberger, *Japan and the United States*, p. 245.

2. Gary Saxonhouse and Hugh Patrick, "Japan and the United States: Bilateral Tension and Multilateral Issues in the Economic Relationship," in Donald Hellman, ed., *China and Japan: A New Balance of Power*, p. 98 (Lexington, Mass.: Lexington Books, 1976).

3. Raymond Bauer, Ithiel de Sola Pool, and Lewis Dexter, *American Business and Public Policy*, p. 60.

4. Hunsberger, *Japan and the United States*, p. 292.

5. United States, *Department of State Bulletin*, June 26, 1955.

6. Jerome B. Cohen, *Japan's Postwar Economy*, p. 152; A. Doak Barnett, *China and the Major Powers in East Asia* (Washington: Brookings Institution, 1976), p. 102.

7. United States, *Department of State Bulletin*, December 26, 1955; interview with Stanley Nehmer.

8. *Ibid.*

9. Quoted in John Lynch, *Towards an Orderly Market*, p. 102.

10. *Ibid.*, p. 90.

11. *Ibid.*, p. 91.

12. United States, *Department of State Bulletin*, April 30, 1956, and July 2, 1956.

13. The Japanese exchanged notes with the United States stating that they would limit fabric sales of print cloth to the U.S. to 20 million square yards and velveteen to 5 million square yards. In June, they also agreed to limit exports of blouses to 2.5 million dozens for 1956 and 1.5 million dozens for 1957. This latter act led to the dropping of an escape clause petition in blouses. *Wall Street Journal*, June 20, 1956; hereafter cited as *WSJ*.

14. *WSJ*, May 18, 1956; *WSJ*, June 14, 1956.

15. Kenneth Dam, *The GATT*, p. 21.

16. Gerard Curzon and Victoria Curzon, "The Management of Trade Relations in the GATT," p. 258.

17. There were also strong economic interests in maintaining trade with Japan. Japan bought more raw cotton from the United States than it sold in manufactured exports. One observer commented that "it would be strange indeed if we should lose the friendship of 90 million Japanese and gain exclusive control of the domestic market for dishrags." David Cohn, "Southern Cotton and Japan," *Atlantic Monthly*, August 1956.

18. *Japan Times*, September 4, 1956; hereafter cited as *JT*. Some of the articles referred to below from the *Japan Times* were based upon articles that also appeared in the American textile industry paper, the *Daily News Record*.

19. Interview with Herbert Blackman.

20. Hunsberger, *Japan and the United States in World Trade*, and Lynch, *Towards an Orderly Market*, discuss the details of the 1930s VER. The only critical difference was that those negotiations took place between the two industries rather than between governments.

21. The industry was particularly concerned about aggregate limits, and the limits for velveteen, gingham, and cotton blouses.

22. *JT*, September 7, 1956.

23. Statement by Mike Masaoka, representative and lobbyist for the Association on Japanese Textile Imports, in United States Senate, *Problems of the Domestic Textile Industry* (1958), p. 1613; see also United States, *Department of State Bulletin*, April 30, 1956; and the statement submitted by the American Importers of Japanese Textiles, in *Compendium of Papers on Foreign Trade Policy*, Committee on Ways and Means (Washington: GPO, 1957), p. 29.

24. Cohen, *Japan's Postwar Economy*, p. 65.

25. Saburo Okita, *The Experience of Economic Planning in Japan*, p. 11.

26. *Japanese Industry, 1955* (Tokyo: Foreign Capital Research Society, 1956).

27. United States Senate, *Problems of the Domestic Textile Industry* (1958), p. 20 1.

28. *Japan Trade Guide* (Tokyo: J.I.J.I. Press, 1957), p. 93.

29. Haruhiro Fukui, "The GATT Tokyo Round," p. 96, and Chalmers Johnson, "MITI and Japanese International Economic Policy."

30. Ezra Vogel, "Introduction," in E. Vogel, ed., *Modern Japanese Organization and Decision-Making*, p. xv; see also T. J. Pempel, "Japanese Foreign Economic Policy."

31. Philip Trezise with Yukio Suzuki, "Politics, Government, and Economic Growth in Japan," in Hugh Patrick and Henry Rosovsky, eds., *Asia's New Giant: How the Japanese Economy Works* (Washington: Brookings Institution, 1976), pp. 800–802.

32. Leon Hollerman, "Foreign Trade in Japan's Economic Transition," in Isaiah Frank, ed., *The Japanese Economy in International Perspective* (Baltimore: Johns Hopkins University Press, 1975), pp. 182–184.

33. Interview with Herbert Blackman.

34. *JT*, September 4, 1956.

35. United States, *Department of State Bulletin*, October 8, 1956.

36. These tactics are consistent with a general pattern associated with Japanese bargaining style. See Michael Blaker's "Probe, Push, and Panic."

37. Interview with Herbert Blackman.

38. *WSJ*, September 28, 1956.

39. *JT*, October 4, 1956.

40. According to documents released under the Freedom of Information Act from the U.S. Department of State, the Japanese said they exported 270 million square yards in 1955, while the United States said it was only 220 million; Japan wanted to export 50 million square yards of gingham, while the U.S. wanted 30; the Japanese wanted a ceiling of 5 million square yards of velveteen, while the U.S. wanted only 1.5 to 1.8 million—and so on.

41. *JT*, November 11, 1956.

42. United States, *Department of State Bulletin*, October 8, 1956. This tariff increase was within the confines of GATT regulations.

43. According to transcripts of the negotiating session, the Japanese clearly perceived these carrots and sticks, and expressed their concern.

44. *JT*, October 8, 1956.

45. Japan reduced its demand on the aggregate limit to 245 million square yards from 270. Meanwhile the Americans continued to insist on 220. The Japanese also discussed a range for velveteen from 3 to 4 million square yards, while again the U.S. held its demand for 1.8 million square yards. *JT*, November 23, 1956; Department of State documents.

46. The compromises included figures of 230 million for the aggregate total and 3.5 million for velveteen. A State Department memo stated that officials believed the final quota would be between 230 and 240 million square yards.

47. Documents released under Freedom of Information Act.

48. The *Japan Times*, which largely reflects the Foreign Ministry's view, continually warned of the dangers of the textile dispute throughout the fall of 1956. On December 17, for example, an editorial warned that if the textile agreement fell

through, "tuna fish, plywood, photographic equipment, stainless flatwear . . . would be the next on the list, and it is critical that the government settle the issue as quickly as possible."

49. According to State Department memos, retaliatory action would also include reducing purchases of U.S. cotton and switching to Canadian markets.

50. *JT*, December 22, 1956.

51. *New York Times*, December 22, 1956; hereafter cited as *NYT*.

52. *JT*, December 22, 1956.

53. *NYT*, January 5, 1957.

54. *Daily News Record*, January 3, 1957: hereafter cited as *DNR*.

55. Interview with Stanley Nehmer; Department of State documents.

56. *DNR*, January 11, 1957; and *ibid*.

57. At a later date, the Japanese agreed to restrain voluntarily a few items of wool. A week after the agreement was signed, however, American manufacturers complained that the omission of wool and synthetics could "prove disastrous" to the American Textile industry. *DNR*, January 21, 1956.

58. *DNR*, January 21, 1956; and Department of State documents.

59. The American Cotton Manufacturers' Institute, the prime mover behind the protectionist drive, stated that the VER was "basically sound and workable." *DNR*, January 18, 1956.

60. *DNR*, January 23, 1956.

61. Gardner Patterson, *Discrimination in International Trade*, p. 273.

62. The Japanese fears were not unfounded. When Senator Pastore of Rhode Island held hearings, in 1958, about the textiles problems, testimony frequently suggested that the Japanese had a pattern of unfair competition which they used for "progressive conquest." See United States Senate, *Problems of the Domestic Textile Industry* (1958), p. 127.

63. *Japan Trade Guide*, p. 305.

64. Lynch, *Towards an Orderly Market*, ch. 6.

65. Transshipments took various routes, ranging from Hong Kong to Rotterdam and South Africa. See Kenneth Bauge, "Voluntary Export Restriction as a Foreign Commercial Policy," and testimony by Mike Masaoka, in United States Senate, *Problems of the Domestic Textile Industry* (1958).

66. *Tokyo Shimbum*, December 20, 1957.

67. *Nihon Keiza*, December 21, 1957.

68. Warren Hunsberger, *Japan and the United States in World Trade*, p. 325.

69. *DNR*, February 20, 1959.

70. Within a year, the Japanese realized that accepting the reduction in flexibility was a mistake. The following year they sought and failed to renegotiate for the flexibility they had lost. *DNR*, March 9, 1960. Through trial and error, Japan was becoming more sensitive to the realities of making quotas work. Also, a precedent was set in 1960 when the U.S. agreed to allow Japan to "carry over" part of its unfilled 1959 quota. The U.S. allowed this only because of unusual circumstances (a typhoon had disrupted trade in late 1959), but carryover provisions would soon become an integral part of the Long-Term Arrangement in cotton textiles. See *DNR*, February 9, 1960.

71. See Hunsberger, *Japan and the United States*, p. 324; and William Lockwood, *The Economic Development of Japan*, p. 631.

72. Haruhiro Fukui, "Economic Planning in Postwar Japan: A Case Study in Policymaking," Asian Survey (April 1972); Richard Caves and Masu Uekusa, Industrial Organization in Japan, and Yasuo Takeyama, "The Outlook for U.S. Japan Economic Trade Relations," Journal of International Affairs (1974), vol. 1.

73. Lynch, Towards an Orderly Market, p. 173.

74. One important difference was that Hong Kong's agreement was negotiated between industries rather than governments.

75. Shik Chun Young, "The GATT Long-Term Cotton Textile Arrangement and Hong Kong's Cotton Textile Trade" (Ph.D. diss., Washington State University, Pullman, 1969).

76. Theodore Geiger and Francis Geiger, Tales of Two City-States, p. 145.

77. South China Morning Post, February 13, 1959; hereafter cited as SCMP.

78. Far Eastern Economic Review, February 12, 1959.

79. SCMP, February 14, 1959.

80. SCMP, February 14, 1959; DNR, February 16, 1959.

81. SCMP, February 15, 1959.

82. SCMP, February 17, 1959.

83. SCMP, February 18, 1959.

84. Interview with Henry Kearns.

85. DNR, April 9, 1959.

86. DNR, May 7, 1959. There was some degree of truth to Kearns' charges. Large retailers and importers, such as Sears, Roebuck, would transmit samples and specifications of garments to be made in Hong Kong. Particularly after the VER with Japan, these organizations actively sought alternative suppliers for their goods. Since Hong Kong already had an industrial base developed from its exports to Britain, it turned out to be the most attractive producer for American firms.

87. SCMP, August 5, 1959.

88. SCMP, August 20, 1959.

89. Hong Kong had accepted the Lancashire Pact with Britain on the understanding that Pakistan and India would also be restrained. The latter two nations, however, backed down on their accords (until 1960) because they felt that Hong Kong had achieved a superior deal. During 1959 Hong Kong manufacturers frequently expressed their feelings about being unfairly burdened by England. SCMP, August 26, 1959.

90. DNR, October 2, 1959.

91. DNR, November 24, 1959; SCMP, November 23, 1959.

92. Young, "The GATT," p. 32.

93. SCMP, November 18, 1959.

94. Interviews with Herbert Blackman and Henry Kearns.

95. SCMP, November 22, 1959.

96. Calculated from United Nations, Yearbook of International Trade Statistics, 1959.

97. SCMP, January 3, 1960; NYT, December 29, 1959.

98. SCMP, December 28, 1959.

99. SCMP, January 8, 1960.

100. The proposed VER covered only five types of garments and would have allowed a 15 percent increase in the first year, followed by 10 percent increases in the next two years. SCMP, December 29, 1959; DNR, December 30, 1959.

101. American apparel executives asked for a reduction in the overall export limit, an early starting date for the VER, more differentiation, and monthly reports. Textile manufacturers insisted on including some categories of textile fabrics.

102. *SCMP*, February 2, 1960; *DNR*, March 1, 1960.

103. One constraint on the American government directly participating in the negotiations was its relationship with Japan. When the Japanese textile industry heard Hong Kong's proposal, there were immediate demands for revision of the Japanese VER. The stronger the U.S. government's association with the Hong Kong negotiations, the harder to justify Hong Kong's generous agreement. See *DNR*, December 31, 1959; interview with Henry Kearns.

104. *SCMP*, January 31, 1960.

105. *The Economist*, January 22, 1960.

106. *DNR*, February 9, 1960.

107. *SCMP*, February 6, 1960; *DNR*, February 8, 1960.

108. *1961 Yearbook and Asian Textile Survey* (Hong Kong: Far Eastern Economic Review), p. 187.

109. *1961 Yearbook* (Hong Kong: Far Eastern Economic Review), p. 189.

110. Fukui, "The GATT Tokyo Round," p. 155.

3. Textiles, Round 2:
The STA and LTA, 1961–1969

1. Raymond Bauer, Ithiel de Sola Pool, and Lewis Dexter, *American Business and Public Policy*, p. 78.

2. Quoted in Hunsberger, *The United States and Japan*, p. 327.

3. *Daily News Record*, June 23, 1961; July 12, 1961; hereafter cited as *DNR*.

4. *DNR*, July 19, 1961; *DNR*, July 24, 1961; and for text of the STA, see United States, *Department of State Bulletin*, August 21, 1961, p. 336.

5. *DNR*, July 25, 1961; July 26, 1961.

6. *Ibid.; New York Times*, July 26, 1961; hereafter cited as *NYT*.

7. *DNR*, July 7, 1961; *NYT*, July 4, 1961; *DNR*, July 11, 1961.

8. *DNR*, October 11, 1961.

9. Established in 1960, the Cotton Advisory Board was supposed to advise the colonial authorities on all textile matters and organize the distribution of quotas. See *DNR*, July 20, 1961; and *Hong Kong Yearbook, 1961*.

10. *DNR*, February 2, 1962.

11. *Ibid.*; interview with Stanley Nehmer.

12. *Wall Street Journal*, March 19, 1962; hereafter cited as *WSJ*: *DNR*, March 19, 1962; *NYT*, March 19, 1962; and *Hong Kong Yearbook, 1962*.

13. *DNR*, March 19, 1962.

14. *DNR*, March 28, 1962; *Hong Kong Yearbook, 1962*, p. 79.

15. *NYT*, June 5, 1962; *DNR*, June 18, 1962.

16. Japanese bargaining had changed since 1956. No longer were Japanese negotiators as insistent upon overall increases. Government and industry officials had become more sensitive to the critical features of individual categories and flexibility. Also, this approach to negotiations, of finding a referent, is similar to the process

described by I. W. Zartman in "Negotiations as a Joint Decision-Making Process," in I. W. Zartman, ed., *The Negotiation Process*. See also *NYT*, June 20, 1961, and June 26, 1961, and *DNR*, June 20, 1961.

17. *DNR*, July 28, 1961. Information on the process and Japanese strategy during this period is somewhat sketchy. Newspaper accounts do not differentiate between Japanese posturing for position, on the one hand, and serious statements on their resistance points, on the other. Also, none of the negotiators interviewed had specific recollections on this set of negotiations. The reconstruction in this chapter is taken largely from the *Daily News Record* and the *Japan Times*.

18. *DNR*, August 16, 1961.

19. *DNR*, August 22, 1961. Japan's strategy during these negotiations was close to an ideal typical "controlled risk" approach.

20. *DNR*, August 17, 1961. Interviews with Stanley Nehmer, Philip Trezise, and Harry Phelan confirmed that internal division was the norm at this time.

21. *DNR*, August 27, 1961, quoted from an American textile adviser to the bilateral negotiations.

22. See *DNR*, August 27, 1961; August 28, 1961; and for the final accord, see Department of State, Press Release, no. 631, September 13, 1961.

23. See *Japan Times* from August 10 to September 15, 1961.

24. *DNR*, September 11, 1961; *NYT*, September 9, 1961.

25. Department of State, *U.S. Treaties and Other International Agreements*, no. 3096.

26. These figures do not correspond exactly to the twelve months of the STA. Japan's bilateral agreement went from January to December, while the STA was from October to September.

27. *DNR*, November 5, 1962; November 8, 1962.

28. *Foreign Trade of Japan, 1963* (Tokyo: JETRO Press, 1963), p. 205.

29. See Kenneth Dam, *The GATT*, p. 311, for a detailed discussion of the system; and United States, *Department of State Bulletin*, May 21, 1962, for the official announcement.

30. For a review and evaluation of the LTA, see Benjamin Bardan, "The Cotton Textile Agreement, 1962–72."

31. Department of Commerce, Press Release, December 20, 1962.

32. *DNR*, December 31, 1962; interview with Nehmer.

33. *DNR*, February 18, 1963.

34. See *Japan Times*, month of February 1963; and *NYT*, February 23, 1963.

35. *DNR*, February 26, 1963; February 27, 1963.

36. *DNR*, February 28, 1963.

37. *DNR*, April 15, 1963.

38. *Ibid.*

39. *DNR*, July 16, 1963.

40. *DNR*, July 15, 1963.

41. *DNR*, August 29, 1963.

42. *DNR*, August 30, 1963.

43. In some cases, such as Japan's 1965 agreement, the Japanese were successful in bargaining for somewhat more favorable terms. In 1965, the Japanese attained more flexibility.

44. Calculated from *Japan Foreign Trade, 1965* (Tokyo: JETRO Press, 1965), p. 159.

45. The reason for this change was the better quality of synthetic products and the increased acceptance of synthetic fibers by consumers. These figures were calculated from United States International Trade Commission, *The History and Current Status of the Multifiber Arrangement*, p. C-3.

46. GATT, *Japan's Economic Expansion and Foreign Trade, 1955 to 1970*, Studies in International Trade, no. 2 (Geneva, 1971), p. 19.

47. Department of Commerce, "Japan: Performance Under the Bilateral Agreement," 1961–70.

48. Bardan, "The Cotton Textile Agreement, 1962–72," p. 26 (emphasis added).

49. Interviews with John Emmerson and Edwin Reischauer; Emmerson was the Deputy Chief of Mission in the U.S. Embassy, Japan, while Reischauer was the Ambassador. Reischauer felt that textile controversies were nothing more than a minor irritant during his tenure in Tokyo.

50. In the text of the LTA it states that cotton is a special case. See *DNR*, August 28, 1963, for discussion of U.S. assurances. The issue of multifiber restrictions is the topic of chapter 4.

51. S. Nehmer, "U.S. Participation in the LTA," in United States, *Department of State Bulletin*, January 20, 1964.

52. S. Nehmer, "Record of U.S. Participation in the Second Year of the LTA," United States, *Department of State Bulletin*, January 11, 1965.

53. Interview with Stanley Nehmer. Nehmer's view of the process was supported by interviews with Harry Phelan, Ron Levin, Philip Trezise, and Herbert Blackman.

54. *DNR*, March 14, 1966, and May 12, 1966.

55. This was the consensus of all the negotiators and advisers who were directly involved in Hong Kong negotiations throughout the 1960s and 1970s, including Stanley Nehmer, Philip Trezise, Seth Bodner, Theodore Geiger, Harry Phelan, Herbert Blackman, Buford Brandis, William Brew, Milan Fabry, Donald Foote, Irving Kramer, Janie Hester, Carl Priestland, Bill Tagliani, and David Kennedy.

56. Interview with Seth Bodner.

57. Department of Commerce, "Hong Kong: Performance Under the Bilateral Agreement," 1961–70.

58. Shik Chun Young, "The GATT Long-Term Cotton Textile Arrangement and Hong Kong's Cotton Textile Trade" (Ph.D. diss., Washington State University, 1969), tables 1.4 and 2.5.

59. *Ibid.*, p. 178.

60. Calculated from U.S. Tariff Commission, *Textiles and Apparel: Report to the President on Investigation No. 332-55 Under Section 332 of the Tariff Act of 1930*, TC Publication 226 (January 1968), table 10.

61. *DNR*, March 4, 1960, and February 23, 1960.

62. *Asian Textile Survey, 1965–66* (Hong Kong: Far Eastern Economic Review, 1966), p. 199.

63. *Ibid.*, p. 197.

64. Economic Research Center of Korea, *Industrial Structure of Korea. Vol. 1: Manufacturing Industries* (Seoul: Pyonghua-hand Printing, 1962).

65. *Asian Textile Survey, 1967–68* (Hong Kong: Far Eastern Economic Review, 1968); and *Asian Textile Survey, 1969–70* (Hong Kong: Far Eastern Economic Review, 1970) p. 176.

66. Interviews with Herbert Blackman, William Brew, Stanley Nehmer, Seth Bodner, David Kennedy, and Donald Foote.

67. Interview with Stanley Nehmer.

68. Documents from the United States Commerce Department suggest that these contingency arrangements were frequent.

69. *Asian Textile Survey, 1967–68*, p. 64.

70. I. M. Destler, Haruhiro Fukui, Hideo Sato, *The Textile Wrangle*, p. 35.

4. Textiles, Round 3:
The Search for Comprehensive Protection, 1969–1982

1. Quoted in Gerald Meier, *Problems of Trade Policy*, p. 98.

2. In 1961 the Japanese extended their VER. They set voluntary quotas on men's suits after the Amalgamated Clothing and Textile Workers threatened to refuse to work on Japanese fabrics. *Daily News Record*, February 16, 1966; hereafter cited as *DNR*.

3. Interview with Stanley Nehmer.

4. *DNR*, December 13, 1962.

5. *DNR*, January 29, 1963.

6. *DNR*, January 21, 1965.

7. After the textile VER between the U.S. and Japan in the 1930s, industry-to-industry talks were proclaimed by the U.S. courts to be an illegal restraint of trade. See Malcolm Smith, "Voluntary Export Quotas and U.S. Trade Policy."

8. *DNR*, April 14, 1965.

9. *DNR*, June 1, 1965.

10. *DNR*, June 9, 1965.

11. *DNR*, September 30, 1965.

12. *Ibid.*, emphasis added; also interviews with Herbert Blackman, Stanley Nehmer, and John Emmerson.

13. Interview with Stanley Nehmer.

14. Interviews with Herbert Blackman, Stanley Nehmer, and John Emmerson indicated that each of these participants remembered vividly what happened fifteen years later. Ambassador Reischauer, however, had no recollection of the dispute.

15. According to American negotiator Seth Bodner, Japanese intransigence with the wool agreement was one factor in strengthening American resolve in the 1969 negotiations. The Japanese also agreed to continue discussions through diplomatic channels. In 1966, they may have agreed to an extension of the VER in men's wool suits. *DNR*, February 16, 1966.

16. *DNR*, July 21, 1965.

17. Japan shipped only 22.7 percent of its total exports to the U.S. in 1955; in 1970, it exported more than 30 percent and imported 29.4 percent of its needs from the U.S. Although Japan was America's second largest trading partner, Japanese im-

ports represented only 14 percent of the U.S. total, and the U.S. shipped only 10.7 percent of its goods to Japan.

18. United States Tariff Commission, *Textiles and Apparel: Report to the President on Investigation No. 332-55 Under Section 332 of the Tariff Act of 1930,* January 1968.

19. Most of the evidence in this chapter on the 1969 to 1971 negotiations is based on my interviews and I. M. Destler, Haruhiro Fukui, Hideo Sato, *The Textile Wrangle.* The bibliography on this episode, however, is extensive. See, for example, Morton Kaplan and K. Mushakaju, eds., *Japan, America and the Future World* (New York: Free Press, 1976); Michael Blaker, "Probe, Push, and Panic"; Jerome B. Cohen, ed., *Pacific Partnership;* Gerard Curzon and Victoria Curzon, "The Management of Trade Relations in the GATT."

20. Interview with Seth Bodner.

21. Destler, Fukui, and Sato, *The Textile Wrangle,* p. 94.

22. In 1961–62, Japan had a number of common interests with the United States—especially in limiting competition from other exporters. In 1969, the Japanese were in a completely different situation, because there were no obvious common interests.

23. Interview with Philip Trezise.

24. *China Post,* May 17, 1969.

25. Interview with Seth Bodner.

26. Some in the American government argued that Japan was more likely to agree to "selective" restraints. But Stans repeatedly rejected this course. He recognized that selective textile barriers merely provide an incentive for the exporter to shift into unrestricted product lines.

27. This section is taken from Destler, Fukui, and Sato, *The Textile Wrangle,* pp. 121–140.

28. The historical record of this meeting is still somewhat unclear. Neither Nixon nor Kissinger discuss this textile issue in their memoirs. Interviews with American officials close to Nixon have nonetheless confirmed that the President believed Sato had promised a textile agreement.

29. Destler, Fukui, and Sato give an in-depth discussion of each of these episodes. The government-to-government negotiations included the Japanese *aide-mémoire* of March 9, 1970, Miyazawa and Stans' meeting of June 1970, the second Nixon–Sato summit of October 1970, and the Flanagan-Ushiba talks in November–December 1970.

30. Kissinger again tried to maneuver a secret deal in March 1970, according to Destler, Fukui, and Sato. As far as transnational efforts are concerned, Donald Kendall, a Pepsi-Cola executive, sponsored his own plan in March 1970; and Congressman Wilbur Mills negotiated a VER with the Japanese textile industry in the spring of 1971.

31. The Okinawa–textiles linkage became a joke among negotiators. In an interview, one negotiator recounted a golf match between the Japanese Foreign Minister and Secretary of State William Rogers in which someone made the remark, "One round for Okinawa and one round for textiles?"

32. The role of transnational actors was especially prominent during this phase. A lawyer-lobbyist named Michael Daniels was hired by Japan and Hong Kong to defend their interests. In addition to lobbying in Washington, Daniels was instru-

mental in the Mills–Japanese industry deal. See Tong Sang Il, *American Domestic Politics and Foreign Policy: A Case Study of the Textile Controversy with Japan 1969–71* (Ph D. diss. University of Washington 1974)

33. According to Kennedy's assistant, Rex Beach, Kennedy believed before his first trip that he could solve the problems within four weeks—one week per country.

34. Interview with David Kennedy.

35. United States International Trade Commission, *The History and Current Status of the Multifiber Arrangement*, p. C-11; and Chen Sun, "Prospects for Sino-American Trade," *Industry of Free China*, July 1977, table 6.

36. According to Rex Beach, the 11 percent figure was unacceptable to the industry and was never formally offered. It was nonetheless discussed as a possible compromise. See *DNR*, June 28, 1971; and *New York Times*, June 9, 1971; hereafter cited as *NYT*.

37. There were few credible linkages available. Besides the Okinawa linkage used with Japan, the only other stick was unilateral quotas.

38. There have been several stories about how this process evolved. David Kennedy thought it was a two-way process. The Koreans and the Taiwanese would say something like: "If we make this concession for you, what will you give us in return?" Rex Beach thought that the chief technical negotiator, Tony Jurich, offered these as carrots as a means to close the gap in textile positions. Undoubtedly, it was a little of both.

39. *China Post*, June 19, 1971; *DNR*, June 28, 1971; *NYT*, June 19, 1971.

40. *NYT*, June 20, 1971; United Nations, *Yearbook of International Trade Statistics, 1971*.

41. Interview with Rex Beach. This was one of the few times this tactic was successful. Whenever the Koreans, Japanese, or the others tried to circumvent Kennedy, the White House would reaffirm that Kennedy had Nixon's full authority. In an interview with David Kennedy, he discussed his effort to prevent these maneuvers. For example, when Vice President Agnew traveled to Korea in early July, Kennedy sent Rex Beach to intercept him and warn the Vice President about Korean textiles. During Agnew's visit, the Koreans *did* try to discuss textiles, but Agnew dutifully told them they would have to talk to Kennedy.

42. The U.S.–Korea cotton bilateral agreement expired in December 1970 and had been extended for six months. According to documents released under the Freedom of Information Act, the Koreans wanted an increase in the cotton growth rate as well as the possibility of renegotiating the agreement if there was to be a multifiber agreement. Since the United States wanted to keep pressure on Korea, it agreed only to a simple extension of the old bilateral accord, with the possibility of renegotiation if a multifiber arrangement was forthcoming.

43. Interview with David Kennedy.

44. According to information obtained from Harry Phelan and David Kennedy in interviews, the United States probably could have pressured Taiwan into an accord, but it was decided in conjunction with Taiwan that this was not the best course.

45. Michael Daniels said in an interview that he went from country to country trying to assure each exporter that restrictions would not come if they could resist collectively.

46. One such example was the Sixth Sino-Korean Economic Cooperation Conference, held in mid-July 1971. Textiles were an important item on the agenda. *China Post,* July 5, 1971.

47. According to the *DNR,* June 22, 1971, and Rex Beach, the industry was very unhappy with the Kennedy terms, and it might have been able to exercise a veto.

48. Stephen Krasner, "U.S. Commercial and Monetary Policy: Unravelling the Paradox of External Strength and Internal Weakness," in Peter Katzenstein, ed., *Between Power and Plenty;* Robert O. Keohane and Joseph Nye, *Power and Interdependence;* Linda Graebner, "The New Economic Policy, 1971," in U.S. Commission on the Organization of the Government for the Conduct of Foreign Policy, *Appendices,* vol. 3 (Washington: Government Printing Office, 1975).

49. Destler, Fukui, and Sato, *The Textile Wrangle,* p. 318.

50. Kennedy was in Guam, close enough to the Far East to maintain good communication with his staff but sufficiently isolated to stay out of sight.

51. *NYT,* September 16, 1971; *DNR,* September 16, 1971; September 17, 1971; and September 20, 1971.

52. Interview with Rex Beach.

53. Interview with David Kennedy. Kennedy would not say precisely what this was. The only thing he would say was that it was not a "fancy plane" or special military equipment.

54. Beach was in charge of the Hong Kong negotiations. Although he had no authority to make this threat, it seemed to have worked.

55. Documents released through the Freedom of Information Act.

56. *DNR,* October 21, 1971.

57. See *NYT,* October 17, 1971, and October 19, 1971; and *DNR,* October 18, 1971; October 19, 1971; and October 20, 1971. Taiwan and Korea were to receive around a 15 percent cotton bonus and Hong Kong about 5 percent.

58. These figures were taken from *NYT,* October 19, 1971, and Department of State, *Treaties and Other International Acts Series,* nos. 7498 and 7499. Rex Beach agreed with this interpretation of the disjuncture in the figures, and David Kennedy said he had no idea what happened after October 15. As far as he was concerned, that date marked the end of the matter.

59. Japan's synthetic exports were 238 million dollars in 1969, and total exports were 4.88 billion dollars. See United Nations, *Yearbook of International Trade Statistics, 1969.*

60. According to documents released by the Department of Agriculture, all but 57 million dollars of the original 776.3 million dollars of P.L. 480 aid was disbursed to the Koreans by the end of 1979. The remainder was to be delivered in 1980 and 1981. The only snag in the implementation came in 1976 when a House of Representatives committee voted to limit agricultural aid to Korea because of increased political repression. At that point, the Koreans reversed the linkage back to textiles, insisting that their quotas had to be raised if the aid were cut. This put the government in an embarrassing position. If the bill passed Congress, the administration would have to admit publicly that it had compensated the Koreans in 1971. Fortunately for the White House, the bill never passed, and the P.L. 480 aid continued to flow.

61. Snyder and Diesing, *Conflict Among Nations,* p. 256.

62. Comptroller General of the United States, *Economic and Foreign Policy Effects of Voluntary Restraint Agreements on Textiles and Steel; DNR,* October 27, 1971.

63. Far Eastern Economic Review, *Asia Yearbook, 1978* (Hong Kong: South China Post, 1978), p. 228. The United States took 33.9 percent; Japan, 20 percent; and Europe, 17 percent.

64. Cheng Tong Young, *The Economy of Hong Kong* (Hong Kong: Far East Publications, 1977), p. 195.

65. Parvez Hasan, *Korea;* C. T. Young, *The Economy of Hong Kong,* calculated from tables 10.8 and 11.1; and Economic Planning Council, *Taiwan Statistical Data Book, 1977,* June 1977, pp. 201–204.

66. *DNR,* May 15, 1971.

67. Interviews with Seth Bodner and Stanley Nehmer. Bodner said that a Hong Kong official admitted at one point that its government was trying to "pull a fast one" on the United States.

68. Interviews with Stanley Nehmer, Seth Bodner, Harry Phelan, David Kennedy, and Herbert Blackman. The compromise was that some of Hong Kong's quota for the next year would be deducted because of the overshipments. Kennedy and Phelan said that they did not want to push Hong Kong too hard at a time when they were trying to negotiate an international multifiber arrangement.

69. United States International Trade Commission, *The History and Current Status of the Multifiber Agreement.*

70. Everyone interviewed in the U.S. government who was involved with textiles in 1975 felt that the United States could have done better. The American failure was generally attributed to tenacious bargaining on the part of Hong Kong, Korea, and Taiwan, and a very accommodating strategy on the part of the United States. Interviews with Ron Levin, Donald Foote, Harry Phelan, Herbert Blackman, William Brew, Irving Kramer, and Florence James.

71. Susan Strange, "The Management of Surplus Capacity," p. 314.

72. GATT press release quoted in International Monetary Fund, *Survey* (1978), no. 1, 7:13. The U.S. and Europe switched roles between 1969 and 1977. In 1969, the U.S. insisted on more restrictions, whereas Europe was not interested. By 1977, the Europeans took the lead by immediately using their greater authority to tighten restrictions more than the United States.

73. United States Special Trade Representative's Office, Press Release, no. 302, February 15, 1979, pp. 3–4.

74. For the pessimistic views about the MFA, see Strange, "The Management of Surplus Capacity"; UNCTAD, *Liberalization of Non-Tariff Barriers: International Trade in Textiles, TD/B/C/.2/155;* and UNCTAD, *International Trade in Textiles: International Trade in Textiles and Developing Countries, TD/B/C.2/174.* It should be stressed that the MFA is potentially more dangerous for latecomers than for countries with well-established industries, such as Taiwan, Korea, and Hong Kong. Just as Taiwan and Korea had much more trouble than Hong Kong under the LTA, countries which enter the market late will have a harder time under the MFA.

75. Interviews with Stanley Nehmer, Ron Levin, and Donald Foote.

76. Interview with Ron Levin. This position was supported by those persons mentioned in note 70.

77. Interview with Buford Brandis.

78. See *DNR*, October 29, 1979; October 30, 1979; and October 31, 1979.

79. *Ibid.* In addition to simple methods of cheating and transshipment, Taiwanese, Korean, and Hong Kong firms have established extensive networks of subsidiaries in countries such as Thailand, Mauritius, and Sri Lanka. As a result, some of the East Asian trade earnings from textiles and apparel may be "hidden" in the service account of the balance of payments. See Krishna Kumar, "Third World Multinationals," *International Studies Quarterly* (September 1982), Vol. 26, no. 3, and K. Kumar and M. McLeod, eds., *Multinationals from Developing Countries* (Lexington, Mass.: D. C. Heath), 1981.

80. Import penetration in apparel grew from 6 percent in 1967 to 22 percent in 1979; in textiles, imports held 10 to 12 percent of the market in 1969. *Business Week*, May 14, 1979.

81. *DNR*, January 18, 1982.

5. Footwear: The Spread of Protection, 1977–1981

1. United States Special Trade Representative's Office, Press Release, no. 247, April 1, 1977; hereafter cited as STR.

2. Previous assistance was almost exclusively trade-adjustment assistance to individual firms. The only time the government provided protection was when it levied countervailing duties and antidumping duties on shoes from various sources, and the possible negotiation of two VERs. According to Ralph Oman, the government tacitly negotiated a VER with Italy, which had very little impact on Italian exports, and there were rumors in Washington that Korea's VER in rubber shoes in 1973 was negotiated by the U.S. See Ralph Oman, "The Clandestine Negotiations of Voluntary Restraints on Shoes from Italy"; and STR, Press Release, no. 183, June 19, 1973.

3. For a review of the footwear industry's industrial problems, see David B. Yoffie, "Orderly Marketing Agreements as an Industrial Policy"; and Comptroller General of the United States, *Slow Productivity Growth in the U.S. Footwear Industry—Can the Federal Government Help?* February 15, 1980.

4. Interview with Harriet Hentges.

5. STR Press Release, no. 222, April 16, 1976.

6. Interview with Roger Porter.

7. See United States International Trade Commission, *Footwear Investigation,* USITC Publication 758, February 1976; and *Footwear Investigation,* USITC Publication 799, February 1977.

8. This discussion is largely based on an article by David Broder that appeared in the *Washington Post,* July 23, 1977. His information came from an executive reorganization project conducted by OMB. I. M. Destler, one of the consultants on this project, verified in a phone interview that Broder's information was "quite accurate." Roger Porter, who also read the report, said that a few of the dates of meetings were inaccurate, but that the remainder of Broder's article was reliable.

9. Three months later, this evolved into an extensive Footwear Industry Revitalization Program. See Department of Commerce, *Footwear Industry Revitalization Program: First Annual Progress Report* (1978).

10. Interview with Faun Evenson.

11. This was the assessment of the Executive Reorganization Project, according to Broder's article.

12. Interviews with Stanley Nehmer, Faun Evenson, Jack Lesley, and Anita Jenson.

13. Interview with Rita Cavenough.

14. Interview with Faun Evenson.

15. Harriet Hentges said that comparisons with the MFA were explicitly avoided. Furthermore, in an unusual interview at the Labor Department, I sat in one room with five negotiators for several different commodities, including steel, textiles, color televisions, and footwear. It was striking that the negotiators had never talked with one another about some of these problems. Some were surprised to learn that they had common problems with a bureaucrat at the next desk. Interviews with Gloria Pratt, Janie Hester, Jorge Perez-Lopez, Howard Dobson, and Florence James.

16. Interviews with Faun Evenson and Jack Lesley.

17. These figures were constructed from several interviews, including those with Jack Lesley, Faun Evenson, Thomas Graham, Gloria Pratt, Bernie Ascher, Stanley Nehmer, and Janie Hester.

18. *China News*, January 8, 1977; hereafter cited as *CN*; *Korea Herald*, January 8, 1977; hereafter cited as *KH*.

19. *CN*, January 28, 1977; *KH*, January 9, 1977.

20. Brimmer and Company, *Trends in the Demand for and the Supply of Nonrubber Footwear*, June 27, 1979, p. 19.

21. *KH*, February 1, 1977.

22. *KH*, January 11, 1977.

23. *KH*, January 4, 1977; *CN*, January 28, 1977.

24. Interview with Bernie Ascher.

25. Albert Hirschman, "Beyond Asymmetry," p. 48.

26. Interview with Thomas Graham. Graham has subsequently differed with my interpretation of Lande's behavior, but he did not deny the facts. Graham felt that Lande was a first-rate negotiator.

27. Most of the specific details about the day-to-day negotiations came from my interview with Thomas Graham. Korean and Taiwanese press accounts served as the basis for all the interviews, and all major points were reaffirmed in interviews with negotiators Gloria Pratt and Bernie Ascher; AFIA representative Faun Evenson; congressional assistants Jack Lesley and Anita Jenson; and industry consultant Stanley Nehmer.

28. Lande's bargaining strategy was identical to the method suggested by I. W. Zartman in "Negotiation as a Joint Decisionmaking Process," in I. W. Zartman, ed., *The Negotiation Process*.

29. Interviews with Thomas Graham, Gloria Pratt, and Bernie Ascher. See also *CN* May 5–7, 1977; and *KH*, May 2–7, 1977.

30. Graham reported that Lande would frequently meet alone with the Korean and Taiwanese chief negotiators. Despite the general coherence of the exporting governments' policies, different ministries sometimes took varying positions. Part of

the open bargaining was as much for internal consumption as for convincing the opponent. By meeting separately, Lande could get more honest information. This is probably the reason that the Americans were confident when they left Korea, while the press reports were very pessimistic.

31. Interview with Bernie Ascher.

32. Interview with Thomas Graham.

33. CN, May 7, 1977.

34. See Department of State, *Treaties and Other International Agreements*, no. 8884, p. 2.

35. Interview with Faun Evenson.

36. Department of State, *Treaties and Other International Agreements*, no. 8884, p. 22.

37. Graham said that if they had returned to Washington, the U.S. would have had definitely imposed unilateral restrictions on Korea.

38. Interviews with Jack Lesley, Faun Evenson, Iver Olson, and Stanley Nehmer.

39. KH, May 19, 1977.

40. CN, May 15, 1977. A Chinese government representative said, "We believe quite a number of our manufacturers will be forced to produce higher-quality shoes in order to raise prices and hedge their losses resulting from the forthcoming restrictions."

41. Department of State, *Treaties and Other International Agreements*, no. 8884, p. 29; no. 8885, p. 33.

42. Data from Volume Footwear Retailers of America, *Bulletin*, no. 7, February 23, 1979. Information regarding transshipments obtained from STR, Press Release, no. 277, September 19, 1978; and interview with Janie Hester.

43. ASP is a complicated system. American manufacturers must demonstrate to the Customs Bureau that an imported shoe is directly competitive with an American equivalent. Since this was the first time Korea and Taiwan had exported these shoes as "rubber," manufacturers had to petition the government before a higher tariff could be levied.

44. Calculated from Commerce Department, *Summary Tables*.

45. Taiwanese and Korean cheating was not limited to transshipment and shifting into rubber. According to the AFIA, both countries violated side letters. Korea, for example, was accused of overshipping leather workboots, which it promised to restrain; and Taiwan apparently shipped large quantities of polyurethane footwear, which they also agreed to moderate. Interview with Faun Evenson; and United States International Trade Commission, *Nonrubber Footwear*, USITC Publication 1139, April 1981, p. A-10.

46. According to the *Footwear News*, April 9, 1979, the shoe industry in Taiwan was pricing itself out of the market. This led to sharp declines in orders. Korea, on the other hand, was unable to keep up with demand.

47. *Footwear News*, April 8, 1979.

48. Comptroller General of the United States, *Slow Productivity Growth in the U.S. Footwear Industry*.

49. *United States Department of Commerce News*, April 26, 1979.

50. Interview with Mary Beasley.

51. Interview with Janie Hester. It seems somewhat suspicious that the fallback position was largely agreed upon before the negotiations. Although this is pure con-

jecture, one might speculate that the two negotiators made a transgovernmental alliance to bring about this result. Also, it appears that Hong Kong probably knew that the United States' threats were empty. See STR Press Release no. 277, September 19, 1978.

52. *New York Times*, February 28, 1980; United States International Trade Commission, *Nonrubber Footwear*, USITC Publication 1139, April 1981.

53. In the ITC report to the President in April 1981, the Commission found that the industry was not in a healthy position. Profits remained low for the majority of firms, capacity utilization had not improved, and five thousand workers had lost their jobs during the OMA period.

54. Interviews with Faun Evenson and Peter Mangione; and *New York Times*, July 1, 1981; *Boston Globe*, July 1, 1981.

55. Unofficial translation of Taiwan's Board of Foreign Trade ruling.

6. The Pattern of Protectionism: Color Televisions, Automobiles, and the Future

1. United States International Trade Commission, *The History and Current Status of the Multifiber Arrangement*; *The Economist*, December 21, 1981, p. 76.

2. I. M. Destler, Haruhiro Fukui, and Hideo Sato, *The Textile Wrangle*.

3. Compared to the outside world, the cultural similarities of these four nations appear to be great. To experts of East Asia, however, the differences are numerous.

4. Gustav Ranis, "Challenges and Opportunities Posed by Asia's Superexporters: Implications for Manufactured Exports from Latin America," in Werner Baer and Malcolm Gillis, eds., *Export Diversification and the New Protectionism*, pp. 204–227.

5. Latin American countries appeared to have suffered from inadequate factor mobility in textiles and other light industries. Yet as I noted in chapter 1, factor mobility is a *sine qua non* for success in world manufacturing trade—with or without protectionism.

6. Morawetz, *Why the Emperor's New Clothes*; Baer and Gillis, *Export Diversification and the New Protectionism*; Hollis Chenery, Montek Ahlvwalia, C. Bell, John Duloy, and Richard Jolly, *Redistribution with Growth* (London: Oxford University Press, 1974).

7. John J. Nevin, "Can U.S. Business Survive Our Japanese Trade Policy?" *Harvard Business Review*, September–October 1978.

8. David B. Yoffie, *Zenith Radio Corporation v. the United States* (Abridged), Harvard Business School, case no. 9-382-128.

9. The quota required Japan to cut exports to 1.56 million sets and 190,000 unassembled units. This compares with 2.53 million sets exported in 1976. However, according to industry sources, Japanese retail sales were only 1.8 million in 1976, and the remainder were for building inventory in anticipation of the OMA. *Ibid.*

10. Interview with David Hartquist.

11. In the letter to Japan's Ambassador, Strauss clearly stated this position on the antidumping suits. This letter was reprinted in *Hearings Before the Subcommit-*

tee on *Trade of the Committee on Ways and Means*, House of Representatives, July 18, 1978, pp. 16–17.

12. *Wall Street Journal*, April 12, 1980; hereafter cited as *WSJ*.

13. United States International Trade Commission, *Color Television Receivers and Subassemblies Thereof*, USITC Publication 1068, May 1980, p. A-6.

14. *Ibid.*, p. D-5.

15. *New York Times*, February 5, 1978; hereafter cited as *NYT*.

16. *Korea Herald*, March 27, 1977.

17. *WSJ*, January 9, 1979.

18. Interview with David Hartquist and William Gladkowski.

19. *Ibid.*; *WSJ*, January 9, 1979.

20. Mexico was excluded from the negotiation of new OMAs because the United States was in the midst of a dispute with Mexico on oil and natural gas imports.

21. Interview with David Hartquist. Confidential notes about the negotiations with Taiwan received from the State Department substantiated Hartquist's observation. According to those notes, the final OMAs seemed to have been designed largely to meet Taiwanese needs.

22. United States International Trade Commission, *Color Television Receivers*. Taiwan exported twenty-five thousand more complete sets than originally allowed in the OMA, while Korea pushed up shipments by 230 percent in the first quarter of 1979. The Special Trade Representative revised Taiwan's quota to permit the overshipments. The only formal Korean violation of the OMA was that it did not evenly space its exports. By the end of the first quota period, Korea reduced shipments to bring its total under the OMA to 99 percent of the allowable level.

23. *Business Week*, January 15, 1979.

24. *WSJ*, May 5, 1981.

25. Richard S. Rosenbloom and William Abernathy, "The Climate for Innovation in Industry: The Role of Management Attitudes and Practices in Consumer Electronics," *Working Paper*, Harvard Business School, January 1982.

26. *TV Digest*, February 15, 1982.

27. *Korea Herald*, March 27, 1977.

28. *Ibid.*

29. It was not until 1981 that Korean color television exports to the United States again reached their highs of 1978. Yet according to the United Nations' *Yearbook of International Trade Statistics* (1981), Korean global exports of color televisions, black and white televisions, and radios increased from 235 million dollars in 1977 to 705 million dollars in 1980; and in the United States International Trade Commission, *Monthly Import / Business Review*, March 1982, it was reported that color television broadcasting started in Korea in 1981 and domestic sales were believed to absorb any of the industry's excess capacity.

30. Confidential notes received from the Department of State.

31. Interviews with William Gladkowski and Howard Dobson; *WSJ*, May 5, 1981.

32. There are numerous political histories of the auto industries. See, for example, Gilbert R. Winham and Ikuo Kabashima, "The Politics of United States-Japan Auto Trade," in I. M. Destler and Hideo Sato, eds., *Coping with U.S.-Japanese Economic Conflicts*, pp. 73–121 (Lexington, Mass.: Lexington Books, 1982): and Mark Fuller, "Ford Motor Company (B): The Automobile Crisis and Ford's Political Strategy," Harvard Business School draft case, 1982.

33. WSJ, February 13, 1980.

34. The ITC unanimously rejected the petition on light trucks, WSJ, November 11, 1980.

35. GM reluctantly supported a VER and was adamantly opposed to all other trade barriers. The only reason GM endorsed this limited position was to gain added bargaining power in its negotiations with the UAW. My thanks to Professor Malcolm Salter of the Harvard Business School for pointing this out.

36. Quoted in Winham and Kabashima, "The Politics of United States-Japanese Auto Trade," p. 115.

37. Interviews with Charles Swinburn and an economist, Council of Economic Advisers; Washington Post, May 26, 1982.

38. Ibid.; and interview with Amy Porges.

39. WSJ, February 13, 1980.

40. According to Charles Swinburn, the Japanese privately communicated to the Carter administration that they felt that a public demand from the United States would help force Toyota and Nissan to agree to a VER.

41. NYT, May 2, 1981.

42. Ibid.

43. Nashiro Amaya, "Rejecting Soap-Opera Naturalism," Bungei Shunji, July 1981, translated in Economic Eye (September 1981), vol. 2–3. Amaya reiterated these views at a lunch in his honor at the Harvard Business School.

44. Ibid.

45. In May 1981, I predicted in an editorial that appeared in the Wall Street Journal that the VER with Japan would be a failure. Basing my prediction on the theoretical framework presented in this book, I summarized my argument by writing that "this agreement with Japan will fail to give Detroit meaningful protection, it will increase prices to consumers, and in the long run it may even exacerbate the threat from Japanese industry." See David B. Yoffie, "Reagan's Mythical Auto Restraint Agreement," WSJ, May 18, 1981.

46. Ibid.

47. Ibid.

48. Interview with Charles Swinburn.

49. James Bush, "Here They Come, Quotas or Not," WARD's Auto World, October 1981, pp. 62–64.

50. Ibid., p. 63; NYT, December 23, 1981.

51. There is no guarantee that this element of Japan's strategy will work. American companies have long held a technological lead in the manufacturing of trucks.

52. NYT, September 25, 1981. Global exports of auto kits from Japan were on the rise as all Japanese manufacturers sought to evade restrictions in Europe and Canada, as well as in the United States. Furthermore, other Japanese exporters have also considered joint ventures that would allow them to set up assembly facilities in the United States.

53. WARD's Automotive Report, February 22, 1982, p. 89.

54. By "large" cars, the Japanese mean their most expensive autos. WARD's Automotive Report, February 22, 1982.

55. Ibid.

56. Consumption was down 12 percent in the first six months of 1982 compared to 1981—yet 1981 was also a bad year.

57. Congressional supporters of the auto industry have also pushed for local content laws, which they trust would force more Japanese investment in the United States. According to Professor Malcolm Salter of the Harvard Business School, the Japanese were very frightened of this prospect during the summer of 1982.

58. See Richard Blackhurst, "The Twilight of Domestic Economic Policies," *The World Economy* (December 1981), vol. 4; and Richard Blackhurst, Nicholas Marion, and Jan Tumlir, *Trade Liberalization, Protectionism, and Interdependence*.

59. The number of petitions in front of the ITC for relief from imports into the United States has grown from 105 between 1954 and 1969 to 364 from 1970 to 1978. See Judith Goldstein, "The State, Industrial Interests and Foreign Policy: American Commercial Policy in the Postwar Period," paper presented to the Annual Meeting of the American Political Science Association, September 3–6, 1981.

60. This fear was expressed by several officials of the GATT Secretariat interviewed in July 1982.

61. Stephen Krasner, "The Tokyo Round"; Charles Kindleberger, *The World in Depression, 1929–39*; Robert O. Keohane, "The Theory of Hegemonic Stability and Changes in International Economic Regimes," in Ole Holsti, Randolph Siverson, and Alexander George, eds., *Changes in the International System* (Boulder, Colorado: Westview, 1980).

62. Most empirical research on this question of trade restrictions across sectors supports the research findings I have presented here. Historically, with a few exceptions such as Smoot-Hawley, trade barriers have been devised industry by industry. See Richard Caves, "Economic Models of Political Choice"; John Pincus, *Pressure Groups and Politics in Antebellum Tariffs*; and James Kurth, "The Political Consequences of the Product Cycle: Industrial History and Political Outcome," *International Organization* (Winter 1979).

63. Robert O. Keohane, "The Demand for International Regimes." In a partial critique of his previous work (cited in footnote 62), Keohane suggests that hegemony may not be as important to regime stability as previously believed. One could conclude from the debate on the role of hegemony that a hegemonic nation may be a *sufficient* condition for the maintenance of free trade, rather than a *necessary* condition. See also Charles Lifson, "The Transformation of Trade: The Sources and Effects of Regime Change," *International Organization* (Spring 1982).

64. Robert O. Keohane, "The Demand for International Regimes." Keohane argues that the demand for regimes, such as a trade regime, would not necessarily diminish with an increasing fragmentation of power. As long as the GATT helps its members overcome problems associated with market failures and uncertainty, the regime may remain stable.

65. The most significant failure of the Tokyo Round of trade talks was the absence of an agreement on VERs and OMAs—known in GATT terminology as "safeguards." Major efforts will be made, however, between 1982 and 1985 to fill this gap. Interviews with officials of the GATT Secretariat; interview with Fred Mackeldowny; Isaiah Frank, *Trade Policy Issues of Interest to the Third World*, ch. 3; Brian Hindley, "Voluntary Export Restraints and the GATT's Main Escape Clause"; and Alan Wm. Wolff, "The Need for New GATT Rules on Safeguard Actions," paper prepared for the Institute for International Economics, June 4, 1982.

66. Joseph Badaracco and David Yoffie, "Why a U.S. Industrial Policy Will Fail," Harvard Business School Working Paper, 1982, no. HBS 83-20.

67. In addition to textiles, American steel companies have also learned how to deal with many of the deficiencies of the new protectionism. In 1982, the steel industry forced the American government to investigate dumping and subsidy charges against European producers as well as several other third world countries. When the Commerce Department found that the steel industry claims were justified, it was compelled by law to levy extra duties on imported steel. To minimize trade tensions, the United States government negotiated a VER with Europe. The Commerce Department hoped that the VER would satisfy the steel industry and lead it to withdraw its suits. Through late September 1982, steel companies refused to accept a VER, despite government pressure. Voluntary restraints in the late 1960s and early 1970s had caused exporters (Japan and Europe) to diversify out of restricted areas into growing segments (specialty steel) of the American steel market. U.S. Steel and other big companies feared that the same result would occur in 1982 because the American government excluded from the VER new growth areas such as pipe and tubing. It was not until the European countries agreed to restrict pipe and tubing products in mid-October 1982 that American steel companies agreed to withdraw their law suits. Interviews with officials of the American Iron and Steel Institute; WSJ, August 24, 1982; WSJ, October 20, 1982.

68. David B. Yoffie, "The Newly Industrializing Countries and the Political Economy of Protectionism," p. 596.

69. In the negotiations on a safeguard code at the GATT in Geneva, most developing nations have advocated a strict code to regulate the use of VERs and OMAs. The South Koreans, however, have remained strangely aloof. The Koreans seem to believe that they would manage better under the present system than under any new set of alternatives that the GATT might produce. Interviews with officials of the GATT Secretariat, 1982.

Selected Bibliography

Interviews

Between 1979 and 1982 close to one hundred open-ended interviews were conducted with policy makers, government negotiators, industry advisers, lobbyists, congressional assistants, and business executives. Whenever possible, interview material from one source was cross-checked with second or third interviews as well as with government documents. In addition to those individuals listed below, several officials interviewed in 1982 wished to remain anonymous. These included members of the GATT Secretariat in Geneva, the European Economic Community in Brussels and Washington, and the Council of Economic Advisers in Washington. I further benefited from conversations with economists and officials from Japan, Taiwan, Korea, and Hong Kong during the Eleventh Pacific Trade and Development Conference held in Seoul, Korea, in September 1980.

Ascher, Bernie. Director, Import Program Office, Department of Commerce. August 31, 1979.
Atkins, Edward. Executive vice president, Volume Footwear Retailers of America. July 9, 1979.
Beach, Rex. Special assistant to Ambassador-at-Large David Kennedy. June 25, 1980.

Beasley, Mary. International Trade Division, Department of the Treasury. August 28, 1979.

Blackman, Herbert. Associate Deputy Under Secretary of Labor for International Affairs. June 28, 1979.

Bodner, Seth. Former Director, Import Program Office, Department of Commerce. July 9, 1979.

Brandis, Buford. Director, International Division, American Textile Manufacturers Institute. June 22, 1979.

Brew, William. Assistant chief, Textile Division, Department of State. June 20, 1979.

Brookhart, Larry. Acting Director, Footwear Industry Team, Department of Commerce. August 28, 1979.

Burkholder, Irving. Former Director, Footwear Industry Team, Department of Commerce. October 9, 1979.

Cavenough, Rita. Senior economist, American Footwear Industries Association. August 27, 1979.

Daines, Kay. Senior vice president, American Retail Association. October 9, 1979.

Daniels, Michael. Lawyer-lobbyist with Daniels, Houlihan & Palmeter. June 28, 1979.

Destler, I. M. Former consultant, Executive Reorganization Project, and senior fellow, Carnegie Endowment. July 2, 1979.

Diroll, William. Special Trade Activities Division, Department of State. June 21, 1979.

Dobson, Howard. TV OMA negotiator, Office of Foreign Economic Policy, Department of Labor. June 25, 1979.

Emmerson, John. Former Minister and Deputy Chief of Mission, U.S. Embassy, Japan. June 7, 1979.

Erb, Guy. National Security Council. June 24, 1979.

Evenson, Faun. Executive vice president, American Footwear Industries Association. August 27, 1979, and December 23, 1981.

Fabry, Milan. National manager, Sears, Roebuck, Import Division. October 3, 1979.

Foote, Donald. Branch chief, International Agreement and Monitoring Division, Department of Commerce. June 29, 1979.

Geiger, Theodore. Senior vice president, National Planning Association. June 25, 1979.

Gladkowski, William. TV OMA negotiator, Import Program Office, Department of Commerce. June 27, 1979.

Graham, Thomas. Deputy general counsel, Special Trade Representative's Office. September 5, 1979.

Groner, Larry. Legislative assistant, Gaylord Nelson (U.S. Senator, Wisconsin). August 29, 1979.

Hartquist, David. Lawyer-lobbyist with Collier, Shannon, Rill and Scott. December 23, 1981.

Hentges, Harriet. Former staff member of Policy Planning, Department of State, and STR; executive director, League of Women Voters. June 22, 1979.

Hester, Janie. Footwear OMA negotiator, Office of Foreign Economic Policy, Department of Labor. June 24, 1979.

Hughes, Anne. Deputy Assistant Secretary for International Trade Administration, Department of Commerce. December 23, 1981.

Jacobson, Clarence. Former president, J. Baker Shoes. June 19, 1982.

James, Florence. Textile negotiator, Office of Foreign Economic Policy, Department of Labor. June 25, 1979.

Jenson, Anita. Legislative assistant, Edward Muskie (U.S. Senator, Maine). August 31, 1979.

Johnson, Ernest. Special assistant to Under Secretary of State for Economic Affairs. July 3, 1979.

Johnson, Joel. Staff member of Policy Planning, Department of State. June 25, 1979.

Kearns, Henry. Former Assistant Secretary of Commerce. October 27, 1980.

Kennedy, David. Former Secretary of the Treasury and Ambassador-at-Large. November 11, 1979.

King, Marge. Office of Cooperative Technology, National Bureau of Standards. August 30, 1979.

Kramer, Irving. Assistant Director, International Commodity Division, Department of Labor. August 24, 1979.

Lavorel, Warren. Deputy Chief of Mission, a U.S. Special Trade Representative's Office in Geneva. July 13, 1982.

Lesley, Jack. Legislative assistant, Edward Kennedy (U.S. Senator, Massachusetts). August 29, 1979.

Levin, Ron. Office of Textiles, Department of Commerce. October 12, 1979.

Mackeldowny, Fred. U.S. Special Trade Representative's Office, Geneva. July 13, 1982.

Malmgrem, Harald. Former staff member, National Security Council. December 22, 1981.

Mangione, Peter. Assistant executive vice president, Volume Footwear Retailers of America. December 22, 1981.

Mannering, Gina. International trade specialist, Import Program Office, Department of Commerce. June 29, 1979.

Milgate, John. Assistant Director, International Division, General Accounting Office. August 29, 1979.

Morse, Edward. Special Assistant to Under Secretary of State for Economic Affairs. July 2, 1979.

Nehmer, Stanley. Former Deputy Assistant Secretary of Resources, Department of Commerce; trade consultant, American Footwear Industries Association. October 11, 1979.

Norman, George. Manager, Import Coordination and Planning, Sears, Roebuck. October 3, 1979.

Olson, Iver. Chief economist, American Footwear Industries Association. August 27, 1979.

Perez-Lopez, Jorge. Office of Foreign Economic Policy, Department of Labor. June 25, 1979.

Phelan, Harry. Former Director, Office of Textiles, Department of State; U.S. representative to Textile Surveillance Board, Geneva. October 11; 1979.

Porges, Amy. Special Trade Representative's Office. December 22, 1981.

Porter, Roger. Former special assistant to President Gerald Ford. October 15, 1979.

Pratt, Gloria. Director, Office of Foreign Economic Policy, Department of Labor. June 25, 1979.

Priestland, Carl. Economist, American Apparel Manufacturers Association. October 11, 1979.

Reischauer, Edwin. Former U.S. Ambassador to Japan. October 15, 1979.

Samuels, Howard. Former Deputy Assistant Secretary for International Labor Affairs, Department of Labor. June 25, 1979.

Siff, Robert. President, B & W Footwear. October 16, 1979.

Swinburn, Charles. Deputy Assistant Secretary of Policy, Department of Transportation. December 22, 1981.

Tagliani, Bill. Staff member of Textile Office, Department of State. October 12, 1979.

Trezise, Philip. Former Assistant Secretary of State for Economic Affairs. October 10, 1979.

Wilson, Bruce. Special Trade Representative's Office. June 14, 1979.

Wiseberger, Leo. Director, Footwear Project, Research Triangle Institute. September 4, 1979.

Selected Books, Articles, and Government Documents

In addition to the selected books, articles, and documents listed below, my research benefited from documents released under the Freedom of Information Act. These included transcripts, cables, and memoranda of the 1956 negotiations with Japan, and a limited selection of these documents from the 1969–71 negotiations with Taiwan, Korea, Hong Kong, and Japan released by the State Department. The Department of Agriculture also released information about the linkage between Korea's P.L. 480 aid and textiles, and the Department of Commerce provided copies of the performance reports of textile bilaterals from 1961 to 1980, and the footwear OMAs. Lastly, confidential notes on the color TV negotiations were inadvertently supplied by the Department of State.

American Apparel Manufacturers Association. *The Apparel Problem.* Alexandria, Va.: American Apparel Manufacturers Association, 1969.

Badaracco, Joseph and David Yoffie. "Why a U.S. Industrial Policy Will Fail." 1982. Harvard Business School, Working Paper no. HBS83-20.

Baer, Werner and Malcolm Gillis, eds. *Export Diversification and the New Protectionism.* Champaign: University of Illinois Press, 1981.

Balassa, Bela. "Export Incentives and Export Performance in Developing Countries: A Comparative Analysis." *Weltwirtschaftliches Archiv* (1978), no. 114.

——— "The 'New Protectionism' and the International Economy." *Journal of World Trade Law* (1978), vol. 12.

Bardan, Benjamin. "The Cotton Textile Agreement, 1962–72." *Journal of World Trade Law* (1973), 7:8–35.

Bauer, Raymond, Ithiel de Sola Pool, and Lewis Dexter. *American Business and Public Policy: The Politics of Foreign Trade.* 2d ed. New York: Aldine, 1972.

Bauge, Kenneth. "Voluntary Export Restrictions as a Foreign Commercial Policy with Special Reference to Japanese Cotton Textiles." Ph.D. diss., Michigan State University, 1967.

Bergsten, C. Fred. "On the Non-Equivalence of Import Quotas and 'Voluntary' Export Restraints." In C. Fred Bergsten, ed. *Towards a New World Trade Policy: The Maidenhead Papers,* pp. 239–271. Lexington, Mass.: Heath, 1975.

——— "Let's Avoid a Trade War." *Foreign Policy* (Summer 1976), 23:24–31.

Bhagwati, Jagdish, ed. *The New International Economic Order: The North-South Debate.* Cambridge: MIT Press, 1977.

Blackhurst, Richard, Nicholas Marion, and Jan Tumlir. *Trade Liberalization, Protectionism, and Interdependence.* GATT Studies in International Trade, no. 5. 1977.

——— *Adjustment, Trade, and Growth in Developed and Developing Countries.* GATT Studies in International Trade, no. 6., 1978.

Blaker, Michael. "Probe, Push, and Panic: The Japanese Tactical Style in International Negotiations." In Robert Scalapino, ed. *The Foreign Policy of Modern Japan,* pp. 55–103. Berkeley: University of California Press, 1977.

Blaker, Michael, ed. *The Politics of Trade: U.S.-Japan Policymaking for GATT Negotiations.* Occasional Papers of the East Asian Institute, Project on Japan. New York: Columbia University Press, 1978.

Caporaso, James, ed. "Dependence and Dependency in the Global System." Special issue of *International Organization* (Winter 1978), vol. 32.

Caves, Richard. "Economic Models of Political Choice: Canada's Tariff Structure." *Canadian Journal of Economics* (May 1976).

Caves, Richard and Masu Uekusa. *Industrial Organization in Japan*. Washington: Brookings Institution, 1976.

Chacholiades, Militiades. *International Trade: Theory and Policy*. New York: McGraw-Hill, 1978.

Chenery, Hollis and Donald Keesing. "The Changing Composition of Developing Country Exports," Working Paper No. 314. Washington D.C.: World Bank, 1979.

Cheng, Tong Yong. *The Economy of Hong Kong*. Hong Kong: Far East Publications, 1977.

Chung, Kae H. "Industrial Progress in South Korea." *Asian Survey* (May 1974), #14:439–456.

Cline, William. *Imports and Consumer Prices: A Survey Analysis*. Prepared for the American Retail Federation. 1979.

Cohen, Benjamin. *Multinational Firms and Asian Exports*. New Haven: Yale University Press, 1975.

Cohen, Jerome B. *Japan's Postwar Economy*. Bloomington: Indiana University Press, 1958.

Cohen, Jerome B., ed. *Pacific Partnership: U.S.-Japan Trade Prospects and Recommendations for the Seventies*. Lexington, Mass.: Lexington Books, 1972.

Comptroller General of the United States. *Economic and Foreign Policy Effects of Voluntary Restraint Agreements in Textiles and Steel*, B-179342, March 21, 1974.

—— "Slow Productivity Growth in the U.S. Footwear Industry—Can the Federal Government Help?" February 15, 1980.

Curzon, Gerard and Victoria Curzon. "The Management of Trade Relations in the GATT." In Andrew Shonfield, ed. *International Economic Relations of the Western World, 1959–71*, 1:143–186. London: Oxford University Press, 1976.

Dam, Kenneth. *The GATT: Law and International Economic Organization*. Chicago: University of Chicago Press, 1970.

Destler, I. M. *Making Foreign Economic Policy*. Washington: Brookings Institution, 1980.

Destler, I. M., Haruhiro Fukui, and Hideo Sato. *The Textile Wrangle: Conflict in Japanese-American Relations, 1969–71*. Ithaca: Cornell University Press, 1979.

Destler, I. M., H. Sato, P. Clapp, and Haruhiro Fukui. *Managing an Alliance: The Politics of U.S.-Japanese Relations*. Washington: Brookings Institution, 1976.

Destler, I. M. and Hideo Sato, eds. *Coping with U.S.-Japanese Economic Conflicts.* Lexington, Mass.: Lexington Books, 1982.

Druckman, Daniel. *Human Factors in International Negotiations: The Social-Psychological Aspects of International Conflict.* Beverly Hills: Sage Publications, 1973.

Druckman, Daniel, ed. *Negotiations: Social-Psychological Perspectives.* Beverly Hills: Sage Publications, 1977.

Eckstein, Harry. "Case Study and Theory in Political Science." In Fred Greenstein and Nelson Polsby, eds. *Handbook of Political Science,* 7:79–139. Reading, Mass.: Addison-Wesley, 1975.

Economic Planning Council (Republic of China). *Taiwan Statistical Data Book.* 1970–79.

Fiallo, Fabio. "The Negotiation Strategy of Developing Countries in the Field of Trade Liberalization." *Journal of World Trade Law* (1977), no. 3, 11:203–214.

Fisher, Bart. "Enforcing Export Quota Commodity Agreements: The Case of Coffee." *Harvard International Law Journal* (Summer 1971), 12:401–435.

—— *The International Coffee Agreement.* New York: Praeger, 1972.

Fishlow, Albert, Jean Carriere, and Sueo Sekiguchi. *Trade in Manufactured Products with Developing Countries Reinforcing North-South Partnership.* A Report to the Trilateral Commission. Triangle Papers, 21, 1981.

Fox, Annette Baker. *The Power of Small States.* Chicago: University of Chicago Press, 1959.

Frank, Isaiah. *Trade Policy Issues of Interest to the Third World.* London: Trade Policy Research Centre, 1981.

Frank, Isaiah, ed. *The Japanese Economy in International Perspective.* Baltimore: Johns Hopkins University Press, 1975.

Fukui, Haruhiro. "The GATT Tokyo Round: The Bureaucratic Politics of Multilateral Diplomacy." In Michael Blaker, ed. *The Politics of Trade: U.S.-Japan Policymaking for GATT Negotiations,* pp. 75–171. Occasional papers of the East Asian Institute, Project on Japan. New York: Columbia University Press, 1978.

Fulda, Carl. "Textiles and Voluntary Restraints on Steel: Protecting U.S. Industries from Foreign Competition." *Virginia Journal of International Law* (1972–73), 13:11–23.

Geiger, Theodore and Francis Geiger. *Tales of Two City-States: The Development Progress of Hong Kong and Singapore.* Washington: National Planning Association, 1973.

George, Alexander. "American Foreign Policy: The Problem of Legitimacy." Talk prepared for the Symposium on U.S. Foreign Policy in the Next Decade. University of Missouri, Saint Louis, April 1977. Mimeographed.

—— "Case Studies and Theory Development: The Method of Structured, Focused Comparison." In Paul Lauren, ed. *Diplomacy: New Approaches in History, Theory, and Policy*, pp. 43–69. New York: Free Press, 1979.

Gershenkron, Alexander. *Economic Backwardness in Historical Perspective*. Cambridge: Harvard University Press, 1963.

Gilpin, Robert. *U.S. Power and the Multinational Corporation*. New York: Basic Books, 1975.

Gourevitch, Peter. "The Second Image Reversed: The International Sources of Domestic Politics." *International Organization* (Autumn 1978), #32:881–913.

Haas, Ernst. "Why Collaborate? Issue-Linkage and International Regimes." *World Politics* (April 1980), 32:357–405.

Hasan, Parvez. *Korea: Problems and Issues in a Rapidly Growing Economy*. Baltimore: Johns Hopkins University Press, 1976.

Helleiner, G. D. "Manufactured Exports from L.D.C.'s and Multinational Firms." *The Economic Journal* (March 1975), vol. 83.

Heuser, Heinrich. *Control of International Trade*. Philadelphia: P. Blackstone's Sons, 1939.

Hindley, Brian. "Voluntary Export Restraints and the GATT's Main Escape Clause." *World Economy* (November 1980), 3(3):313–341.

Hirschman, Albert. *National Power and the Structure of Foreign Trade*. Berkeley: University of California Press, 1945.

—— *The Strategy of Economic Development*. New York: Norton, 1958.

—— "Beyond Asymmetry: Critical Notes on Myself as a Young Man and on Some Other Old Friends." *International Organization* (Winter 1978), 32:45–51.

Hollerman, Leon. *Japan's Dependence on the World Economy*. Princeton: Princeton University Press, 1967.

—— "Foreign Trade in Japan's Economic Transition." In Isaiah Frank, ed. *The Japanese Economy in International Perspective*, pp. 168–207. Baltimore: Johns Hopkins University Press, 1975.

Hong Kong Yearbook. 1959–68.

Hopmann, P. Terrence. "Asymmetrical Bargaining in the Conference on Security and Cooperation in Europe." *International Organization* (Winter 1978), 32:141–179.

Hunsberger, Warren. *Japan and the United States in World Trade*. New York: Harper & Row, 1964.

Iklé, Fred. *How Nations Negotiate*. New York: Harper & Row, 1964.

—— "Negotiation." In *International Encyclopedia of the Social Sciences*, 2:117–120. New York: Macmillan, 1968.

Jackson, John. "Orderly Marketing Arrangements." Proceedings of the 72nd Annual Meeting of the American Society of International Law. Washington. April 27–29, 1978.

Johnson, Chalmers. "MITI and Japanese International Economic Policy." In Robert Scalapino, ed. The Foreign Policy of Modern Japan, pp. 227–281. Berkeley: University of California Press, 1977.

Johnson, Paul. "Washington and Bonn: Dimensions of Change in Bilateral Relations." International Organization (Augumn 1979), 33: 451–480.

Katzenstein, Peter. "International Relations and Domestic Structures: Foreign Economic Policies of Advanced Industrial States." International Organization (Winter 1976), 30:1–47.

Katzenstein, Peter, ed. Between Power and Plenty: Foreign Economic Policies of Advanced Industrial States. Madison: University of Wisconsin Press, 1978. Also published as special issue of International Organization (Fall 1977), vol. 30.

Keesing, Donald. "Developing Countries' Exports of Textiles and Clothing: Perspectives and Policy Choices." Washington, D.C.: World Bank, 1978. Processed.

Keesing, Donald S. and Martin Wolf. Textile Quotas Against Developing Countries. London: Trade Policy Research Centre, 1980.

Keohane, Nannerl O. Philosophy and the State in France: Renaissance to Enlightenment. Princeton: Princeton University Press, 1980.

Keohane, Robert O. "The Big Influence of Small Allies." Foreign Policy (Spring 1971), 2:161–182.

—— "The Demand for International Regimes." International Organization (Spring 1982), 36:325–355.

Keohane, Robert O. and Joseph Nye. "World Politics and the International Economic System." In C. Fred Bergsten, ed. The Future of the International Economic Order: An Agenda for Research, pp. 115–179. Lexington, Mass.: D. C. Heath, 1973.

—— "Transgovernmental Relations and International Organizations." World Politics (October 1974), 27:39–62.

—— Power and Interdependence: World Politics in Transition. New York: Little, Brown, 1977.

Kindleberger, Charles. Power and Money: The Economics of International Politics and the Politics of International Economics. New York: Basic Books, 1970.

—— The World in Depression 1929–39. Berkeley: University of California Press, 1973.

Krasner, Stephen O. "State Power and the Structure of International Trade." World Politics (April 1976), 28:317–347.

—— Defending the National Interest: Raw Material Investments and U.S. Foreign Policy. Princeton: Princeton University Press, 1978.

—— "The Tokyo Round: Particularistic Interests and Prospects for Stability in the Global Trading System." International Studies Quarterly (December 1979), 23:491–532.

Krasner, Stephen O., ed. "International Regimes," special issue of *International Organization* (Spring 1982), 36:2.

Lasswell, Harold D. *Politics: Who Gets What, When, How.* Cleveland: Meridian Books, 1964.

Lijphart, Arend. "Comparative Politics and the Comparative Method." *American Political Science Review* (September 1971), 65:682–694.

Lockwood, William. *The Economic Development of Japan.* Princeton: Princeton University Press, 1968.

Luce, Robert and Howard Raiffa. *Games and Decisions.* New York: Wiley. 1957.

Lynch, John. *Towards an Orderly Market: An Intensive Study of Japan's Voluntary Quota in Cotton Textile Exports.* Tokyo: Sophia University Press, 1967.

Machiavelli, Niccolò. *The Prince and the Discourses.* New York: Modern Library, n.d.

March, James. "The Power of Power." In David Easton, ed., *Varieties of Political Analysis,* pp. 39–70. New York: Prentice Hall, 1966.

Meier, Gerald. *Problems of Trade Policy.* Oxford: Oxford University Press, 1973.

Meier, Gerald, ed. *Leading Issues in Economic Development.* 3d ed. New York: Oxford University Press, 1976.

Metzger, Stanley. "Injury and Market Disruption from Imports." *United States International Economic Policy in an Interdependent World.* Washington: Government Printing Office, July 1971.

Ministry of International Trade and Industry (Japan). *Japan Trade Guide 1957.* Tokyo: J.I.J.I. Press, 1957.

—— *New Long Range Economic Plan 1958–62.* Tokyo: J.I.J.I. Press, 1958.

—— *Medium Term Economic Plan 1964–68.* Tokyo: J.I.J.I. Press, 1964.

—— *White Papers on Foreign Trade.* Various years.

Mintz, Ilse. *U.S. Import Quotas: Cost and Consequences.* Washington: American Enterprise Institute for Public Policy Research, 1973.

Morawetz, David. *Why the Emperor's New Clothes Are Not Made in Colombia.* London: Oxford University Press, 1981.

Morton, Kathryn and Peter Tulloch. *Trade and Developing Countries.* New York: Wiley, 1977.

Odell, John. "Latin American Trade Negotiations with the United States." *International Organization* (Spring 1980), 34:207–229.

Okita, Saburo. *The Experience of Economic Planning in Japan.* Center Paper no. 23. Tokyo: Japan Economic Research Center, April 1974.

Oman, Ralph. "The Clandestine Negotiation of Voluntary Restraints on Shoes from Italy: An Augury of Future Negotiations Under the Trade Reform Act of 1974." *Cornell International Law Journal* (1974), no. 7, vol. 6.

Organization of Economic Cooperation and Development. *The Impact of* the Newly Industrializing Countries on Production and Trade in Manufactures. Paris: OECD, 1979.

Overseas Development Institute. "Protectionism in the West—The Third World Link." Briefing Paper. London, April 1978.

Oye, Kenneth. "Towards Disentangling Linkages: Issue Interdependence and Regime Change." University of California, Davis, 1977. Mimeographed.

Patrick, Hugh and Henry Rosovsky. Asia's New Giant: How the Japanese Economy Works. Washington: Brookings Institution, 1976.

Patterson, Gardner. Discrimination in International Trade: The Policy Issues, 1945–65. Princeton: Princeton University Press, 1966.

Pempel, T. J. "Japanese Foreign Economic Policy: The Domestic Bases for International Behavior." International Organization (Fall 1977), 30:723–775.

Pincus, John. Pressure Groups and Politics in Antebellum Tariffs. New York: Columbia University Press, 1977.

Plesch, Phi Anh. "Statistical Trends in Developing Countries: Exports and Imports of Manufactures." Washington, D.C.: World Bank, 1979. Processed.

Pressman, Jeffrey and Aaron Wildavsky. Implementation. Berkeley: University of California Press, 1973.

Rapoport, Anatol. Fights, Games, and Debates. Ann Arbor: University of Michigan Press, 1960.

Rothstein, Robert. Global Bargaining: UNCTAD and the Quest for a New International Economic Order. Princeton: Princeton University Press, 1979.

Sawyer, Jack and Harold Guetzkow. "Bargaining and Negotiation in International Relations." In Herbert Kelman, ed. International Behavior: A Social-Psychological Analysis, pp. 466–520. New York: Holt, Rinehart & Winston, 1965.

Saxonhouse, Gary. "The Textile Confrontation." In Jerome Cohen, ed. Pacific Partnership: U.S.-Japan Trade Prospects and Recommendations for the Seventies. Lexington, Mass.: Lexington Books, 1972.

Schattschneider, E. E. Politics, Pressures, and the Tariff. New York: Prentice-Hall, 1935.

Schelling, Thomas. The Strategy of Conflict. Oxford: Oxford University Press, 1960.

Shonfield, Andrew. Modern Capitalism: The Changing Balance of Public and Private Power. New York: Oxford University Press, 1965.

Shonfield, Andrew, ed. International Economic Relations of the Western World, 1959–1971, vol. 1. London: Oxford University Press, 1976.

Smith, Malcolm. "Voluntary Export Quotas and U.S. Trade Policy—A New Nontariff Barrier." Law and Policy in International Business (1973), no. 10, 5:10–54.

Snyder, Glenn and Paul Diesing. *Conflict Among Nations*. Princeton: Princeton University Press, 1977.

Strange, Susan. "What Is Economic Power and Who Has It?" *International Journal* (Spring 1975), 30:207–224.

—— "The Management of Surplus Capacity: How Does Theory Stand Up to Protectionism, Seventies Style?" *International Organization* (Summer 1979), 33:303–334.

Strauss, Anselm. *Negotiations: Varieties, Contexts, Processes, and Social Order*. San Francisco: Jossey-Bass, 1978.

Taake, Hems-Helmut and Dicter Weis. "The World Textile Arrangement: The Exporter's View Point." *Journal of World Trade Law* (1974), 8(6):624–654.

Thucydides. *The Pelopennesian War*. New York: Modern Library, 1951.

Tong, Sang Il. *American Domestic Politics and Foreign Policy: A Case Study of the Textile Controversy with Japan, 1969–71*. Ph.D. diss., University of Washington, Seattle, 1974.

Trezise, Philip. "Japan and the European Economic Community." In *The New Japan: Prospects and Promise*. Proceedings of Princeton University Conference, November 16–17, 1962.

Trout, Thomas. "Rhetoric Revisited: Political Legitimation and the Cold War." *International Studies Quarterly* (September 1975), 19:251–285.

Tsoukalis, Louka and Antonio da Silva Ferreira. "Management of Industrial Surplus Capacity in the European Community." *International Organization* (Summer 1980), 34:355–377.

Tumlir, Jan. "The Protectionist Threat to International Order." *International Journal* (Winter 1978–79), 34:53–64.

United Nations. *Yearbook of International Trade Statistics*. New York: U.N. Statistics Office, various years.

United Nations Conference on Trade and Development. *Growing Protectionism and the Standstill on Trade Barriers Against Imports from Developing Countries*. TD/B/D.2/194, May 1978.

United States *Department of State Bulletin*, 1955–72. Various issues.

United States International Trade Commission. *The History and Current Status of the Multifiber Arrangement*. USITC Publication 850, January 1978.

—— *Reports to the President*, on textiles, apparel, footwear, and color TVs, various years.

United States Senate, 86th Congress, 1st session, Committee on Interstate and Foreign Commerce. *Problems of the Domestic Textile Industry*. Senate Report no. 2. Washington: GPO, February 4, 1959.

Vogel, Ezra, ed. *Modern Japanese Organization and Decision-Making*. Berkeley: University of California Press, 1975.

Walton, Richard and Robert McKersie. *A Behavioral Theory of Labor Negotiations: An Analysis of a Social Interaction System*. New York: McGraw-Hill, 1965.

Waltz, Kenneth. *Theory of International Politics.* Reading, Mass.: Addison-Wesley, 1977.

Westphal, Larry. "The Republic of Korea's Experience with Export-Led Industrial Development." *World Development* (1978), 6(3):347–382.

World Bank Report. Washington, D.C.: World Bank, various years.

Yoffie, David B. "Orderly Marketing Agreements as an Industrial Policy: The Case of the Footwear Industry." *Public Policy* (Winter 1981).

—— "Reagan's Mythical Auto Restraint Agreement." *Wall Street Journal,* May 18, 1981.

—— "The Newly Industrializing Countries and the Political Economy of Protectionism." *International Studies Quarterly* (1981), 25(4):569–599.

Zartman, I. W. *The Politics of Trade Negotiations Between Africa and the EEC: The Weak Confront the Strong.* Princeton: Princeton University Press, 1971.

Zartman, I. W., ed. *The 50% Solution.* New York: Anchor Books, 1976.

—— *The Negotiation Process: Theories and Applications.* Beverly Hills: Sage Publications, 1979.

Zysman, John. *Political Strategies for Industrial Order: State, Market, and Industry in France.* Berkeley: University of California Press, 1977.

Selected Newspapers and Periodicals

Business Week.

China Herald (Taipei).

China News (Taipei).

China Post (Taipei).

Daily News Record (daily newspaper of the textile and apparel trade, Fairchild Publications, New York).

The Economist.

Far Eastern Economic Review (Hong Kong).

Far Eastern Economic Review Asian Textile Survey (Hong Kong).

Far Eastern Economic Review Yearbook (Hong Kong).

Footwear News (daily newspaper of the footwear trade, Fairchild Publications, New York).

Japanese Press Translations (U.S. Embassy, Tokyo).

Japan Times (Tokyo).

Korea Herald (Seoul).

New York Times.

South China Morning Post (Hong Kong).

TV Digest (weekly publication of the consumer electronics trade).

Wall Street Journal.

WARD's Automotive Report (weekly publication of the automotive trade).

Washington Post.

Women's Wear Daily (daily newspaper of the fashion apparel trade, Fairchild Publications, New York).

Index

THE POLITICAL ECONOMY
OF INTERNATIONAL CHANGE
JOHN GERARD RUGGIE, GENERAL EDITOR